Slowth

Slowth

The Changing Economy and How You Can Successfully Cope

MARTIN KUPFERMAN

MAURICE D. LEVI

JOHN WILEY & SONS   New York • Chichester • Brisbane • Toronto

Published by John Wiley & Sons, Inc.
Copyright © 1980 by Martin Kupferman and Maurice Levi

Library of Congress Cataloging in Publication Data:

Kupferman, Martin, 1948-
    Slowth: the looming struggle of living with
less.

    1.   United States—Economic conditions—1971-
2.   Social values.   I.   Levi, Maurice D., 1945-
joint author.   II.   Title.
HC106.7.K86   330.973′0926   80-18863
ISBN 0-471-08090-X

Printed in the United States of America

10 9 8 7 6 5 4 3 2 1

With love to our parents—Karl and Louise Levi and Celia Kupferman, and to the memory of Joseph Kupferman

Acknowledgments

This book evolved out of some long-held beliefs and ideas of Professor Levi about the existence and causes of slow economic growth. These ideas have been developed jointly by both of us, and we extend thanks to a number of people who aided in developing this book. They are: Kate Birkinshaw, Michael Charters, Albert Dexter, Don Donovan, Jim Forbes, Mike Goldberg, Bill Harrington, Tracy Herrick, Alan Kraus, Celia Kupferman, Iza Laponce, Peter Lusztig, Joanna Rood, and Bernard Schwab. Gerald T. Papke of John Wiley & Sons provided valuable encouragement from the earliest stages of the manuscript's development to the completion of the book. We believe the term slowth, standing for slow economic growth, was originally coined by an anonymous staff member of the Paris-based Organization for Economic Cooperation and Development.

We would also like to thank Kathryn Gamble and Janice Lupul, who prepared the manuscript. We are especially thankful to the Faculty of Commerce and Business Administration of the University of British Columbia and to Currie, Coopers & Lybrand Ltd. for providing the encouragement and the facilities used in the preparation of *Slowth*. The views that are expressed are, however, our responsibility alone.

M.K.
M.D.L.

Preface

A cynic, as the sardonic wit of Oscar Wilde would have it, is one who knows the price of everything and the value of nothing. With this simple definition, Wilde unwittingly captures the spirit with which many of us view the economic reality of the 1980s. Disappointment over stagnant living standards is widespread; cynicism about the reasons for our declining economic fortunes is rampant. Yet as we face the reality of slowth, or slow economic growth, we know something of the price it will demand of us, but little about why it exists or how we will ultimately pay for it. In this book we show why the new reality of slow growth has come to be and how we are subtly making the adjustment to it. *Slowth,* written in nontechnical language, establishes the contours of the economy and helps its readers find places for themselves within it. In so doing it helps alleviate this common experience of cynicism and helps us all escape the barbs of Wilde's spirit.

Slowth traces the roots of the economic malaise afflicting people in the United States today: our own values. It describes the way American consciousness has grown alongside our rising national income and shows why this consciousness is no longer compatible with rapid growth. The adoption of nonmaterial values—the rise of American consciousness—is slowing the system that produces our goods and services. Indeed, we shall be shifting into lower economic gear throughout the 1980s as the result of our very own choice.

The suggestion that we ourselves block the path to improvement in our own living standards is neither common nor easy to accept. Instead, many reluctantly lean for explanation on false but popular notions that gain currency. Inflation is one phenomenon to which we attribute these tougher times, although few people understand much more about it than its status in our language as a nine letter word meaning rising prices. *Slowth* challenges the importance attributed to inflation. It explains why it is not money that matters in determining our living standards, but output of real goods and services. In the first part of the book we offer the reader a comprehensive framework to aid in understanding how the living standards of the nation are determined. It is an account of our productive system and why it is now faltering. This framework establishes the meaning of "supply side" economics, a concept that has begun to receive wide attention in the press. It affords a simple, coherent explanation for a variety of phenomena that now plague our economy: trade deficits, a declining currency, the rise in protectionism, and the revolt against paying taxes. The end result is an unmistakably clear snapshot of an economy in slowing motion.

Slowth is also written to enable its readers to find the best place for themselves within that new picture. It affords a global view of the economy and how it will affect our lifestyles, psyches, and our institutions of government and business. We examine the rising level of political conflict, both in our society and within ourselves, which is a result of living standards that do not grow. A reading of *Slowth* demonstrates what to expect in the way of services from government, what sacrifices will have to be made for a higher standard of living, and how other people will be making the financial adjustment to a harsher economic reality. The related psychological adjustment is also discussed, because it will be a common experience that we all shall share from our separate, and perhaps isolated, perspectives. The ultimate objective is to aid our readers in adjusting to tougher economic times.

We do not suggest that slowth is a permanent or even long-term reality. We do not write as soothsayers, enjoying a glimpse of the twenty-first century. But we do suggest that slowth is an immutable reality to which we must adjust during the next decade.

The readers of this book undoubtedly include many without technical training or even schooling in the field of economics. The broad and encompassing scope of *Slowth* is aimed at a broad audience, including perhaps the manager of a small business, the member of a large corporation, the homemaker, civil servant, political activist, those who have retired, students planning careers, journalists, and educators. We are writing for an ever widening audience of the bewildered—those who are concerned about the economic trends of the 1980s and how these trends affect them.

In our writing we forgo the usual formal structure of argument with its careful qualifications and consequent detail that is the economist's normal stock-in-trade. We do this in the hope of sharpening the understanding of a problem that is fundamental in nature.

We write as we do from a conviction in what we see. To proceed otherwise would require mountains of evidence to support our claims. Indeed it is hard to see how many of our ideas would gain unanimous support. But we move beyond these difficulties to alert our readers to the nature of the current economic trends that are challenging their living standards. In so doing we hope to go some way in helping make the choices we face in adjusting to slowth.

MARTIN KUPFERMAN
MAURICE D. LEVI

Vancouver, British Columbia
July 1980

Contents

chapter 1

Introduction

Slowth is not some misspelled word describing the indolence of the human condition. Nor is it the sluggish, three-toed creature that inhabits tropical forests. Rather it is the name we use to describe our current economic state—slow economic growth. Slowth lies behind the difficulties each of us faces in achieving the standard of living we desire. The national struggle to move ahead has become the increasingly futile effort each of us makes to stretch our budgets to suit our aspirations. Although that stretch has never quite fit, not even in the decades of the 1950s and 1960s, we are now seeing the emergence of forces that will stretch our budgets to the breaking point. These forces herald the era of slowth.

The roots of slowth date back to the 1960s at the earliest, when we began to adopt a new set of values that are now acting as a barrier to expanding production. These new values unwittingly support the slow growth in our national and individual economic well-being. In this era of slowth, we shall see reality continue to drift ever further from our material aspirations. The cause is not the limited although generous endowment of resources provided by nature. It is not the drain of dollars, siphoned off by Arab nations charging higher and higher prices for their oil. Nor does slowth stem from inflation. As we show, the battle of spiraling prices could indeed be fought and won while as a nation we would be no better off materially. Instead, slowth results from limits we ourselves are imposing on the vital materials, people power, and machines that we require for production.

Slowth has a very real meaning. It is not a product of the declining value of money so painfully apparent in the inflation statistics. Rather, slowth is the reality that lies behind those statistics. It is a slowing of the rate at which we generate new homes and haircuts, automobiles and airplane rides—the sum of all the goods and services that fill our national basket and provide our means to consume. Inflation threatens the value of our wages. Yet it is not inflation but instead a decrease in the amount we produce that forces us to make the adjustment to less.

Slowth has a very personal meaning for many of us. We find it increasingly harder to improve our living standards even with added dollars in the monthly paycheck. But despite our too familiar understanding of our own economic problems, we are unable to grasp the widespread nature of our plight from the myriad of economic statistics. Although the statistics do trace real and often complex phenomena—output, unemployment, inflation, and measures of the balance of trade and payments—exposure to too many statistics can confuse essential and simple facts. Like blind men vainly groping individual parts of the elephant's anatomy in an effort to discern the whole, many who seek meaning in statistics are unable to grasp the true essence of the subject. Yet the basic factor that determines living standards, like the shape of the elephant, is quite obvious. It is the level of output we collectively produce. And slowth means we are adding to our output of goods and services at a pace slower than that to which we have become accustomed.

Among the welter of economic statistics are those on output. They are simple to understand. During 1947–1973 real gross national product (GNP) per person, for all its weaknesses as a precise measure of gains, rose at an annual rate of 2.4 percent. This was cut in half, to 1.2 percent, during 1973–1977. Between these two periods, growth in real disposable income per person showed a similar decline, from 2.5 to 1.3 percent. When adjustments are made for increased federal government debt per person the average annual gains in the period up to 1973 fell from 2.2 percent to a paltry 0.1 percent. At this rate, each person in the United States improves his or her real buying power by a mere $8 per year!

In short, the standard of living has scarcely budged since 1973.

This is commonly attributed to a rampaging inflation that has wiped out monetary income gains. But the problem is not inflation itself; rising prices merely veil the truth. The essential cause is the drop in output growth or material production. As expressed by Senator Lloyd Bentsen, "You hold down the cost of living by producing more goods and services more cheaply."[1] We are just not producing the goods.

This emphasis on the rate of *production* as the determinant of continued growth in our living standards defies the conventional wisdom of post-Depression economics. The bedrock of policy since John Maynard Keynes has been the belief that the maintenance of real growth requires only the clever management of *demand*. Supply receives scant if any attention; the potential to produce a rising national output is viewed as ever present and naturally available. Keynesians are not the only ones to concentrate on demand while downplaying supply. Virtually all post-Depression economists fail to consider the nation's potential to produce, assuming that if demand is present, output will continue to grow. The difference between Keynesians and other theorists lies instead in the different policies they propose to influence demand.

All these policies stem from the false notion that demand is the only force that can hold our economy back. Ultimately, policies rooted in this belief contribute to inflation and the economic malaise in which we find ourselves mired. They aim to fine tune the level of demand and ignore the real supply constraints. Such misguided demand-oriented policies produce only inflation, currency crises, and continued deterioration of the country's balance of trade. But we intend to show more than the existence of the problem of slow growth. We aim to demonstrate that it is consciousness—our determination to pursue nonmaterial goals in defiance of their price—that is keeping our growth rates low. Slowth is the condition that we as a nation have allowed ourselves to choose.

This assertion that we have made such a choice is not a common view. Much of the economic performance of the 1970s has been dubbed a recession, implying that we have temporarily failed to advance our material standards. But how long can a recession last before we reduce our expectations, resigned to a lower rate of growth? In other words, how long must a recession last before it is no longer called a recession? This fundamental question must be answered within the 1980s as we are forced to shift economic gears downward to a state of slower growth. This claim is based on the advent of trends that transcend the cycles of business. The consciousness we have come to embrace is the chronic and deep-seated cause of slowth. And as we examine its nature, we see why it is emerging as a fundamental and long-term factor shaping the economic landscape.

By consciousness we mean the growing concern for the quality of the physical environment, for the welfare and well-being of our fellow citizens—particularly the sick and the old—and for a degree of safety from technological disaster in our own and future generations. The level of concern about the environment and technology has been raised over the course of the 1970s with the help of such institutions as the Sierra Club and the Club of Rome. It is during the 1970s that we saw the emergence of such vaguely defined concepts as "Small is Beautiful" and "Limits to Growth" and the evolution of such intangible goals as self-sufficiency and self-fulfillment. Concern for the welfare of our fellows has an institutional base that has been nurtured during recent years.

Institutionalized concern for the well-being of other members of society in preindustrial days was clearly a notion unconsidered; over the course of two wars and a depression it was an effort unaffordable. Today, welfare and social services are viewed as only a small part of a vast largess. Joblessness is now deemed so insufferable as to warrant unemployment insurance and a developed level of job protection.

"In the 1960's," commented Joseph Califano, former U.S. Secretary of the then Department of Health, Education and Welfare, "all these social programs didn't seem to cost the American people anything because we were all making more real income."[2] Califano's HEW—recently renamed and reorganized—stands as a monument to the enormity of our efforts to minister to our social consciousness. Its estimated budget in fiscal 1980 was almost $200 billion—the third largest budget in the world, exceeded only by the total budgets of the U.S. and Soviet governments. HEW expenditures, consuming almost 38 percent of the federal budget, are largely directed toward outlays that are appropriately called "entitlements." Califano estimated that nine of every ten HEW dollars are now spent in this manner, over which the government has limited effective control. Entitlement programs, including most major welfare programs—Social Security and Medicare, for example—are obligated to dispense benefits to all those who meet eligibility requirements.

Examples of our environmental consciousness are even more dramatic. The movement that embodies this concern has made striking gains in momentum and level of support. "Environment has become the Viet Nam of the middle class,"[3] observes one political scientist. The movement's accomplishments have been large indeed. Cars and factories are required to reduce air emissions. Dumping of sewage and wastes into our nation's rivers and streams has been sharply reduced. Offshore drilling and coal mining are closely monitored, regulated, and highly constrained.

The tightening of regulation and the process of monitoring is also the result of a longer term and wider concern about the potential dangers of new technology. The stagnation of the nuclear power industry is one of the more obvious results of the enforcement of our safety consciousness through the regulatory and judicial system. But opposition to technological risk has worked in many quieter ways through government bodies, such as the Environmental Protection Agency, which has, among other moves, curtailed the use of many pesticides that help protect the nation's food crops.

American values have been transformed during the 1960s and 1970s, leaving us with a legacy of noble concerns. The society we have created is indeed more compassionate for those who are old, in trouble, or are yet unborn. We have become more cautious, perhaps more responsible. But these good deeds and intentions are not without a price. We shall pay for them through slowth. That price can be expressed not only monetarily but also in our feelings of well-being, emotions that we still measure in very concrete and individual ways. For us as individuals, slower growing material standards arising from these values will mean disappointment, a loss of confidence, and an eclipse of hope. The way rising living standards have become intertwined with our identities makes this an unavoidable consequence of any protracted economic slowdown.

Ultimately, the price we pay is the adjustments we are making in our life-styles and institutions because of the reality of slowth. We trim our aspirations and settle for less than we had grown to expect. Those who maintain their material goals are forced to pay with harder work, as perhaps both husband and wife find it necessary to hold jobs. Working to an older age becomes a more common practice for those who are spending more of their current incomes and reducing their savings in an effort to maintain or improve current standards. Large families are becoming less affordable. Individuals are continually uprooted in the geographic scramble for job advancement. Our universities are being transformed into high-powered vocational institutes teaching "professions" and recycling those whose education does not equip them to compete in the harsher struggle for material well-being.

Passive acceptance of ill fate is not common to the American heritage. Indeed, there are those who use slowth as an instrument for positive change in their lives. Their efforts to cut consumption spur a more creative use of leisure time, involving more personal input and less spending. Bicycle and hiking outings replace trips to Europe and Disneyland. Some of us are developing our personal skills more fully, doing more reading and crafts, learning about the arts, developing our bodies and minds.

For others in this society, the reaction to slowth will be venomous. Strife and turmoil will spread as disappointment and frustration are vented on the system that no longer provides the goods. Indeed, isolated skirmishes have already begun. In July of 1979, most of the U.S. independent truckers went on strike to protest a variety of grievances. It was a brief but violent episode in which more than one person was killed, and a number were beaten and threatened. The truckers were striking over a number of long-standing issues, including diesel prices and onerous regulation of their industry, which they claimed jeopardized their financial viability. Although this anger appears to have stemmed from conditions specific to the industry, the sentiments expressed by one trucker will be echoed by the many and varied interest groups that fall victim to a slowdown of the economy. Says George Sullivan, organizer of one truckers association, in referring to diesel prices and bothersome regulation, "When the truckers are making money, they can put up with all that. But when they're not making money, they get very hostile."[4] We see an alarming potential for the spread of hostility.

The truckers' strike of July 1979 is just one of the early episodes in a series of struggles that we call the slowth skirmishes. There will be other conflicts that have no direct link to broad concepts such as growth, consciousness, or national income. They will appear on the nightly news as isolated, often parochial issues. Yet it will be the frustration and heat of slowth that will spark them. Slowth skirmishes will surface in any number of communities over nuclear power, pesticide use, taxes, or the price of a key commodity, such as oil. They will be rooted in the personal disappointment and frustration brought on by the era of slowth. And they will feature hostility between those who feel materially deprived and those who find greater value in less tangible concerns.

For most Americans, taking their frustrations to the streets seems decidedly foreign. Political expression is still normally channeled in wars of concepts. In such a political forum the reaction to slowth can be seen in another guise, the rise of anger over inflation. The present elevation of inflation to Public Enemy No. 1 is not the first time it has enjoyed such lofty status. This time, though, something is very different. Americans, on balance, will turn against this culprit for one essential reason: they see inflation as the phenomenon that holds them back from higher material standards, keeping them in continual motion on some economic treadmill. As we show in the arguments that follow, the public enemy, at least as far as living standards are concerned, is not inflation, but the slow growth of output that keeps these standards lagging behind what we have come to expect.

chapter 2

The Real Essentials

A few obvious targets are now receiving a large share of the hostility over stagnant living standards and the inflationary form in which slowth is disguised. Among them are the sheiks of the Organization of Petroleum Exporting Countries (OPEC) and the mandarins of the federal bureaucracy. Although they are obviously part of the problem, the roots of slowth go far deeper. Slow growth would be an increasing part of our scene even without our present-day bogeymen.

One descriptive notion by the great Scottish economist Adam Smith provides a good perspective. In his book *An Inquiry into the Nature and Causes of the Wealth of Nations,* which is exactly as old as the United States, Smith posits the existence of an invisible guiding hand that brings together the materials, people, and machines that work to provide a nation's products. What we produce, therefore, is a direct result of these three inputs. Technology is another key to production, since it influences the dexterity with which these inputs are combined and determines the productive capacity of each. Our national output only grows as the result of greater application of these inputs and technologies. What we are finding, though, is that our expanding consciousness is now acting to hold them back. The process of production is being constrained through controls on all inputs and technology, eliminating the means through which output can continue to grow.

Resource use is inhibited by our environmental consciousness.
The oil crisis of 1973 forced us to take inventory of our untapped
wealth. The huge jump in the world price of oil has been used to
justify drilling off our shores, most notably off the coasts of New
Jersey and California. Under the huge and beautiful states of Montana, Wyoming, and North Dakota lie deposits of what may be our
energy salvation—coal. Suddenly it has become imperative to divide
the state of Alaska and speed oil through a pipeline and in the
bellies of supertankers that skirt our western shores.

Yet the exploitation of all these forms of wealth has stirred a
level of environmental indignation and opposition that has arisen
out of the queasy realization that the dirty process of energy extraction can less and less be confined to barren deserts or the
frozen tundra of a foreign land. It is happening here, near our
homes. This concern has led to political pressure and a maze of
legislative enactments and lawsuits aimed at retarding the supply
of fuel our economy requires for growth.

Our access to Alaskan oil and gas was held back by debate
about extractive methods and routing. And coal, America's vast
energy resource, is rendered less economical to extract and use as
a result of a growing body of environmental protection laws and
regulations.

The effect of environmental consciousness in restricting resource inputs is in no way limited to energy. "The public must be
made aware of *all* resource crunches," warns Northwest Mining
Association President Marvin Chase, "not just the energy crunch,
before the lack of metal stops auto production. And before the
lack of lumber causes housing shortages or the lack of rangeland
use drives food prices even higher. The United States has enough
resources to sustain us at home and to trade in world markets. But
we don't have the national will to produce them."[1]

Evidence of the flagging national will strikes especially close
to home for Chase and the mining industry in the congressional
plan to carve out vast protected wilderness areas in Alaska. Opposed by mining, oil and gas, and forestry interests, that bill would
hit hard at Alaska's potential for providing natural resources.

From the seas, forests, and surface of the earth, we have taken
much of what is choice and easily reached. Resources are now

more remote from final markets, and the cost of continuing growth is higher both in dollars and in the environmental degradation required.

The harvesting of our nation's trees reveals how large the full extraction costs have become and why they will remain so. Logging is restrained by efforts aimed at preserving existing stands from the abuses inflicted in the past and protecting our threatened wilderness. Public opposition to clearcutting the nation's forests and exploiting the rich stands remaining on public lands have reduced our supply of available timber. But as we slow the rate at which we feed raw materials into the productive process, we shall find it harder if not impossible to get more out at the other end.

Our collective effort in work is falling victim to the system established by our social concern. We provide welfare, disability, and unemployment assistance to those who have trouble coping, and the rest of society pays. In the end these programs create a scissors effect that cuts at human effort with both its blades. The first cutting edge is the way the welfare system enables those who find little nonmonetary reward in work to reduce their effort and still survive. This is true not only for those who abandon work altogether, but also for those who apply less effort on the job. This trend is glaringly apparent in the declining level of effort exhibited in much of America at work. It is present in the level of service we experience at the bank, post office, supermarket, or government office. It is present on the factory floor. Often the result is a mere inconvenience to which we can adjust. But magnified in the giant national production process, this decrease in human input can only mean slower growth in output and therefore in what is available to each of us.

The other edge of the scissors formed by welfare and unemployment benefits is a reduction in the incentive to work among those who pay the taxes to maintain the programs. High taxes prevent real producers from receiving a full level of monetary reward. On one side, then, we have lost the output of those choosing the path of easier existence; and on the other, the reduced effort of those paying the taxes that provide the system with its financial support. The result is lower effort by both those who choose the easier path and those who are left to pay the bill.

Technological innovation is declining because of our unwillingness to accept the risks that are involved. The mechanism of steam was apparent to anyone who boiled water in a kettle. An understanding of the combustion engine might come easily to those who have been shaken by a bang. But laser beams, microwaves, quartz circuitry, and the splitting or combining of atomic particles are foreign to our daily experience. Moreover, their potential effects extend far beyond the realm of those who knowingly and willingly risk their use. Technological risk, as a result, is not only greatly enlarged but also, in the minds of many, completely unconscionable.

Technological innovation in a number of areas is under siege. Nuclear power has been all but blocked as a viable energy option because of severe doubt about its implications for our own future and for those yet unborn. The reaction against technological agriculture is rooted in the same concern. Opposition on an item-by-item basis to key pesticides and growth hormones has restricted their use, rendering the job of producing our food increasingly complex and expensive.

Confidence in controversial technology is difficult to achieve in the face of disagreement among scientists about its threat to our safety. As a result we grow increasingly fearful. This fear was summarized by economist Herman Daly in his reworking of a popular economic paradigm, Pascal's Wager. "We can err in two ways: we can accept the omnipotent technology hypothesis and then discover that it is false, or we can reject it and later discover that it is true. Which error do we wish most to avoid? If we accept the true hypothesis, the result will be catastrophic. If we reject the true hypothesis, we will forego marginal satisfaction."[2] Even when our technological advance has come in a form with no obvious environmental or safety risks, a different form of consciousness has helped hold us back. Our orientation toward saving jobs and preventing the displacement of those whose careers and work are at stake has at times checked the adoption of the optimal technology. Clean and safe technologies like those becoming available in offices and in the typesetting rooms of some of our daily newspapers have met with strong resistance from those who have the most to lose—their jobs. Yet again these well-motivated concerns do little to enhance output. Along with environmental and safety checks, they hold back much of what we could produce. But if these constraints were confined to existing technology alone, they would not cause the drag on production we are now experiencing. However, regulation invoked for our protection has also weakened the prospects for innovation.

The adoption by regulatory agencies of conservative policies mitigating against technological risk has cut away at investment in research and development. The technology of the future will inevitably suffer, and, along with it, growth rates of national output will decline. For each of us, therefore, the growth in our individual standards of living will turn downward alarmingly. Even if dollar wages rise, inflation must inevitably wipe real gains away.

Investment is discouraged by our regulated consciousness. Our concerns for the environment, human safety, and social welfare have been transformed into a maze of complex government regulations and controls. Both the regulations themselves and the proliferation of civil litigation that has ensued have added to the uncertainty and ultimate cost of a wide range of investments. In some cases specific projects already have been abandoned. In other cases projects even fail to make it past the corporate boardroom as a direct result.

The proliferation of regulation has cast a cloud of uncertainty over the key business decision of whether to invest. Not only is total investment reduced in the process, but much of the investment that does take place is not for machines that contribute to production, but rather for those that minimize the way production violates our consciousness. Investment in antipollution and safety equipment forms a big part of investment in the most important productive sectors of our economy—electric utilities, petroleum, chemicals, paper, and steel. As a result, not only is the amount of investment constrained by our consciousness-enforcing effort, but a substantial part of what is invested cannot produce the output we desire.

The subversion of the productive process is the point of origin of the new era of slowth. While this era is being ushered in by talk of inflation, recession, or inappropriate government policy, the basic truth is that we have constrained the growth of our production to rates that are too low to satisfy our collective material aspirations. Growth of output is being slowed by a reduction in growth in *all* the types of input that are necessary—materials, human effort, and machinery—as well as by the barriers we have placed on the advance of technology. If there is slower growth in the number of goods we can enjoy, any income gains we separately experience must on average be offset by the higher prices of what we buy. We have all seen how easily this can occur.

The aim of this book is to render the causes and consequences of slowth clear, rather than to decry the evolution of consciousness. In the process it traces the nature of the modern economic dilemma that baffles most economists and government policymakers. Their failure to recognize slowth and its *roots in the constraints on supply* have contributed to our poor economic state. Whatever the outcome of the struggle between those favoring growth and those advocating a consciousness-led improvement in the quality of life, our collective welfare stands to be improved from the recognition of the existence and causes of slowth. The lack of understanding has led governments to construe slowth as recession and has led to economic tinkering on a broad scale.

As part of the knee-jerk reaction to anything resembling a downward turn of the business cycle, public spending is stepped up or taxes reduced. As the attempt is made to spend our way out of our dilemma, the public sector grows, and more people are hired as part of an expanding range of government programs. Other efforts to breathe life into the economy have unfortunately expanded the money supply, thus causing inflation to exist alongside slowth—an economic condition known as stagflation. Yet none of these demand-oriented policies will correct the real cause that lies behind our failure to produce. They will, however, result in an ever larger government sector, which is intractable, essentially irreversible, and costly to maintain. The result of all this will be inflation as the government continues to ignore, and tries to spend its way out of, slowth.

But these are not the only side effects of slowth. It has also played havoc with the foreign exchange value of the U.S. dollar. Americans are still trying to raise their living standards at rates equal to those of the past, oblivious to the slowdown in the rate at which we produce. The only way we can consume more than we produce is by supplementing our own production with the output surplus of other nations. It is not coincidental that these are nations whose production is less hampered by a national consciousness like ours. From them we supplement our own inadequate production of steel and oil, cars and bicycles, cameras, stereos, clothing, and other items we continue to buy. In this way we trade off the longer term and less tangible substance of financial strength for the real items that provide our material "needs." The immediate result has been immense balance of payment deficits and the fall in the value of the U.S. dollar. This pattern stems not only from our failure to produce (or conserve) sufficient oil, as popular mythology would have it, but also from the fact that as a nation we are not producing the gamut of goods we desire at internationally competitive prices.

The result of the costly shackles on production is that in those cases where domestic goods actually compete in quality they fail to measure up in price. But a visit to the department store reveals an even more frightening trend: foreign televisions, stereos, cameras, and sporting goods and clothes are often all there is to purchase.

The process of supplementing our own inadequate production with foreign goods cannot go on without end. In the long run we can consume only as much as we ourselves produce. Immutably, a nation whose production slows will also have to slow the rate at which it adds to what it consumes. One result of our effort to live beyond our own productive means (and one we have seen) is a cut in the foreign exchange value of our dollar. Sinking with the dollar is our ability to afford the products of other nations that prop up our consumption habits.

Theories abound that purport to explain our puzzling economic circumstances. Most trace our dismal condition to the lack of some single vital input. Included are those theories that beat the energy drum and those that indict the ballooning nonproductive bureaucracy. There are theories claiming that we tax and regulate away the incentive to invest or that we don't innovate as we did in the past. Some maintain that we let interest rates rise too high; others say that the work force is being swelled with the unskilled. But to suggest that any one factor is responsible is to raise the hopes of a quick and easy remedy. Such suggestions stem from a failure to perceive the bind we have placed on *all* our productive inputs in an effort to secure a higher quality of life. And they ignore the looming battle between an expanding national consciousness and our standard of material life.

chapter 3

Environmentalism and the Material Input

Ecotopia, published in 1975, is a popular account of an environmentalist's vision. Fred Callenbach opens his story as the more environmentally conscious states—Washington, Oregon, and northern California—secede from the United States and form a new country called Ecotopia. Hydroelectric dams are dynamited to allow for recreational use of rivers; the aluminum industry is abandoned and the automobile completely banned. The population is dispersed to the countryside.

Callenbach presents the following balanced assessment of his land of make-believe: "Ecotopian air and water are everywhere crystal clear. The land is well cared for and productive. Food is plentiful, wholesome and recognizable. All life systems are operating on a stable-state basis, and can go on doing so indefinitely. The health and general well-being of the people are undeniable. . . . On the other hand, these benefits have been bought at a heavy cost. . . . The Ecotopian industrial capacity and standard of consumption [are] markedly below ours, to a degree that would never be tolerated by Americans." This reference is to the halving of the incomes of individual Ecotopians, a condition that most of us would have trouble associating with a utopia of any kind.

In spite of an undoubtedly negative reaction to such an extreme state of affairs, many Americans have come to support the cause of clean air and water, less noise, clean beaches, and a host of other concerns aroused by an environmental consciousness. Included under the broad umbrella of environmentalists are people with vastly different concerns. Some worry about pollution. Others want to protect the earth from the ravages of resource extraction. Another group is concerned about the "greedy" consumption of resources and the threat it poses for future generations. Common to all these concerns is the singular potential effect they have on our material standard of living. Translated into action—as indeed they have been—they slow or render more expensive the process of extracting and using our material resources. In this role environmental consciousness, and the movement it has created, is a prime contributor to slowth.

"The environmental movement is growing stronger in the sense that it is becoming institutionalized. It's out of the streets," remarked one observer, an official of the U.S. Environmental Protection Agency (EPA). The date that marks the change in the movement from one of isolated protest to a cohesive and powerful political force may be Earth Day—April 22, 1970. On this day millions of Americans demonstrated simultaneously in all parts of the nation. These events drew upon the spirit of the anti-Vietnam War movement and established a legitimacy of numbers. Today there is no doubt that "the environmental lobby" is a major political force in the United States. It is hard to believe that the institutionalized environmental movement is so young, and that the EPA, the largest federal regulatory unit, was established only after Earth Day, on December 2, 1970.

Today's environmental organizations are no longer solely ad hoc groupings of single-minded individuals. They are more often slick public-relations-minded operations, which employ techniques characteristic of the nation's largest corporations. Their major tool is no longer public protest. "They have had a tremendous influence in shaping the laws,"[1] says EPA Administrator Douglas Costle in reference to environmentalists. This influence is drawn from the American public's widespread support. One survey estimates that from 5 to 8 million Americans belong to at least one environmental group. Clearly, the size and budget of such groups indicates an established support.

The Sierra Club has been the most visible and well-known environmental protection group. It is now one of the strongest. Its membership has grown at the rate of 7 to 8 percent every year for the past six years. But its strength comes not only from numbers— members are almost 200,000 strong—but also because of its influence as a lobbying group. "To be effective we must be in their [legislative] offices and committee rooms when crucial decisions are being made,"[2] says Raymond Sherwin, a former President. And indeed a number of Sierra Club campaigns have been highly effective, including those advocating environmental protection in the process of energy extraction and those opposing supersonic transport and the cutting of timber in the national forests.

The Sierra Club is but one of a large number of other like-minded organizations. U.S. environmental groups now number over 3000, and almost all have sprung up since the mid-1960s. Among these are the Environmental Defense Fund, the Friends of the Earth, the Environmental Law Institute, the League of Conservation Voters, and the Natural Resources Defense Council.

All the environmental groups would be markedly less effective without a particularly powerful weapon that the environmental movement lobbied for and obtained. This is the National Environmental Policy Act of 1969, also known as the EPA Act after the agency that enforces it. Its enactment as a federal statute, virtually without opposition, indicates the perception by our officials of the ground swell of environmental support. Its passage came on the heels of the oil-well leakage in Santa Barbara, which blackened that area's beaches and darkened the American public's view of environmental risk-taking. The function of the act is to incorporate into important economic decisions safeguards against the befouling of our air, land, and water by requiring that wide-ranging impact statements be included to quantify prospective government actions potentially affecting the environment.

The National Environmental Policy Act has had enormous implications. Its effects have been unforeseen. "Under this hopeless confusion, the environment is running the government," commented *Oil and Gas Journal,* a business publication. But the EPA Act does not, as implied, include environmentalists within the decision-making process. It doesn't have to.

The potency of the EPA Act comes in its providing environmentalists a tool, a tangible focal point, with which to take the government to court. Says one member of an environmental group, Denis Hayes of World Watch Institute, "In the past, environmentalists would dump diseased fish on the rug of corporate headquarters. Now we take the corporation to court to force them to stop water pollution."[3] The greatest number of legal cases involve highway construction and, to a lesser degree, urban renewal projects, dam construction, and nuclear power projects. Based on objections to, or alleged errors and inadequacies of, the environmental impact statements, concerned groups have succeeded in arresting or delaying a great deal of economic activity. Foremost among these was the tie-up of the Alaska oil pipeline, delayed for over three years before Congress intervened in the wake of the 1973 Arab Oil Embargo.

Court challenge of the environmental impact statement has also thrown roadblocks in the path of the nuclear power industry. In the case of the Vermont Yankee plant, the U.S. Circuit Court of Appeals ruled that before granting a plant's operating license, the Nuclear Regulatory Commission (NRC) must consider the weighty matter of the environmental impact posed by nuclear waste disposal. In a striking decision, that same court ruled with regard to a Michigan plant that the NRC was obliged to consider energy conservation as an alternative to nuclear power as part of the impact statement. A number of states have followed the lead of the federal government in requiring impact statements, many of which are concerned with air and water quality.

Environmental groups are using the courts more and more frequently and, according to one estimate, have some 600 full-time lawyers on their staffs, with a war chest of $25 million for litigation. Two large groups, the Environmental Defense Fund and the Natural Resources Defense Council, draw on their membership of more than 80,000 to financially support their sizable court activity. These and other groups have scored some impressive victories.

Lost in thirteen years of legal wrangling was a coal-fired generating plant to have been built on Kaiparowitz Plateau in southern Utah. It would have been the nation's largest such development. Environmentalists feared that pollutants would destroy ancient and scenic rock formations, and they carried their case to the courts. Many years of delay drove the estimated cost of the plant from $780 million to $3.5 billion, a cost that became prohibitive for the members of the proposed consortium. Lost was a 300 megawatt plant, which would have powered the homes of 3 million people for a very long time indeed.

Those familiar with the case of the Kaiparowitz Plateau plant are well equipped to answer the following question: what do the snail darter fish, the Furbish lousewort, the Virginia fringed mountain snail, and the orange-bellied mouse have in common? Answer: they have all imparted a case of shivers and headaches to major construction project planners across the United States. As forms of life alleged to be endangered by specific projects, they have caused the delay or abandonment of some projects, a few of which were major in magnitude.

The most celebrated case was the use of the courts to invoke the Endangered Species Act to protect the 3-inch snail darter fish against extinction by the construction of the Tellico Dam on the fish's Tennessee habitat. The act states that no federal funds may be spent on a project that will obliterate any plant or animal species. At stake in the environmental plea, sustained by the U.S. Supreme Court, was the fish's home, which would have been transformed into a stagnant lake by the dam. The Tellico Dam, already partly complete, has become, in the words of former Tennessee Governor Ray Blanton, "the world's largest monument to the world's smallest fish."[4]

The three other creatures have had smaller impacts, but ones that are by no means inconsequential. The orange-bellied mice are little fellows who crave salt and make their homes in marshes like the property considered for a 1.6 million kilowatt coal-fired generating plant in the San Francisco Bay Area. A report prepared by the local regulatory commission suggests that the site be moved to an alternate, if less suitable, location.

The Virginia fringed mountain snail is a creature 3 millimeters in length, which, because of its endangered species status, managed to halt the widening of a highway in Virginia that was slated

to run through the snail's only known habitat. The Furbish lousewort, named after the botanist who first discovered it, is a small
plant with fernlike leaves and yellow flowers. The existence of the
lousewort was threatened by the Dickey-Lincoln Dam on the St.
John River in Maine. The fate of both the lousewort and the dam
are being decided by the courts. As symbols of our environmental
concerns, and the cost of these concerns, the importance of these
creatures far outweighs their size. They demonstrate the evolution
of the United States from a nation obsessed with production and
growth to one with interests that now include protection of even
the smallest forms of life. Such a shift in values is not without its
ramifications for each of us, one of which is the constraint it imposes on inputs required for the production of our goods. As we
enact these concerns, we hold back the output that determines our
material standards. With a slowdown in the production of what we
demand, inflation must gain on our incomes to restrict what we
can buy to what is available.

Congress's commitment to the Endangered Species Act seemed
to falter in the fall of 1979. The Tellico Dam episode was too
much for legislators to accept, and an exemption for the dam was
passed as a rider to a piece of unrelated legislation. Nevertheless,
renewal of the Endangered Species Act seems possible, much to
the disadvantage of the large multinational Monsanto Company.
Monsanto operates a chemical plant in Muscatine, Iowa, home of
the brown Illinois mud turtle. The distinct prospect of having the
plant area declared a "critical habitat" for the creature has Will
Carpenter, the Director of Environmental Operations, very worried; "It could shut down the plant or just mean further bureaucratic delays every time we need a permit."[5]

To allay that prospect, Monsanto has been sending teams of
scientists into the field to track the turtle's activities. The sum of a
half million dollars was spent to trap, tag, and take a turtle shell
count. For the purpose of learning about their nesting and feeding
habits, radio transmitters were placed on the backs of some of the
creatures. Raccoons and skunks in the area were trapped to keep
them from disrupting the turtles' nests. The study's results revealed
that the area contained more turtles than originally thought, some
2000 rather than the 150 that the U.S. Department of the Interior

believed present. "We're glad they found more turtles," replied the Department's Kenneth Dodd, Jr., "but that doesn't mean it's not endangered."[6]

"We are now in the middle of a long process of transition in the nature of the image which man has of himself and his environment. Primitive men, and to a large extent also men of early civilizations, imagined themselves to be living in a virtually illimitable plain," wrote economist Kenneth Boulding as we entered the 1970s. Up to the time that Boulding wrote those words, few people would have foreseen the blossoming of environmental consciousness. Our economy and standard of living were fed by prodigious use of our forests, minerals, fossil fuels, and hydroelectric sites. Boulding dubbed this a "cowboy economy," that image denoting "the illimitable plains . . . [and] reckless, exploitative, romantic, and violent behavior."[7] A prudent, watchdog approach was clearly not the order of the day.

Today times have indeed changed. We are in the midst of Boulding's transition to what he calls a "spaceship" economy "in which the earth has become a single spaceship, without unlimited reservoirs of anything." Even television advertising, with its spongelike absorption of every fad and trend, uses concepts such as "inner space" and "limited space" to sell its more environmentally conscious fare. And although there may not be a cheerful embrace of such a concept, there is undoubtedly a growing awareness of it all.

Today's environmental consciousness is far different from the movement of the early 1900s that gave meaning to the term "conservation." This distinction is made clear by historian Samuel Hays, of the University of Pittsburgh, who points out that the heroes of yesterday's conservation movement are among today's environmental villains. They include the Tennessee Valley Authority, the U.S. Forest Service, and the Bureau of Reclamation. Hays attributes this to a vast difference in the philosophies that underlie both movements. The conservation movement was, in Hays's words, "dominated by the perspective of 'efficient production.' "[8] Much of that movement was designed to eliminate waste in our use of resources. Hays thinks the conservation movement gave way, beginning in the 1960s, to an environmental ethic "with a strong connotation of 'quality' or 'amenity' rather than efficient economic development. . . . Clean production is not enough; basic production goals must be restricted to make way for 'quality of life' goals."

The environmental ethic is apparent in our attitude toward the production of our fossil fuels and, in particular, coal. Despite the talk of "energy crisis," and the Jimmy Carter Administration's exhortation to pursue conservation with a fervor that is "the moral equivalent of war,"[9] it is accurate to say that America does not face a shortage of fossil fuels. Rather it is a shortage at the price we are willing to pay. And that price has come to include American environmental consciousness.

The United States, coal company officials are fond of saying, is the "Persian Gulf" of coal. In the strict sense they are correct. Coal reserves are said to be sufficient to last several hundred years at our present consumption level. But this is only a matter of potential and not of fact. In reality, while coal comprises more than 75 percent of U.S. fossil fuel reserves, it supplies less than 25 percent of our fossil fuel needs. One reason for this is clear: coal bears too high an environmental price tag. When the price of environmental protection is included in the cost of coal, far less can be profitably used. That high price of environmental concern has been ensured through a number of pieces of federal legislation.

Almost half of today's 600 million ton production of coal is extracted by strip, or surface, mining. This is the cheaper method of removing coal from the top down, rather than burrowing underneath the earth. Open-pit mining has become increasingly efficient with the development of a remarkable family of giant earth-moving equipment, which can peel off layers of earth more than 200 feet thick to get at the beds of coal.

One of the largest earth-moving machines is called, with a mixture of awe and affection, "Big Muskie." It weighs 27 million pounds, stands thirty-two stories high, and runs on 170 electric motors. Other earth-moving machines, like one in Egypt Valley, Ohio, have interiors so large that they have shower and dressing rooms for the crew.

Naturally, these machines visit an enormous ecological trauma upon the countryside. They notch hillsides and decapitate mountains to expose the coal seams. They denude an area of its vegetation and poison its water with acid drainage from the sediment that is being constantly eroded. That is the environmental legacy of the Appalachian region, where most of the nation's strip-mined coal is extracted. That legacy predates reclamation, which today is a mandatory part of surface coal mining.

But the real coal bonanza—particularly of low-sulfur seams lying close to the surface—is in the great American West. The Great Plains states of North Dakota, Montana, and Wyoming have vast reserves that are yet untouched. Higher costs of substitute fuels now render these reserves economically exploitable despite the high costs of transporting the coal to areas where it is used.

The potential for environmental degradation, however, is as large as the size of the coal reserves themselves. With this in mind Congress and the Carter Administration, amid much debate and controversy, enacted a bill aimed at preventing the strip mining excesses of the past. The new law requires stripped land to be restored to the approximate condition that existed before the mining process began. In the steeper areas of Appalachia now being mined, these requirements will raise production costs sharply. However, in areas of the West, because of the low moisture conditions, reclamation may not be possible at all, according to a study done for the Ford Foundation. Moreover, removal of coal seams that act to trap underground water would disrupt the region's water supply and remove a source of valuable moisture. Cheap strip mining of coal in fact may not be a viable option in parts of the West.

The utility of alternate coal sources has also been reduced by our concern for the environment. Coalfields in Illinois, Indiana, and western Kentucky are blessed by abundant rainfall and seams that lie close to the surface. Extraction is cheap and reclamation possible. But the difficulty lies in the quality of the coal, which is of a polluting high-sulfur variety—the type that produces acid rains. Rainwater tested recently in New England bears more likeness to acidy vinegar than normal rainwater. Claims have been made that the growth of the area's forests and the life in its lakes have been choked off by the acidic rain. The Clean Air Act of 1970 and a 1977 amendment have reflected environmental concern by imposing emission standards and requiring scrubbers and other devices to be installed in coal-fired plants. These are rendering the use of coal more expensive. As a result, some electric power plants east of the Mississippi River have switched from coal to oil as their source of generating fuel. This is directly contrary to the goals of the administrations since Richard Nixon, all of which encouraged the conversion from oil to coal. During the Nixon Administration, seventy-four utility boilers were ordered to convert, yet few did so. The Carter Administration has enjoyed only limited success in getting utilities to convert. The major reasons why coal use has failed to catch on are environmental ones. Not only does mandatory federal antipollution equipment make conversion to coal a costly prospect for utilities, but a number of state and local air pollution standards are actually stiffer than federal ones.

Environmental constraints on the use of coal do not stop here. The U.S. Department of the Interior has proposed a five-year moratorium on surface mining on prime agricultural land. Depending on how such land is defined and how restrictions are enforced, mining in the coal and farm regions of Illinois, Indiana, and Kentucky may be seriously curtailed. As a result of our environmental concerns, the use of coal has scarcely risen in importance as a part of the U.S. energy picture. The demand for coal increases marginally each year, yet it falls far short of supply. Some producers have cut work schedules at their mines and are laying off miners. Since the Arab Oil Embargo, the use of coal as a percentage of the U.S. energy requirements has risen by something in the order of a paltry 1 percent.

The problems limiting the use of coal also prevail in the case of another major potential source of fossil fuel—oil shale. Resources located in Colorado, Utah, and Wyoming can be extracted using methods similar to those of coal mining. The problems of reclamation, however, are even greater because of the larger volumes of spent shale and the limited water resources in these mountainous regions.

Another potential source of energy is found in oil and gas reserves that lie off our shores. Offshore fuels have been a growing source of U.S. energy supplies. Offshore oil now amounts to almost 20 percent of domestic production, most of that coming from wells in the Gulf of Mexico. The oil and gas industry has had high hopes of large new strikes in basins that lie along the outer continental shelf. The primary areas of exploration lie adjacent to the populated East Coast and California and along large areas of the southern Alaska coast.

One major exploration area is the more than 800,000 acres of deep trench off the coast of eastern New Jersey known as the Baltimore Canyon. Estimates of its potential vary sharply, as does reaction to drilling so close to such a densely populated region. Environmentalists, again using the National Environmental Policy Act as their tool, mounted a court challenge to the impact statement that was required before drilling could begin. This action was sufficient to delay the start of exploration for eighteen months, resulting in a cost to the industry of some $130 million for interest on funds required to secure the lease. Although drilling has finally begun, further obstacles to offshore drilling remain. In an effort to incorporate local and state consultation into the granting of offshore leases, amendments are pending before Congress to change the leasing process; delays may become longer and the procedure more expensive.

To the many people living near potential drilling sites, it is essential to have greater input of opinion to ensure care in granting leases. They have seen too many graphic examples on the nightly news of well blowouts and tanker spills. The massive ecological traumas of Santa Barbara and Ekofisk (in the North Sea) are still vivid in their minds. But such events, as dramatic as they seem, are insignificant when compared with chronic routine discharges that emanate from wells and oil tankers. While still at a very low level, such chronic discharges are thought to harm salt marshes and estuaries, which are important biological breeding grounds.

In the eyes of many people, offshore drilling poses a far more direct threat to the environment than the shipment of oil past their shores. Should exploration prove successful, a frightening scenario may be realized for residents of these areas. According to the Ford Foundation in its study *A Time to Choose, America's Energy Future,* "Once production of oil and gas begins, the storage tanks, pipelines, terminals, refineries and gas producing plants must be ready. In addition, petrochemical complexes and electric power plants may be attracted to the region by the green light for industrialization that offshore drilling signals."

Few communities have been able to halt drilling and the environmental changes it brings, but one state may have a good portion of its land declared off bounds for development. In May 1979 the House of Representatives passed Bill HR 39, which would, if passed by the Senate, establish 116 million acres of land as park and refuge. That bill would set aside an area in Alaska the size of California and in one step double the acreage of the federal park system.

The bill has stirred up controversy that extends well beyond the borders of Alaska. Two thousand people gave testimony before the House—a turnout greater than any single piece of legislation since the Civil Rights Act of 1964. A number of them agreed with Representative Morris Udall, the act's sponsor, who provided this wistful statement supporting the bill: "Suppose that a century ago, Abe Lincoln sent you West, that he said 'go bring me 100 million acres to preserve!' What would you have picked? Jackson Hole? The Grand Tetons? All of Arizona? Before they burned the land, before they chopped the timber? What would you pick if you could turn the clock back, see the tall grasses blowing on the prairies in Kansas; see the Rockies looming; see the land the way God made it? If we save parts of Alaska, people can have that experience."[10]

It was probably not statements like these that led to passage in the House, but a fit of political reaction against the big oil companies suspected of manipulating gas supplies. The oil companies argued against the loss of potentially valuable reserves that might lie in a number of areas, such as the 13.5 million acre Arctic Wildlife Refuge near the oil-rich Prudhoe Bay. United States Energy Department officials estimate that the area has one of the largest potential onshore petroleum deposits in the United States. Says Jay Mitchell, Atlantic Richfield Company's Public Lands Coordinator, about the Refuge, "If the oil companies had only one more well to drill, that is where it would be."[11] The resource potential of Alaska, quite apart from this one area, is enormous in items of oil, gas, coal, and a number of minerals. Those opposing the parks bill claim that even resources on the land beyond the proposed patchwork wilderness boundaries are inaccessible.

Those advocating the preservation of Alaskan land have a markedly different perspective from those who focus on economic growth and the extraction of resources. Writes Susan Schiefelbein in a *Saturday Review* feature story, "There are deeper questions at the heart of the Alaska problem than how much land to develop and how much to preserve. First, what is progress? If it is a studied march toward a mechanized, profitable but undesirable and uninhabitable world, some of us may wish to fall out of the parade."[12] Those falling out, and the resource potential that they take with them, are a key part of the slide into slowth.

Even the transport of Alaskan oil is a victim of growing environmental concern. It is the height of irony that after several years of debate, three years of pipeline construction, and outlays of $9 billion, Alaskan oil has had nowhere to go. Export abroad has been forbidden by Congress and its availability on the West Coast has exceeded refining capacity. Yet alternative plans to transport the oil to areas of need in the Midwest have been stymied by a string of environmental objections. Plans for a superport of call were vigorously opposed by residents and elected representatives of two proposed sites—Port Angeles, Washington and Kitimat, British Columbia.

The following statement articulates the dilemma of those who value both a high-quality environment and growing living standards. It was made by Andrew Thompson, Chairman of the Canadian commission investigating the building of a Kitimat port. "Whether they be motel operators, sport fishermen, shore workers, naturalists or just plain citizens, people are indignantly outspoken. Some have been pessimistic; they think what the oil companies want, they get. Some have spoken about the contradiction between the dependence on petroleum products to heat their homes and power their cars, on one hand and their opposition to an oil port on the other."[13]

That same dilemma was addressed in California, where environmentalism is institutionalized by regulatory bodies that preclude the need for ad hoc commissions like Thompson's. One such group, the California Air Quality Resources Board, blocked efforts by Standard Oil of Ohio (Sohio) to convert 800 miles of unused natural gas pipeline into a mode of transport for the oil. The line would have run from Long Beach, California, to Texas, where oil would have been refined and transported east. "It would be tantamount to ending all efforts to restore healthy air to the Los Angeles area,"[14] said the Chairman of the Board, Thomas Quinn, in reference to pumping oil from tankers into the pipeline. A compromise was reached that committed Sohio to removing more air pollutants than those that its port and pipeline activities would inject. Sohio agreed to do this, partly by reducing in some way the hydrocarbon emissions of thirteen local dry-cleaning plants. Work on the terminal for receiving the oil might one day commence, but the delay will mean that the pipeline planned since 1974 will not be pumping oil to Texas for some time to come.

The heat set off by the Sohio pipeline debate became unusually intense. "The State blessed it. I annointed it with holy water. The company does not want the pipeline; they want to sell the oil to Japan," cried California Governor Jerry Brown. Sohio's President, Alton Whitehouse, retorted at a Senate Energy Committee meeting in March 1979 that his company was tired of being "the skunk at the lawn party."[15] Federal politicians also added color and took sides in the raucus debate. "I believe the State of California, not the company welshed. Governor Brown and his air quality board welshed,"[16] cried New Mexico Senator Pete Domenici.

The significance of the battle between Sohio and the California Air Quality Resources Board is not trivial. Without a pipeline, the Alaskan oil that cannot be used by refineries on the West Coast must be hauled through the Panama Canal to the Gulf ports at an extra cost of up to $1 for each barrel of oil. This involves shipping no less than 600,000 barrels this way each day. Yet the delays were allowed to drag on. "Our institutions are paralyzed," said Washington Senator Henry Jackson. "We simply cannot seem to make a decision any more."[17] The decision here is between the environment and growth. It is not an easy one to make.

A similar example—again concerning that precious input, oil—can be found north of Los Angeles in Kern County, part of California's San Joaquin Valley. Enhanced recovery methods of the area's heavy oil reserves are becoming more attractive at high world oil prices. These reserves could contribute as much as an additional 40,000 barrels a day to domestic production. Since the crude oil is thick, the recovery procedure involves using steam pressure to make the oil flow. Prospects for production dimmed in late 1978, when a temperature inversion dramatically worsened the region's air quality. The steam generators used in the heavy oil process were found to violate the state's environmental regulations and were shut down. Since that time a number of generators were enjoined from resuming operations without pollution-reducing scrubbers. As this makes the heavy-oil process uneconomical, production has been steadily declining.

It has been said of our energy prospects that no one energy source is liable to be sufficient. This was the conclusion of a major study by the Ford Foundation, *A Time to Choose, America's Energy Future.* "In this same post-1985 period, some supplies can be expected from unconventional sources, including solar energy, geothermal energy, and solid organic wastes. However, total energy requirements even at the lower rate of growth will be so large as to require continued expansion of conventional supplies. We must either make major commitments to at least two of the four troublesome energy sources noted earlier—oil imports, nuclear power, the Rocky Mountain coal and shale, and drilling off the East and West coasts—or we must go ahead with all four on a more moderate scale."

Our environmental consciousness goes well beyond its influence over coal, oil, and other forms of energy inputs into our national production process. Environmentalism extends to another important material input, timber, which helps us generate our nation's output. Some of the most crucial inputs into housing, paper, furniture, and many other important products are derived from our nation's trees. Our newly found appreciation of the value of our timber resources provides another powerful example of the constraint that expanded consciousness has placed on inputs that determine our national output and standard of living.

Although our trees are a renewable resource over time, they need a long growth period to regenerate. Awareness of this has made us more conscious of the dangers that forest mismanagement poses to this national heritage. The harvesting of timber by means of clearcutting, the disregard of the need for reforestation, and the depletion of genetically superior stands loom large among the excesses of the past. These excesses have given rise to enactment of new forest management policies, which constrain the growth of the timber harvest, and entail a rejection of our old "cowboy" ways. Today our new forest management policies also deprive us of the remaining rich and accessible timber stands. This restriction first became a problem during the 1970s. Until that time the supply of softwood timber from private sources was amply supplemented by the harvest of trees from within the national forests and other public lands.

Since then, however, supply from some of the timber-rich western United States has been placed out of reach by the pressure on the U.S. Forest Service to convert national forests (and some private land) into untouchable wilderness areas. According to *Forbes,* "Estimates are that in the early 1980's timber harvested on privately held Northwest forest lands will begin declining, making forest products companies even more dependent on what is known as the 'Forest Service game.' "[18]

Today the national forests contain the last sizable untapped source of high-quality, older timber. The U.S. Forest Service controls an estimated 50 percent of the existing potential softwood supplies. Nevertheless, the government has failed to expand the harvest from these areas, which are largely in the Rockies and the Pacific Northwest. According to the National Forest Products Association, only 27 percent of the nation's timber supplies come from our national forests, as opposed to the 34 percent obtained from the much smaller timber inventory (16 percent) under private sector control. Instead of expanding the use of the federal forests, pressure from environmentalists has led to the further removal of national forestry acres from production. A decision made by Carter to designate over 15 million acres as wilderness will supplement the present 19 million acres placed out of bounds for commercial use. Other measures before Congress may result in the protection (or loss) of a great many more acres than those already set aside.

Timber supply has not been limited only by the withdrawal of new wilderness land. The U.S. Forest Service, an arm of the U.S.

Department of Agriculture, has employed a technique for managing its producing stands known as "even flow, sustainable yield." The technique limits the timber that can be harvested to the amount that can be replaced by replanting. One result, in an extreme case, is that even dying trees cannot be harvested without violating this form of quota. Eliot Cutler, Associate Director of the Federal Office of Management and Budget, maintains that this is "a classic example of how difficult it is to fight inflation within government. We and other non-Agriculture Department agencies can analyze and fulminate but as long as the Forest Service treats the forests as wilderness or semi-wilderness areas . . . there is going to be no increase in timber." Although President Carter has proposed steps to change this policy, environmental opposition will result in a long delay in implementation.

However noble the effort to correct the errors of past abuse, the fruits of environmental concern for our forests come at a cost to our national output. The limitations on supply have been the major factor helping to push prices of lumber up three and one-half times what it was twelve years ago. Moreover, the wholesale price index of all lumber and wood products is expected to double over the next few years, according to a study for the U.S. Commerce Department by Data Resources, Inc. "The nation," the study continues, will "find itself faced with a mounting famine which in the eighties would severely curtail the production of homes, creating European-style, chronic housing shortages."[19]

If the recent past is any indication, the United States will seek to head off these chronic shortages, not by producing more timber, but by importing it. Since 1975 forest product imports have risen dramatically, whereas exports have languished. Over the course of the 1970s, the U.S. trade deficit in forest products tripled, to a level where it accounted for almost 8 percent of the $39 billion trade deficit in 1978. All this is taking place despite the huge reserves of timber present on U.S. soil, particularly in the Pacific Northwest. "This area is a Persian Gulf of wood," says forestry professor Barney Dowdle of the University of Washington, Seattle. "The American people are letting a trillion board-feet of timber sit there without producing the economic activity it should."[20] The "Persian Gulf" label has become a form of hyperbole in the resource field. But its attribution to both coal and timber resources effectively highlights the vastness of America's resources. Yet with both timber and fossil fuels, we seem content to import what we can produce at home.

From the coalfields of Montana to the drill platforms off New Jersey, from the timber stands of the Northwest national forests to the vast mineral reserves of scenic Alaska, the conflict has begun. Americans are approaching a choice between a reduction in the growth of their material consumption and the abandonment of an environmental consciousness in favor of a higher level of output and standard of living. This choice will not be easy. There is no simple solution that will rescue our living standards while saving us from the need to sacrifice at least part of our environmental concern.

In spite of the extra cost imposed on resource extraction and in some cases even jobs, Americans appear to retain their environmental consciousness. A Harris poll in mid-1977 found that the vast majority of respondents prefer to "live in an environment that is clean rather than in an area with a lot of jobs." Although such noble intentions are no doubt sincere, provided that the respondents themselves have jobs and rising incomes, a different picture is likely to be drawn when tough environmental controls mean a loss of jobs, income, and the conveniences of life.

If we could make up for slowth in our input of materials with more human effort, better machines, or finer technology, then Americans might not have to sacrifice anything in maintaining their environmental ideals. Unfortunately, as we shall see, these other options for maintaining growth are also being foreclosed by our mounting consciousness. The rise of environmental awareness is only part of a wider trend that is closing all the doors to continued growth. Slowth is the sole remaining outcome. It is the inevitable price of our expanded national values.

chapter 4

People Power: Living with Compassion

A story from the times of slavery has it that one day a plantation owner was touring his property looking for signs of indolence. He found one—a slave sound asleep at the border of his fields. Without passion he raised his whip and began to beat the startled man, who protested, "Don't beat me sir, I was meant to sleep here." To this the master replied, "Yes and I was meant to beat you."

Any theory of work and reward requires a model of motivation. The one inherent in this story, employed during the period of slavery to reinforce slave owners' ideas of that institution, has lasted well through North America's Industrial Revolution. It is still alive in a somewhat more refined form—an unimaginatively named theory of industrial behavior—Theory X, advanced in 1960 by an industrial psychologist, Douglas McGregor. Theory X believers hold that the average human being has an inherent dislike of work and will avoid it whenever possible. Others maintain that motivational behavior corresponds more closely to McGregor's Theory Y, the centerpiece of which is the belief that the average person works as naturally as he plays or rests. External control and punishment, it is held, are unnecessary since individuals are capable of acting in a self-directed manner.

Theory X type beliefs enjoyed their high point during the early days of industrialization when coercion, fear, and insecurity were the prime motivators of the workplace. Stress on productivity and the concept of the "fair day's work," accompanied by warnings about the evils of goofing off, reflected management's underlying belief that a good employer has to counteract the basic human tendency of workers to avoid work. Buttressed by codes regulating proper job behavior and attendance, setting strict measures of productivity, and the ever present threat of dismissal, many an employer elicited his due. In short, fear was used to extract work.

How strange today's workplace would appear to a manager of those days! A deep-rooted consciousness has moved our system far away from the use of fear as a spur to output. A large part of this change was initiated by the organized labor movement. Advocating goals such as the fair work day, fair pay, and job guarantees, labor leaders pressed management and government on behalf of the rank and file. Their success is a hallmark of our society and the wealth it contains. The rights that unions sought were first written into American consciousness, and then into its laws, to be shared by union and nonunion employees alike. To a large extent unions have been part of a process that has gone a good way toward guaranteeing our fellows certain basic rights—to life and to work.

Many of us have accepted the existence of certain "job rights," whether explicitly provided by legislation or labor contract or implicity expected as part of a fair and civilized society. It is largely these rights that help alleviate fear and insecurity in today's working person. Although they have been won to different degrees in different locales and circumstances, they increasingly creep into our assumptions about the kinds of things an affluent society owes its citizens; in short, they have molded our consciousness about our fellows.

The job rights to which we now feel entitled include:

* A measure of job protection. This pertains especially to those in a union shop or civil service position where dismissal is a tough option for an employer to exercise.

- Industrial protection from inhuman conditions at work, particularly danger to life and limb. Some of these rights are derived from the Occupational Safety and Health Act and the regulatory agency that administers it.

- Protection in hiring and promotion against discrimination on the basis of race, religion, creed, or sex. This protection exists in the form of affirmative action programs, federal contract conditions, the Civil Rights Act, and the actions of the Equal Employment Opportunity Commission.

- Guarantee of a minimum level of financial reward for work. This means minimum hourly wage laws, guaranteed income, and wage maintenance programs, which are negotiated as part of union contracts or enacted through legislation.

- Insurance, in the event a worker is unemployed because of circumstances outside his control, provided through unemployment insurance laws.

- Opportunity for relaxation and leisure pursuits through breaks at work, shorter hours, and longer vacations.

In addition to these job rights most Americans enjoy certain "life rights," which include:

- An education not limited by financial means, at least through the secondary level.

- Health care available to many who cannot afford it.

- A reasonable standard of living, even if the individual is unable to produce. In the United States this is provided nationally in the form of welfare programs, disability compensation (which grew from $1.5 billion in 1965 to $13 billion in 1977), and care for the handicapped. Handicaps may even include emotional disorders such as depression, rather than strictly physical problems.

- The right to a respectable standard of living when economic contribution is limited by age. This, of course, is the aim of the Social Security system.

Provision of these rights has grown over the past fifteen years, most graphically in the monetary sense. The former U.S. Department of Health, Education and Welfare, which ministered to these concerns, had its budget increased from $5.4 billion in 1953 to $182 billion in 1978—a growth of well over 3000 percent in twenty-five years! Its spending became greater than that of the U.S. Defense Department and about equal to that of all fifty state governments combined.

Such a massive shift in priorities would have provided a stiff challenge to the best of imaginations during the 1940s and 1950s. In the 1980s our imaginations are tickled by another prospect with a decidedly science fiction flavor—the prospect of all work being performed by machines and powerful computers. But until that unlikely day when button pushing alone provides all our material desires, human input will remain essential. And with constraints on other inputs, the less people power we provide, the smaller the output we derive. As we have seen in our analysis of raw materials, human input is also being undermined by regulatory measures originating in the finer values of our national consciousness. These restrictions are to be found in our job and life rights, which have allowed Theory X individuals to reduce their work involvement. Job and life rights can have different effects.

Life rights, when fully achieved, allow those with a particularly strong aversion to work to opt out altogether and indulge in their preference for nonwork, namely leisure. The demand for leisure behaves in a manner similar to many other desirable commodities. If the price goes down, demand will go up. In the words of economist Milton Friedman, when unemployment benefits rise, "the demand for unemployment will increase." This is also the conclusion reached by two other economists, Herbert G. Grubel and Michael Walker, who collected various studies on the subject in a volume entitled *Unemployment Insurance: Global Evidence of Its Effect on Unemployment*. Their introduction, which summarizes their work and that of others, includes the following:

> There are certain types of workers who are characterized by a strong preference for leisure and who have no family or other obligations. Such people have always existed in every society. In the past their numbers were kept small because indulgence in those kinds of preference involved begging, vagrancy, dependence on charity and low social status. The availability of unem-

ployment insurance at high levels and changing public attitudes have permitted larger proportions of people to pursue their preference for an independent life of leisure.

Evidence points to a growing breed of males in their prime years who are choosing not to work. The number of men outside the labor force grew, according to Bureau of Labor Statistics, by 71 percent over the nine years prior to 1977, until some 2.2 million neither held nor sought jobs. Nearly half these men were classified as disabled and have benefited greatly from generous Social Security and other disability programs. Among the various pieces of life right legislation is a Michigan disability law stating that a health problem that is merely aggravated rather than created on the job qualifies a worker for benefits.

Although growth in the ranks of men who do without work may not seriously affect an economy with a work force benefiting from more working women, the trend has symbolic significance. "Our society's attitude toward work appears to be changing," says Joseph Califano, former Secretary of the U.S. Department of Health, Education and Welfare. "Accepting public benefits no longer bears the stigma it once did, and this change affects the growth in the number of beneficiaries."[1] As the ranks of job and life right beneficiaries grow, pockets of individuals who choose not to work spring up. On the ski slopes in Colorado and Idaho, in sunbelt marinas like those in the Florida Keys, or merely at home with their families, more people of working age—both men and women—are finding better things to do than work.

"We just can't seem to motivate people any more," complains Klaus Berger, Manager of the Canada Farm Labor Pool. Berger's objections came after a tough week trying to recruit berry pickers in British Columbia's Fraser Valley. The short, intense strawberry season had just passed, leaving a good portion of the crop rotting in the fields for lack of labor.

"The kids don't say 'no thanks' to a picker's job. No siree— they're much blunter than that. To them it's demeaning,"[2] says Berger. A number of growers point their fingers at the lucrative alternative to a picker's wages—Unemployment Insurance checks ranging from $48 to $240 a week. Grubel and Walker attribute events such as these to a change in attitude among the youth, which results from government paternalism. "This is undoubtedly due to the radical change in the perception of the rights and responsibilities that has occurred in the last thirty years—largely as the result of the evolution of paternalistic governments. This factor may, to some extent, explain why, in Canada, about 40 percent of all UIC [Unemployment Insurance Compensation] beneficiaries are less than 24 years of age."

Similar findings are seen in the work of George Katona and Burkhard Strumpel who, in their research at the University of Michigan Survey Research Center, conduct surveys on trends in work, consumption, and economic expectations. They say, "Young workers who are confronted with a difficult labor market and, moreover, tend to be disappointed by their jobs, and who can expect sizable financial benefits in case of unemployment, may well be tempted to accept longer periods of unemployment."

If growth in the ranks of the happily unemployed were the sole result of life rights, the price for those rights might be small. In an economy with less than 10 percent unemployed, it is hard to imagine that more than a few percent of these would be working even if job and life rights did not exist. Potentially far more damaging to the ultimate productive output and our standards of living is the opportunity that job and life rights provide to those still remaining on the job to exercise their aversion to work. It is this more subtle reduction in human input that threatens our material standards of life.

Job rights enable those who enjoy the protection of union contracts, affirmative action, or civil service status to put less than full energy into their jobs and still avoid dismissal. Reduction of effort and energy on the job can, in extreme cases, allow a contagious indolence to spread through the workplace. "Why should I continue to work hard when others get away with doing a great deal less?" is a typical reaction that stems from exposure to those who set a bad example.

If these examples lead to a widespread reduction of effort, the job security that initially set off the process eventually becomes unnecessary to protect anyone. Once all have lowered their input of effort, managers are unable to single out any particular culprits. The lower level of energy spreads until it becomes the norm. Eventually, this serves as a basis for further reduction of effort, setting in motion a continuous process with no apparent end.

It would be wrong to overestimate the significance of job and life rights in the process of declining human input. Job and life rights only *allow* a reduction in human input. Even before these rights were established, some on-the-job idleness would have appeared, given the chance. Even despite them, well-motivated Y-types would not be lulled into a reduction of effort whatever the alternative to work.

Most individuals probably do not fit into a strict Theory X or Theory Y category but lie somewhere between. Work avoidance will become a pattern only if motivation or incentive is lacking. Other trends, however, also originating in our consciousness, are eroding work motivation. These trends are reducing the level of monetary and nonmonetary satisfaction derived from work.

chapter 5

People Power: Taxes and the Incentive to Work

The rising level of taxation is the center of loud protest and hot debate. A great deal of the heat is directed toward the evils of seemingly irreversible government bureaucracy and waste, but more serious factors underlie the debate. The protest is really an outcry against the erosion by taxes of incentives for each of us to save, take risks, and most of all to work.

Taxes clearly reduce the monetary reward from labor. Its effect on incentives is the subject of a theory advanced by economist Arthur Laffer. It is his position that once tax rates climb above a certain point, the incentive to work (and invest) is destroyed, with the result that total tax receipts are actually reduced. There is little agreement whether the points on his "Laffer Curve," which depicts this relationship, resemble reality. It is a proposition, however, that has some credibility with the many who complain about taxes.

Taxes have another debilitating effect that is, however, much more direct and easy to observe. Paycheck deductions can serve as a symbol of the payments made to support the indulgence of others. Very high deductions act as a disincentive and are often the target of tax protests. Governments bear the brunt of this anger and seem to be under attack for the little good they do with tax revenues. But it is the great deal they have done that causes the most concern among some of the tax protestors. Over the past fifteen years U.S. federal and state programs have worked, to a limited degree, to transfer a higher proportion of income to the elderly and those with lower earnings. Job and life right payments from the federal government—through welfare, food stamps, housing, and medicare—amounted to $41.9 billion in 1976, up from very modest levels of 1964. Over the prior ten years the entire range of government transfer payments doubled and now constitutes over 12 percent of the GNP.

In talking about the tax revolt and government redistributive schemes, *Newsweek* reports that "these were sufficient to raise the share of the bottom 20 percent of American families from their traditional 5 percent of total national income to almost 8 percent. In the same period, the upper 40 percent of the nation saw its share of the pie shrink from 76 percent to 65 percent."[1]

Although the protest registered in California's Proposition 13 was against property taxes, it was also an expedient way of objecting to the level of transfer payments—monies that go toward redistributing income., A survey conducted by the *Los Angeles Times* immediately after the California Proposition 13 balloting revealed that many voters expected that the proposed tax cut of nearly 60 percent would not result in any cut in local government services. The same proportion, when pressed further, said that if cuts were necessary, welfare payments should be the hardest hit./ According to a Gallup Poll conducted in California at the same time, by far the greatest number of respondents objected to the level of social services (listed by Gallup as welfare, counseling, mental health, etc.), rather than any other services (including schools, fire and police departments, road repairs, libraries, parks, sanitation, and hospitals). The movement against taxes is in part the protest of middle-class working men and women against a burden that undermines their work effort. Continually rising taxes, by reducing individual disposable income, do not permit workers to fully enjoy the fruits of their labor. Thus, although the polls and often-voiced expectations of the people of California revealed that many protestors expected and desired a minimal cut in public services, the voters were fully prepared to do away with paycheck deductions that support those who do not work.

Taxes are one disincentive to effort; the seeds of others were planted well before the taxpayers' revolt. The growing emphasis on the importance of self-actualization is one such trend that mitigates against the effort expended in work. Well into the 1960s the motivation to expend human energy in work came through the incentive system—the rewards of money and status. But our material comfort has provided us the ability to concern ourselves with nonmonetary phenomena—including self-fulfillment or "self-actualization," as psychologist Abraham Maslow termed it in his writings of the 1950s.

Maslow maintained that a hierarchy of needs confront the individual, beginning with the basic physical needs for food, water, and sex. As these physical needs are met, other more abstract requirements arise such as self-esteem, independence, and, ultimately, the need to self-actualize. According to Maslow, "Even if all these needs are satisfied, we still may often expect that a new discontent and restlessness will soon develop, unless the individual is doing what he is fitted for. A musician must make music, an artist must paint, a poet must write, if he is to be ultimately happy. What a man *can* be, he *must* be. This need we may call self-actualization."[2]

For many, consciousness in the 1970s and 1980s is a search for self-actualization—a search for what we can and must be. A desperate striving to make contact with our innate being is very evident today. Nighttime education courses, new spiritual disciplines, and the rise of self-analysis and psychoanalysis are all props in this search. The last place many of us would expect to discover our inner selves is at work.

There are indications that a sizable portion of American workers feel demeaned by their jobs. In a periodically updated survey of a large sample of all major demographic and occupational groups, the University of Michigan Survey Research Center found a steady increase in worker discontent. Based on its 1977 survey, the center suggests that 32 percent of U.S. workers feel that their skills are underutilized, 32 percent classify themselves as "overeducated," and over 50 percent resent the lack of control they exercise in their work situation. Part of this discontent lies in the high expectations that are nurtured by increasing levels of education. "Jobs aren't getting worse," says Stanley Seashore, Director of the Michigan Center Program, "but people are getting better."[3]

This has led to the use of what psychologist Daniel Yankelovich calls a "New Breed" of individuals, who cherish a personal identity apart from what is provided by work. "People will often start a job willing to work hard and be productive. But if the job fails to meet their expectations—if it doesn't give them the incentives they are looking for—then they lose interest. They may use a job to satisfy their own needs but give little in return. The preoccupation with self that is the hallmark in New Breed values places the burden of providing incentives for hard work more squarely on the employer than under the old value system."[4]

Indulgence in self-realization is a comfort our society feels it can afford. Indeed there are those who could forcefully assert that it is the raison d'être of our system and standard of living. This is a hard point to fault. But it is just as difficult to ignore the possibility that concern with personal developments of this sort may be incompatible with our contribution to the workplace as it is currently structured. Clearly there are those who are self-fulfilling themselves right out of a growing standard of living.

The impact of the drive toward self-fulfillment is the subject of discussion in many of the writings of George Katona and Burkhard Strumpel. "If people do not seek fulfillment mainly in material goals, in consumption and production, but rather in those areas generally referred to as the 'quality of life'—a humane work environment, friendly treatment by supervisors and coworkers, perhaps artistic and educational activities—one might surmise that they would demand more free time, do more for their education, be less willing to change their residence in the interest of their career, and be less motivated to work for the purposes of acquiring more consumer goods." The proposition tested by Katona and Strumpel in their surveys is whether the shift in workers' motivations is being matched by a change in the workplace in the direction of this higher "quality" experience. The results from surveys in both Germany and the United States are disappointing. "There is no harmony between trends in values and trends in job characteristics. . . . Unfortunately, their [workers'] changed aspirations are not being met by a corresponding enrichment in the nature of most occupations. More and more often people are being disappointed by their jobs."

The growing level of disappointment is also fostered by the educational system, media, and popular mythology. All of these set up lofty expectations and raise the possibility of ultimate disappointment and job dissatisfaction by exploiting a basic cultural trait of American society: the feeling that success and status are open to all. Vertical mobility, as it is more formally called, is an important part of the motivational apparatus of our schools and workplace, indeed of our entire economy. To be upwardly mobile in this society is in fact easier than elsewhere. Numerous examples exist, in nearly every branch of endeavor, of the self-made individual, men and women who through sheer energy and insight reached their goals.

Nevertheless, vertical mobility for the vast majority is a myth—and for some a highly destructive one. It is obviously impossible, given the work that must be done in American society, for everyone to obtain and maintain a high status. Clearly a society of lawyers, airline pilots, doctors, teachers, and businessmen could not provide for all our varied needs. The prospect of success open to everyone, through attainment of professional status, is clearly a myth. Yet lofty professional status is a goal that has been widely promoted, entirely apart from the standards of material comfort such status would provide. High living standards alone, as measured by the size of the house, the number of cars, or the manner of leisure enjoyed, are not entirely substitutes for professional status.

The belief that anybody can succeed, and the aggregate impossibility of this happening, leads to the creation of casualties—those who feel cheated, finding themselves in lower status jobs, stuck behind a desk, or facing a bench. The lack of pride and interest in their work, which some of these people might experience, is nothing new. Status expectations and disappointments have long been part of the American scene. But today's job and life rights allow an individual to indulge any disappointment and resentment with a reduced level of effort. As a result, the more society preaches the virtues of status without providing the means for more of us to succeed, the more job and life rights will be used to allow a reduction of effort. The potential cost for all of us is very large. It will mean slower growth in the availability of goods and services for us to consume.

The end result of any gaps between reality and expectations is the weakening of the motivation of the individual. "As a consequence, not only do [the workers] withdraw emotional involvement from the job," comments Yankelovich, "they also insist upon steady increases in pay and fringe benefits to compensate for the job's lack of appeal. The less they give to the job, the more they seem to demand—a process that cannot continue for long without breaking down."[5]

This situation is even beginning to create problems for labor union leaders who are being forced by rank and file members to address "quality of work" in negotiations as well as hard money issues. In part of the University of Michigan Survey Research Center's poll of organized workers, over 60 percent said they wanted some emphasis placed on nontechnical labor issues, such as the provision of more job interest or more say in the operations of the workplace. According to Thomas Kochan, associate professor at Cornell University, this creates a problem for unions, as "in some places they will have to address quality-of-work issues as well as the bread-and-butter issues, and that means they can no longer apply a standard program to all workers."[6] Until the needs of working people for a higher quality work experience can be met by union management, the level of human input will be threatened. Slowth is a partial but direct consequence of job dissatisfaction and the resultant reduction in effort at work.

Yankelovich's conclusion was also reached by economist Strumpel. As part of a study designed to probe blue-collar workers' satisfaction with their jobs and standards of living, he and his colleagues questioned nearly 600 men. They concluded that the individual's expectations for wage increases ran high, but that such expectations were not reflected in any effort made to secure them. Says Strumpel, "Apparently the link between the need for or expectation of financial increases and the motivation to work for these increases has at least become tenuous."

The result of all this may be the societal breakdown to which Yankelovich alludes. Reduced individual effort—enabled by job and life rights, motivated by job dissatisfaction and a decline in incentives through high taxes—will mean a drop in the input of people power. It is yet another vicious circle so common to economic affairs. Human input is required to pay for the job and life rights that are so central to the new consciousness.

Sweden, a country that has served as a model provider of job and life rights, now serves as a model of another sort. In 1978, for the first time in memory, the living standards of the average Swede declined. Part of the problem, according to some analysts, is the high level of rights enjoyed by workers. The Swedish government, through hourly subsidy payments toward the wages of any worker who would otherwise be laid off, keeps people on the job. Additionally, the government pays 90 percent of the salary of workers who become ill—a hefty sum as absenteeism on account of sickness runs as high as 20 percent in some factories.

The result of all this is the twin problem of high absenteeism and the high cost of government and supporting taxes. "We have come to consider the economy as a machine which produces money without effort," says Axel Iveroth, Chairman of the International Council of Swedish Industry. "It seems that people must suffer before they realize the need to work, but now it is becoming clear that some of the social system will have to go. We can't afford it all."[7]

The problem of absenteeism, a rising phenomenon in many western nations, is a high concern to those in Swedish industry. Says Volvo President Peter Gyllenhammer, "It is no longer a question of whether individual Swedes can afford to be sick and still receive pay, because this is an obvious right. It is a question of the country's ability to pay for the level of absenteeism we have reached."[8]

Absenteeism is not a problem confined to Sweden. In 1977 Canadian business paid wages estimated at $4.9 billion for work that was not performed owing to absenteeism. This was approximately 25 percent more than the amount the country's unemployment insurance bill provided for and almost twenty-five times the value of the labor lost during strikes! In the United States, absenteeism runs still higher than in Canada—at about 4.5 percent of total working time. Aside from its economic importance, absenteeism is also a symbol of the basic fact that motivation has not expanded as fast as our desire to indulge in leisure. Provision of job and life rights is now elevating this to a problem of critical proportions.

Developments brought about by our rising consciousness have not been easy for the individual to digest. On the personal level, economic security provided by job and life rights reduces fear and stress. People have less anxiety about being arbitrarily dismissed and have more confidence in their ability to cope without a job. In the long run, however, society's problem of the ability to pay, posed by Gyllenhammer, will come to haunt the individual. As human energy and input, reduced by this rising consciousness, cut into the total production of goods and services, the individual will in the final analysis be faced with the need to sacrifice added material comfort for economic security. This sacrifice might not be necessary if the decline in human input were compensated by an increased investment in machines and new technology, which would allow us to indulge in our concern for our fellows and enjoy the fruits of a push-button society. But we are not moving any closer in this direction. The rate of adding new machines and production technology is itself being threatened. Once again it is our burgeoning consciousness that lies directly behind this disturbing trend.

chapter 6

Our Machinery Input

The business community in this country is conducting an investment strike. The rate at which we add to our existing machines and other forms of capital—that is, the rate of investment—is undergoing an alarming contraction. It is clear from this rate that business leaders are not comfortable with the existing investment climate. A good deal of their general dissatisfaction can be traced to the proliferation of business regulation and to their perception that they are being made to pay a disproportionate amount to support America's burgeoning consciousness.

The trend is clear. Whereas the fraction of the gross national product (GNP) devoted to *gross* investment has moved within a relatively narrow range during recent years, the rate of *net* investment is dramatically down. Data prepared by R. David Ranson and Charles Babin in an article entitled "What's Holding Up the Capital Investment Boom?"[1] show that as a fraction of net domestic business product, net nonresidential fixed investment by nonfinancial corporations fell during the 1960s and 1970s by more than a third, from 2.2 percent to a meager 1.4 percent. In down-to-earth terms, this means that the rate at which the United States is setting aside its current production to provide the mechanical means of producing for tomorrow is on the decline.

"Growth of the high-employment net capital stock per worker

has practically halted when compared with the trend rate of growth of 2.9 percent per year from 1950 to mid-1972"[2] is the way the investment strike has been put into recent historical perspective by John Tatom of the Federal Reserve Bank of St. Louis. Tatom computes that the level of capital per worker by mid-1979 was about 17 percent less than would have existed had investment continued along its earlier trend. This means a loss for the economy of over $200 billion of capital stock—and this was measured in the more valuable 1972 dollars.

It is necessary to examine net rather than gross amounts because the net investment figures exclude the expenditures required to take care of the normal wear and tear of capital stock. But even the higher gross investment statistics are alarming when placed in a global context. The United States has been devoting a smaller fraction of its national product to gross investment than almost every other major industrialized nation. Whereas Japan has set aside over 30 percent, Germany 25 percent, and France 24 percent, the United States has been investing only about 17 percent of its GNP.

It would be difficult to overstate the contribution of machines to our present standard of living. A rapid glance around the home should make this abundantly clear. But it is even more apparent in our places of work. Machines, along with the technical know-how required to operate them, are the basis of the traditionally high productivity levels enjoyed by the American worker. Without a carefully maintained high-quality machine input, national output will undoubtedly suffer.

This is the threat we now face. The figures on investment levels mentioned above disclose at least part of the extent of the problem. What they do not reveal is the force that lies behind the numbers, the ever tightening noose of government and legal restrictions. Yet it is the hassle of complying with government agencies, the long and costly court battles, and the preparation of endless documents that are contributing to this investment strike today.

"Government officials keep asking us 'Where are the golden eggs?' while the other part of their apparatus is beating the hell out of the goose that lays them,"[3] says Sam Tinsley, Director of Technology of Union Carbide Corporation. The apparatus to which

Tinsley refers is a result of our efforts to impose broad and noble concerns on those who we fear respond only to a narrow interest in profit. Our concerns for our fellows, our environment, and our ultimate safety from technological mishap have found their way into a bewildering number of legislative fiats and regulatory requirements.

That apparatus includes no less than eighty-seven federal agencies that regulate business. They distribute 4400 different forms, and it has been estimated that the completion of these requires a whopping 143 million hours of executive and clerical time. The *Federal Register* that kept records of these regulations with 45,000 pages in 1974 had expanded to 65,000 pages by 1977 and could soon reach 100,000. These agencies, specializing in the multitude of regulations governing a wide range of corporate life, employed 64,000 people in 1976, with all budgets totaling $2.9 billion.

All this red tape is reflected in the statistics and reality of less business investment. This becomes evident to those familiar with the procedures today's businesses undertake when considering a major investment. The investment is judged by its ability to generate cash, with the timing of those flows an all-important consideration. Although a certain level of costs can be built in to cover the costs of compliance with regulatory or legal requirements, other detrimental factors can still arise. For example, undue tie-ups may be encountered while projects are being defended in court or hauled before regulatory bodies, and these can delay the flow of cash and reduce return on an investment. General uncertainty about the cost of regulatory compliance in dollars and delayed start-up time, as well as the possibility of eventually falling victim to some new agency or regulation, work against investment. With all else equal, a general increase in uncertainty tends to reduce the number of projects considered worthwhile. "If businessmen could at least be certain that the rules of the game would remain the same, they could incorporate government mandated expenditures into standard capital-budgeting calculations," is the way Sanford Rose expressed the uncertainty problem in *Fortune*.

Uncertainty also grows as businesses become increasingly aware of projects that have become ensnarled or lost in legal or regulatory wrangling. The reduction in investment stemming from the examples of these projects has an added impact on their actual loss or delay of output. Electricity is not generated by the Tellico Dam or the Kaiparowitz plateau power plant in Utah, nor is oil flowing through the Standard Oil of Ohio (Sohio) pipeline in California. It is impossible to know how many other projects were never even begun because of the costs and uncertainties of government control and regulation. We tend to see only the damage to projects that get past boardroom approval. There are many more hidden costs we do not see.

One project that did receive boardroom approval, only to face inordinate delay, is the Sohio pipeline proposal, which we have already mentioned. The wrangling over the Sohio pipeline provides the clearest evidence of the cost of imposed uncertainties and regulatory red tape. Sohio management spent five years seeking 700 federal, state, and local government permits, at a cost they estimate at $50 million, in an attempt to win final government approval for the plan. According to Sohio's Chairman, Alton W. Whitehouse, the pipeline proposal became "a prisoner of the system." It was the delays as well as the costs that caused successive threats of cancellation. "What has happened," said Whitehouse, "is that time has run out on this project."[4] Sohio's complaint of "endless government permit procedures" and overlapping regulation of multiple government agencies combined with threatened lawsuits to give the board second thoughts about its original plans.

Today these costs are being recognized, and regulation has come under limited attack. Agencies for the reduction of paperwork have been features of both the Gerald Ford and Jimmy Carter Administrations. It may be possible to reduce paperwork and make regulation more efficient, but it is doubtful that a renunciation of the underlying reasons for regulation will take place. As pointed out by a *Time* essay: "Most of the excesses that are drawing fire were born in the mid-1960's and early 1970's when the focus turned from industry control to social reform and a large number of bureaus were formed, including the Environmental Protection Agency, the Occupational Safety and Health Administration, the Equal Employment Opportunity Commission and the Consumer Product Safety Commission."[5]

In referring to these types of agencies that were designed to realize social objectives, *The Economist* is quick to remind its readers of their origins. "This type of agency began to appear in the 1960's, when an activist Congress came to see regulation as a means of implementing social measures: Nearly a third of the existing regulatory agencies were brought into being between 1969 and 1974—when the White House was in Republican hands."[6] We shall continue to change our leaders in the White House and Congress. And at times we shall no doubt shift our emphasis away from these social entitlements, but they are not likely to be abandoned.

Of all the regulatory agencies, two most embody the emphasis on protection of the public entitlement. The most visible is the Environmental Protection Agency (EPA), which, since its birth in 1970, has grown to become the largest regulatory agency, employing over 10,000 people. This agency is charged with administering a host of environmental legislation ranging from the Clean Air Act to the Toxic Substances Control Act. In a study conducted for the Business Roundtable, a group of the largest U.S. companies, the EPA was identified as being responsible for 77 percent of their total direct costs of regulation.

The other agency, which attempts to regulate a safer workplace, is the Occupational Safety and Health Administration (OSHA), an arm of the U.S. Department of Labor. It is easily one of the most visible—and controversial—regulatory agencies. Its job is to monitor and regulate noise levels and procedures for operating dangerous machinery and to ensure worker health and safety. These tasks take OSHA inspectors across a large cross section of business in search of regulatory transgressions, some of which carry costly price tags to correct. A visit by OSHA inspectors has not usually been regarded as an auspicious occasion by recipient plant managers. Often it comes unannounced, a condition OSHA deems necessary to guarantee seeing typical working conditions. The right of OSHA inspectors to show up at will has been challenged in the courts after some companies refused them admission. Undaunted, OSHA obtained special warrants, which have also been challenged.

The growth of OSHA's regulatory role is reflected in its expanding budget. In 1979 it was authorized to spend over $170 million, a dramatic boost from the $70 million budget in 1974. Industry expenses to comply with OSHA have undoubtedly risen as well, although reliable estimates are not available. One company, Dow Chemical, estimates that it spent almost $100 million for health and safety between 1975 and 1977. It labeled more than $35 million of these amounts as spent to comply with "unnecessary laws or regulations." According to the Business Roundtable Study, 7 percent of the total regulatory bill was spent on OSHA compliance.

A small portion of these costs is for the services of a particular professional who is in increasing demand—the industrial hygienist. This is one type of occupational health professional whose prospects for livelihood have been given a sizable boost by OSHA regulations. In fact such people are in short supply. One source has it that only 5000 industrial hygienists are practicing in the United States today and that another 5000, were they available, could be employed in industry, government, and unions.

One example of the role of such professionals came in investigating bizarre circumstances, such as the one that took place in 1977 at the Kinney Shoe Corporation's Perry-Norvel plant in Huntington, Virginia. Over a period of four days, fifty workers visited local hospitals, complaining of nausea, headaches, faintness, and chest pains. Hygienists and industrial psychologists from OSHA were sent to investigate. Their diagnosis: "mass psychogenic illness"—a kind of workplace hysteria triggered by perceived, but not real, danger. Occurrences such as these are increasing in today's regulated workplace. An account of the event in *Industry Week* included a summary of that magazine's interview with Michael Colligan, research psychologist with the National Institute for Occupational Health and Safety.

> Dr. Colligan and others in the field believe that one reason for the increasing frequency of outbreaks is a heightened awareness that the work environment can contain disguised dangers. A major thrust by the Occupational Safety and Health Administration (OSHA) has been to identify toxic elements in the workplace—and to make workers aware of them. This campaign may be leading to greater worker fears of exposure to toxins. Workers do not always understand the difference between safe and

unsafe levels of exposure to chemicals, Dr. Colligan notes. All a
worker may know is that he or she is working with a substance
declared harmful by the government, and although the actual
exposure level may be within safe limits, the element of danger
has been implanted in the worker's subconscious. At that point,
any unusual workplace event can stimulate the symptoms of assembly line hysteria.[7]

Whatever the reasons for worker hysteria, the action of OSHA
has been known to touch off a hysteria of sorts among employees.
This is particularly true when its rulings conflict with other regulatory agencies. The case of one Iowa packinghouse provides a
glaring example. At the insistence of OSHA it installed safety rails
only to be told by the U.S. Department of Agriculture that they
were unsanitary and had to be removed. When OSHA tried to reduce the level of noise in a food packing plant by requiring insula-
tion material, the Food and Drug Administration held that they
were the potential habitat of bacteria. When the Department of
Agriculture required that kitchen floors at the Parks Sausage Co.
be repeatedly washed to maintain standards of hygiene, OSHA
ruled that floors must remain dry at all times. Nevertheless, OSHA
remains steadfast. "Worker safety and health," asserts Administrator Eula Bingham, "are to be heavily favored over the economic burdens of compliance."[8] Contradictions between government agencies and regulatory authorities are not confined to a
single plant or business. Indeed, regulatory counterthrusts may in-
flict uncertainty and expense on entire industries. One such example
is the use of coal, which is emphasized by the Department of
Energy and discouraged by the EPA because of the way that fuel
source conflicts with the standards of the Clean Air Act.

One regulatory nightmare stems from a certain vagueness with
which standards are imposed. The Consumer Product Safety Commission has been taken to court several times because of its decision to remove Tris, a chemical used as a flame retardant for children's pajamas. The commission alleges that the product is cancer
inducing. A judicial donnybrook developed over who should bear
the costs of the product's removal—the chemical manufacturer, the
clothing producer, or the government. This noteworthy case high-
lighted another element of uncertainty common to a great deal of

regulation—namely, a failure to establish who bears its cost. In those cases where costs and benefits are actually identified at all, in an effort to determine whether a regulation is generally beneficial, an economic or legal framework is not established to allocate the disbenefits. The result, as with Tris, is a full-scale involvement of the courts with all the cost and uncertainty this entails.

The burdens of compliance, whoever bears them, have certainly not been light. Yet the burden is not readily apparent in the statistics that show the declining rate of investment. On the contrary, the burden of compliance often results in capital outlay, which actually constitutes investment. Yet complying with regulation represents outlays on account of consciousness rather than for creation of productive capacity. Despite the prospect they hold for improving the overall quality of life, outlays to stem plant pollution or promote industrial safety will cut into output by diverting investment funds from conventionally productive use. Ranson and Babin sum up the results of their detailed analysis of the investment dilemma as follows: "That society benefits as environmental quality and health improve is undeniable. The question is, at what cost? . . . Under present policies, people in general attain a higher quality of life, but the cost of generating this improvement falls disproportionately on the productive elements of society. The loss of production is not quantifiable, but does imply a reduction of living standards."

Although, as Ranson and Babin state, the total true cost of regulation is not readily quantifiable, certain partial estimates provide an indication of its immense magnitude. Washington University business economist Murray Weidenbaum estimates that businessmen spend over $100 billion per year to meet new pollution and safety regulations. *U.S. News and World Report* estimates the cost of regulation in terms of what people buy at a slightly higher level: $130 billion per year or $2000 for each family in the United States. Who among us willingly gives up $2000? And this cost excludes the taxes each of us pays to support the regulatory agencies themselves with their 64,000 employees.

Antipollution spending constitutes an increasing share of investment. The Federal Council on Environmental Quality, a body designed to monitor trends in that area, estimates that in 1977 over

$40 billion was spent on pollution abatement programs—over 2 percent of that year's GNP. Of this amount, business was paying about one-half. By 1985, that body predicts, the cumulative costs directly related to compliance with federal antipollution regulation will total $289 billion for the previous ten years.

These figures take on additional meaning in the context of specific industries for which the burden of compliance is relatively high. Spending is especially heavy in those industries producing goods that are essential to our standards of material comfort—paper and pulp, iron and steel, petroleum products, electric power, and chemicals.

In two years alone (1976–1977) the slumping steel industry was required to spend nearly $1 billion to meet federal water and air pollution abatement standards. These expenditures were imposed on a sick industry, one experiencing heavy foreign competition, reduced profit levels, and an aging and deteriorated physical plant. A 1977 *Business Week* special report sums up the state of the steel industry by saying that it "appears [to be] on the brink of partial liquidation"[9] due to the shutdown of old plants and lack of investment in new ones. The report quotes one economic consultant who raises a dramatic specter for U.S. production: "If steel companies are unable to continue to plan for new expansion, we could be importing all of our steel by 1985."[10]

A similar warning is also being voiced by those whose bias and concerns may lie in a direction different from that of current members of industry. According to former Treasury Secretary Michael Blumenthal, "We are now devoting a very sizable chunk of our private investment to meeting government regulatory standards . . . and in some of these areas we may well be reaching a breaking point."[11]

For many businesses the breaking point has been exceeded. Between 1974 and 1977 some 143 plants (or portions of plants) were closed owing to pollution abatement standards. This statistic (provided by the U.S. Commerce Department Bureau of Economic Analysis) is another figure not reflected in lower investment. Rather, it represents a shrinking of current capacity, which must be met by greater investment if output is to be maintained. Plant closings are by no means confined to big business. One manufacturing sector hit hard by regulation is the nation's electroplating industry, which includes many small independent shops. By its own admission, the EPA says that 20 percent of such shops may be put out of business by strict water emission standards. Representatives of the National Association of Metal Finishers were quick to condemn the standards, which they claim will mean capital outlays of $100,000 to $250,000 per plant. This, the association estimates, is more than the worth of a number of smaller plants.

Shrinking of individual capacity may mean little until it starts to affect us directly. The struggle to provide needed machines and capital in face of growing regulations and red tape now appears academic. But that will change. In the electric power industry, the time of our awakening has been graphically projected by George Christy of North Texas State University. "We may not get a real test of regulatory attitudes," says Christy, "until people start flicking the switches and the electricity doesn't come on."[12]

The costs of regulation are also clearly demonstrated in the case of one company alone, mammoth General Motors. Preparation and actual compliance with government regulation cost a whopping $1.3 billion in one year, 1974, according to GM's research laboratories. This included the salaries of the full-time equivalent of 25,000 employees who complied on behalf of GM with the Civil Rights Act, the Occupational Safety and Health Act, the Clean Air Act, and the Federal Water Pollution Act, among others. Almost one-half of the research and development budget of General Motors is devoted to compliance with regulatory fiats regarding safety, emission, and fuel economy standards. A portion of this research, GM is quick to admit, would be done without regulatory insistance. It is proud of experiments such as the ones it has conducted to isolate the psychological nuisance factor distinguishing noise pollution from ordinary sound. Yet according to GM Vice President Paul Chenea, "much of our regulation-related research we feel shouldn't be necessary."[13] Chenea labels a good deal of this effort as "unnecessary defensive research," which includes testing and compliance with certain emission standards that are unjustifiable on a cost-benefit basis.

Regulatory cost is indicated in yet another way—as part of the price tag of a car itself. Weidenbaum estimates that the cost of mandatory pollution control equipment for automobiles constitutes $666 of the average price of a 1978 car. Thomas Murphy of GM estimated the cost at $800 by the early 1980s.

Specific measures are also seen to have a cost attached to them. Edward Denison of the Brookings Institute has examined, among other issues, the cost of safety in one of our nation's most hazardous occupations, coal mining. The Coal Mining Health and Safety Act of 1969 was an effort to introduce greater safety into the industry. In its administration of the act, the Mine Enforcement and Safety Administration is given some credit for reducing losses from mine fires and explosions. But the cost, acording to Denison, is not negligible. Prior to 1968, productivity was growing at 6.8 percent. Denison's figures show actual 1976 productivity to be less than half what it would have been had this trend continued beyond 1968. Regulating our concern for those who do the dirty work of extracting coal means lower productivity, and hence higher prices, for those whose electricity needs are powered by coal.

Despite the varied estimates of the costs of regulation, its true effects on economic output cannot easily be established. Regulatory impact comes in a variety of shapes and sizes. It includes curtailed investment because of increased uncertainty, loss of productive capacity owing to plant closures, disruption of specific planned projects, and diversion of investment funds away from providing new and vital machines. The impact of a regulated consciousness could indeed be massive.

In an effort to combat what it sees as the excesses of regulation, the business community with the help of economists has begun to fight back. With the aid of cost-benefit calculations, businesses have challenged the worth of specific regulations. In one such effort, the chemical industry took OSHA to court, challenging the agency's standards regarding the exposure of workers to the carcinogenic chemical benzine. The industry contended, and was upheld by the U.S. Circuit Court of Appeals, that the tough standards would likely eliminate one case of leukemia every six years at a cost of $300 million each.

The use of cost-benefit analysis in such cases requires some valued judgment of the worth of the health, safety, or, ultimately, the life of a human being. The process begins with the assessment of the risk of a given activity. For example, for every million miles that lethal chlorine is shipped about in rail cars, the probable loss of lives from accidents resulting in the escape of the gas will be calculated. In cases where few data exist, as with the case of nuclear power plant accidents, elaborate computer models simulate, or statistically construct, estimates of the risk involved. Calculations are then made of the expense required to reduce various levels of risk. Critics of regulation, particularly in the auto industry, go to these lengths to illustrate that the closer regulation comes to enforcing zero-risk conditions, the greater is the cost for each incremental unit of safety, a cost that is then added to the price tag of the automobile.

Although cost-benefit calculations are useful in comparing the effectiveness of various regulations, they ultimately require some valuation of human life if a specific regulation is to be evaluated. In specific cases estimates of the value of a life is made. For example, the National Highway Traffic Safety Administration estimates that for each person who is killed on the highway, society loses an average of $287,175 in production, hospital bills, funeral expenses, and other costs. Highway safety programs costing, on average, less than this amount are apt to be considered worthwhile. However, the value of life goes well beyond the measure of the economic significance that an individual has in society. Indeed it is impossible to know what value society should place on a human life. Yet if the broad cost of the existing level of regulation bears any relationship to such a value, it is extremely high.

One powerful result of regulation is what *Time* magazine calls an "innovation recession."[14] It might have just as easily been labeled an "innovation strike." There has been an alarming decline in an all-important form of investment, that for research and development. Although it does not directly result in an increase in plants and equipment, R&D expenditure is crucial to the survival of our economy. It provides the basis for the manufacture and sale of high-technology items on which U.S. industry relies for sales both at home and abroad.

The direct result of a decline in the rate of spending on R&D is a decreasing rate of innovation. According to a National Science

Foundation study, as quoted in *Time,* the number of patents granted U.S. inventors abroad declined by 25 percent between 1966 and 1976, whereas the number of foreigners granted U.S. protection doubled. These figures should come as little surprise since R&D spending, which amounted to 3 percent of the national income in 1964, had dropped to 2 percent by 1978. This decline in the fraction of national income can instead be expressed in terms of the decline in the annual growth rate of such expenditures. In the period from 1955 to 1968 average annual growth of R&D expenditures was 7.6 percent, which well exceeded the inflation rate of that time. From 1969 to 1976 the level of expenditures grew more slowly than inflation, so that by 1976 the amount was reduced in real terms. And during the same period, many other countries were spending more.

More than one observer lays blame for the slump in R&D spending at the same door as the trend of declining overall investment rates—government regulation and legal entanglements. According to Senator Orrin Hatch, there have been fewer major breakthroughs in the last twenty-five years than in any other comparable period during the previous seventy-five years. "Industry is being required to devote an increasing portion of funds it would normally spend in R&D to comply with Federal regulations on such things as pollution control, worker safety and product safety to mention a few." Hatch adds that "the fantasmagoria of costly Federal controls and bureaucratic red tape have grown to the point where they are strangling not only our ability to pay for R & D but our creative spirit as well."[15] Denison, quoted in *Forbes,* advances the same theme. "The weight of government regulation has become so heavy," he says, "that businesses are no longer trying to match their competitors but instead are trying to outwit the government."[16]

Another even less tangible effect of regulation is the danger of institutionalizing older, less useful technology by directing both funds and attention from more innovative, less encumbered research. The mechanical workings of automobiles are an example. They have not changed in any major way in response to the need for fuel economy or clean air, a fact bemoaned by U.S. Senator Harrison Schmitt. "Instead of looking at pollution controls, if we were looking at building a more efficient and therefore less polluting engine, we would not only be solving our environmental problems, but we would be producing a new thing for export."[17] This is inhibited, however, by the overall declining rates of investment in truly productive capacity and in research and development.

The R&D problem is hampering the ability of the United States to maintain its record of technological innovation, which is required to enlarge today's output. But that is only one facet of the problem. Even currently *known* technology resulting from past R&D is not being fully implemented. The reasons for this lie entirely apart from a lack of investment. They stem from an enlarged safety consciousness, which leads to control and regulation even over innovation with relatively low risk.

The drop in the growth of our human input, as well as a drop in the use of materials and machines, makes slowth inevitable unless we are ready and willing to employ the most advanced workable technology. The only route to the maintenance of a growing national output in the face of declining growth in the input of materials, people power, and machines is through improvement in the way we use these inputs. This can come only through improvements in technology. Yet even this only remaining door to continued growth is being closed by our expanded consciousness.

chapter 7

Blocking the Technological Path to Change

"It's like an endangered species. When it gets below a certain level, it cannot reproduce."[1]
—A description of the present state of the nuclear power industry by Anthony Z. Roisman, a National Resources Defence Council lawyer.

America is in a quandary about nuclear energy. The debate surrounding its use is a strange mixture of probability statistics, scientific facts, and sheer rhetoric. But the confusion remains. The nuclear debate has significant implications that reach beyond our standard of living. It is important as a symbol. It is a bold-faced statement of our love-hate relationship with technology and a symbol of the qualms we experience in trading off material comfort for freedom from technologically wrought danger.

Consider the findings of a poll conducted by the Gallup Organization in 1976. When asked about the importance of nuclear plants in meeting the future power needs of the nation, over 70 percent of those polled responded that it was indeed important. When confronted with the prospect of having such a plant built within 5 miles of their homes, 45 percent—a majority of those with a view—said they would object. These included nearly four of every ten people who felt that such plants were important. Americans feel they need nuclear plants but don't want them in *their own* backyards.

Similar findings were reported in a *New York Times*–CBS News Poll following the Three Mile Island accident, which involved the nuclear power plant near Harrisburg, Pennsylvania. These revealed that national opinion is still divided, although now only a minority of those expressing an opinion (46 percent) favored the development of more plants. Still fewer of those questioned (38 percent) approved of having plants in their own communities.

These confused feelings arise from a deep-seated mistrust of powerful technology, and they have resulted in a virtual standstill in development. Despite the high priority attached to the development of the nuclear power industry by the federal government, over twenty cancellations of plans for plants have taken place since 1975. The prospects for nuclear energy have deteriorated so much that in a Congressional appearance, former Energy Secretary James Schlesinger pleaded for a relaxation of federal licensing requirements in order to reduce the lead time for nuclear plants from the present ten or twelve years. This lead time for regulatory approval has grown from less than eight years during the 1960s. More important, Schlesinger appealed for a separation of the issues of nuclear waste disposal, perhaps the area of greatest industry and public concern, from the license application process. Without such facilitating measures, Schlesinger warned, nuclear power will fade as an energy option.

There are signs that this is already taking place. Only two new reactors were ordered from 1976 to 1979. In light of the Three Mile Island incident, some utilities are reconsidering past orders. The Virginia Electric Power Co., for example, is trying to decide whether to convert two planned reactors from nuclear fuel to coal. For critics of nuclear power, this represents a very positive turnaround. But for others it clearly spells problems in satisfying the voracious energy appetite that fuels the comforts of our daily lives.

"One by one, the lights are going out for the U.S. nuclear

power industry," says a 1979 *Business Week* special report on nuclear power. "Reactor orders have plummeted from a high of 41 in 1973 to zero this year. Nuclear power stations are taking longer to build, and the delays are tacking hundreds of millions of dollars onto their costs. Waste disposal, which was supposed to be solved by now, is not. The export market is already glutted and shrinking fast. And the cumulative effect of these and other troubles has been a severe erosion of both public and political support for nuclear power."[2]

Although fear of the consequences of nuclear power serves to darken our attitudes toward it, the benefits nuclear power provides are typical of those we have come to expect from our technological culture. Technology is the great frontier of American production. It has been the cure for whatever production problems we face—be it a shortage of resource inputs or a decline in labor availability. In short, we have become reliant on the technology fix—a supplement for whatever we lack in the ongoing attempt to add to our material comfort. And technology has come through for us time and again. The telephone, radio, life-extending drugs, and of course the automobile and jet plane have all transported us to new levels of comfort and well-being. This is the story of our love affair with technology.

Such developments, though, have not always come naturally. Indeed the very newness of technology imparts almost a fear of the unnatural. A story has it that when electric lights became a common household feature in the 1890s, many Americans were reluctant to turn them on or off for fear of receiving shocks. Only servants and the very brave were ultimately responsible for getting the lights on.

But what in former times was a healthy measure of distrust has today developed into a full-blown skepticism and, in extreme cases, even hatred of technology. The key differences lie in the Armageddon-like consequences we have come to fear from technological mishap and the apparent disagreement among scientists in assessing the degree of danger we face. No longer is the consequence of employing a technology confined to the individual who experiments with it. Today's technological developments affect far more people than it did in the days when a few brave souls turned on the first electric light or cranked the first automobile. Now the results of many technological developments extend to whole segments of society to include those who do not even give their assent. The risk is that greater technological mishap could extend even to future generations, to those yet unborn.

A classic example of the "time bomb" effect lies in the unknown dangers inherent in the disposal of radioactive wastes. This is a thorny issue, which the government and the nuclear industry have yet to resolve. After nuclear fuel is expended to turn electricity-generating turbines, unburnt uranium and plutonium are recovered, leaving an unused residue of radioactive wastes. Various storage depositories for these wastes have been proposed but the half-life of the substance may be as much as 24,000 years. The Ford Foundation in its energy report *A Time to Choose, America's Energy Future* summed up a concern for the future posed by the very existence of such material. "The question is, how can we be sure that *any* storage 'vault' will remain intact for so long? The wastes must be stored in a place that will be immune from floods, earthquakes or man-caused intrusions (in case knowledge about the hazards involved is lost). It is very difficult, of course, even to list all potential uncertainties because it is almost impossible to think in terms of a million-year future." To this the foundation's report adds a rather chilly note: "Non-technical considerations, such as the stability of the future societies and our responsibilities to them, are key factors that must be considered." It is no small wonder that with the injection into the nuclear debate of considerations like million-year futures and stable societies, Americans grow weak at the knees.

The waste disposal problem that incites this reaction threatens not only the construction of new plants but the continued production of existing ones. "The waste disposal problem is killing us,"[3] says George Gleason of the American Nuclear Energy Council, which is the lobbying arm of the industry. The industry has been frustrated over Congress's inability to agree about how to dispose of nuclear waste. Nuclear proponents want the government to play a major role in taking over the spent fuel from the reactors. The fact that Congress has authorized no plan or site for permanent disposal is an indication of its reluctance to further involve itself in the industry's problems.

"If inaction [on nuclear waste disposal] continues," says U.S. Senator Gary Hart, "in the next two or three years we can start shutting things down."[4] The basis of the Senator's statement is the fact that spent fuel is beginning to fill the temporary storage cavities that were made available. That storage was built under the assumption that more permanent disposal or reprocessing facilities would soon be developed and built. "All it takes to convert a nuclear advocate into a cautious opponent," says Hart, "is to propose dumping waste in his state." To 1980, movements in three states— California, Iowa, and Wisconsin—have had some success in challenging further reactor construction until the waste issue is resolved. Should Congress fail to agree on the issue by the mid-1980s, some plants whose temporary facilities will then be filled face the prospect of a shutdown.

The raging debate within the scientific community offers little reassurance about our own safety in nuclear matters, much less that of future generations. Given a consensus among scientists that nuclear power was totally safe, presuming no problems of waste disposal, meltdown, potential theft of radioactive material, or problems of dismantling, popular concerns would be minimal. The fact is that both pro- and antinuclear forces have marshaled a respectable scientific following, an indication that much has yet to be resolved.

The closest claim to a zero-risk level in the nuclear industry was made in a 1974 update of a study done by Massachusetts Institute of Technology (MIT) professor Norman Rasmussen. According to Rasmussen, the chance of dying as a result of an atomic accident is one in 5 billion. The study is the subject of endless claims and counterclaims, all supported by varied and extensive statistics.

It is not the numbers, however, but the adaptation of the logic expounded by the French philosopher Blaise Pascal that is the ultimate weapon used by nuclear foes. According to Pascal, even the smallest of odds favoring an event of great consequence can be used as a basis for action. Applied to the nuclear debate this logic dictates that the utter horror of nuclear mishap makes any but a zero-risk level unacceptable. It is this logic, combined with horrific speculation about the prospects of a reactor accident, that has stymied the nuclear industry. The fulfillment of such an event, even though it is associated with such a small probability, could, according to a 1965 Brookhaven Institute report, possibly result in 45,000 deaths, $17 billion worth of property damage, and nuclear contamination of an area the size of Pennsylvania. It is no surprise to see people registering their disapproval with bumper stickers reading "Better Active Today than Radioactive Tommorrow" and "No Nukes Is Good Nukes."

The U.S. public has, almost fifteen years after the Brookhaven study, been frightened by the accident at Three Mile Island. Yet are we any closer to a resolution of our ambivalence toward the peaceful use of the atom? Take, for example, the prime form of fallout that emanated from that incident, the conflicting statements of those designed to regulate nuclear power safety. "We cannot have an acceptable nuclear power program in this country if there is any appreciable risk,"[5] said Joseph Hendrie, then the Chairman of the Nuclear Regulatory Commission (NRC), before a Senate subcommittee investigating the accident. However, a major element of the entire Three Mile Island threat was unforeseen by the regulators and the industry alike. NRC officials admitted that they had never anticipated the large volatile hydrogen bubble that threatened the cooling system and contributed to the potential meltdown. According to a statement made at the time by NRC's man on the scene, Harold Denton, the bubble "isn't part of our standard assumptions; it's a new twist."[6] This kind of truth is very painful and will greatly complicate the nuclear dilemma. We are told that no appreciable risk will be tolerated, yet we are shown that risk is an unavoidable part of this infant technology.

Some people working in the nuclear power industry see themselves as victims of a technology backlash. "Whether the force of public disapproval is simply a carryover from antiwar activism of the 1960's," says *Business Week,* "as some industry leaders feel, or if it is part of a greater popular disenchantment with a technological society, it is beginning to have impact in state capitals as well as in Washington."[7] Part of that impact came in the form of a number of antinuclear referenda that were held in 1976. The nuclear issue was big during that year in a half dozen states, with Montana and Hawaii voters actually opting to restrict nuclear power development. In a number of communities, like New York City, New London, Connecticut, and Shaker Heights, Ohio, the through-shipment of radioactive material is banned altogether.

Using some of the protest tactics of the 1960s, at least one antinuclear group has achieved widely publicized success. Construction of New Hampshire's Seabrook reactor plant has been delayed by a group known as the Clamshell Alliance. Over the more than three years during which construction was delayed, the price of plant completion almost doubled. According to Frank Shants, New Hampshire Public Service's Projects Manager, the delay has provided "a splended example, in all its glory and horror, of the regulatory process run amuck."[8] This reference is to numerous appeals and reversals involving the plant's license that have been imposed on the project by the Environmental Protection Agency (EPA), the NRC, and the courts. And although the Clamshell Alliance has been the most publicized local antinuclear group, it is by no means the only one. "Seabrook was rather like Rosa Parks refusing to move to the back of the bus,"[9] claims antinuclear activist Norie Huddle, a member of the Philadelphia-based Mobilization for Survival. The reference to Parks is a reminder of how she became, in 1955, a symbolic figure of the civil rights movement by refusing to surrender her seat on a Montgomery, Alabama, bus. The arrest of Parks led to demonstrations that helped trigger the civil rights movement. The symbol of the Clamshell has similarly sparked a rise in antinuclear activism, now sponsored by groups like the Abalone Alliance in California, the Crabshell Alliance in Washington, the Oyster Alliance in Louisiana, the Paddle Wheel Alliance in Kentucky, and the Palmetto Alliance in South Carolina.

"More and more sound thinkers I talk to," says Representative Morris Udall, who chairs the House Interior Committee, which has responsibility for overseeing regulation of the industry, "are coming to believe that nuclear is one of those kinds of technologies that get so complex they fall of their own weight—technologies that are not really compatible with democratic society. Maybe the Soviets can have nuclear power and we can't, because they simply announce that it is going to be done."[10]

The numbers who share mounting concern over the danger of nuclear power have made it potentially suicidal for U.S. politicians to take a firm stand favoring its development. The public's concern, when converted into political reality, makes all but the most politically secure official lean on the safe side toward the delay or cancellation of nuclear projects. The network of antinuclear organizations, estimated at 185 with 35,000 members, has developed into a major political pressure group. Nuclear power is now a big political issue.

Before the Three Mile Island incident, a majority of the nation's governers called, in a common statement, for a "more positive commitment to nuclear energy by the administration. . . . The President must take the lead and rally public support"[11] It is doubtful that after the accident of Harrisburg such a commitment will be forthcoming or even that the same number of governors' signatures would have appeared on that statement. Not only does a pronuclear stance run counter to the painful memories of Three Mile Island, but it defies a chilling warning issued by the Kemeny Commission, which investigated the accident. After calling for a series of regulatory reforms, its report stated, "We must not assume that an accident of this or greater seriousness cannot happen again, even if the changes we recommend are made."

If nuclear power is to proceed, it requires the continued commitment of the federal government. The industry grew on the wings of government support that came in the form of a benign regulatory system and a commitment to undertake disposal of nuclear wastes and through a government ceiling set on the liability of utilities in the case of nuclear accidents. That support is now in doubt. Not only has Congress failed to establish a more permanent disposal procedure, but it has offered no guidance to regulators or utilities for balancing risks against the cost of reactor safety improvement.

A shift in Congressional attitude toward nuclear power now appears to have taken place. "My position used to be that I was for nuclear power unless somebody showed me it wasn't safe," says

Representative Mickey Edwards, a conservative who had previously supported the nuclear industry in Congress. "My position now is I am for nuclear power if somebody proves it is safe."[12]

Should the federal government turn its back on nuclear power, it would mean death to the industry. The prospect entails much more than withdrawal of legislative support. It would mean the end of a key moral prop that the industry requires to surive in the face of innate public concern about nuclear safety. That concern stems from the fact that the risks from nuclear technology are not ones we voluntarily accept. We do not as individuals assess its risks and benefits based on our own experience and judgment. Rather, with nuclear (and a great deal of hard) technology, the decisions are made for us by industry and government. At the inception of the nuclear option and throughout this very shaky period the active approval of government authorities was and is indispensable. Strong political approval and a regulatory authority that appears sound and credible are necessary to overcome the public's opposition to being exposed to a risk of this type, which is not of its own choosing.

One researcher into public attitudes toward risk was Chauncey Starr, Dean of the School of Engineering at the University of Southern California. Starr attempted to quantify the benefits and risks involved in various activities. He concluded that the public is willing to accept voluntary risks that are 1000 times greater than involuntary ones. Furthermore, he made some observations that are very relevant to the nuclear industry. "It is important to recognize the perturbing role of public psychological acceptance of risk arising from the influence of authorities or dogma. Because in this situation [of involuntary risks] the decision-making is separated from the affected individual, society has generally clothed many of its controlling groups in an almost impenetrable mantle of authority and of imputed wisdom."[13] As that mantle wears thin, our politicians are beginning to shed it. In the process, prospects for nuclear power will cease to exist.

Bear in mind the economics of nuclear power. These plants, and in fact all power plants, are fantastically expensive. The U.S. electric power industry undertakes one-fifth of the new industrial construction of the nation, a huge component of total capital outlay. The local utilities that must raise these vast sums have difficulty committing themselves without the assurance of the political support necessary to push their projects through. Utilities cannot afford massive outlays only to have to sit with partly complete plants on their hands. And the cost of these plants is rising all the time. According to the Edison Electric Institute, the average cost of a nuclear power plant has risen from $165 per kilowatt-hour in 1970 to over $1800 for plants being started at the end of the decade. For coal plants the costs have gone from $145 to $1100.

With these capital cost needs, a utility requires near secure knowledge that its projects will not be halted or delayed once underway. Yet at the very time that costs are rising, the sensitivity of the issue and the wavering stands of uneasy politicians have nibbled at the confidence of the power companies. This has altered both the nature and extent of their plans. Indeed, according to surveys made in the spring of 1979, almost 50 percent of the planned capacity needed for 1987 has not been begun. With a lead time of something between eight and twelve years, that capacity is in great jeopardy.

Heightened levels of concern about technology and environmental safety have provoked grave doubts about the alternatives to nuclear power as well. Coal, particularly, may have two major drawbacks that would have gone relatively unnoticed in a less conscious era. One of the undesirable properties of coal is its emission of significantly more carbon dioxide than other fossil fuels. Attention has recently focused on the properties of carbon dioxide that provide a one-way filter for the rays of the sun, containing the waves of heat within the earth's atmosphere. This is known as the "greenhouse effect," a condition that may alter the earth's climatic conditions and disrupt patterns of agriculture.

Greater use of coal will also increase the sulfur emissions from power plants, creating the acid rain phenomenon that is now receiving attention in the press. Although sulfur emission levels can be cut using expensive scrubbers, coal will be more costly to burn as a result. But the prospect of acid rains may be a negative feature also of new programs to extract the large tar sands and heavy oil deposits that are buried in the nation's Southwest, primarily in California and Louisiana. These deposits, which are considered as alternatives to nuclear power and imported oil, require huge utility operations. Coal, gas, or oil is needed to power the mining process or to generate the steam required for injection into the ground. This source of heat is required to cause heavy oil or sands to flow to the surface. Fossil fuels are also needed in the refining or upgrading process. The authorities in the province of Alberta, Canada, site of two pioneering tar sands plants, have recently become aware of the threat posed by these operations. Large-scale use of fossil fuels to exploit these reserves in western Canada and the United States contains the prospect of afflicting these areas with the rains, which until now have been confined to the industrialized East. The question of whether the threat to lakes and vegetation from these rains is preferable to the danger of nuclear power is one that these regions may have to answer if growth in the supply of energy is to be maintained.

The vast destructive potential of a wide range of modern technologies, with complexity sufficient to confuse scientist and lay person alike, has created a new concern. Many wonder whether we can place actual limits on the risk that technology may pose for our future. Even were such risk defined, it is questionable whether any but a nonzero level would be accepted.

"With synthetic substances that have never existed before . . . the tissues and cells of the body have no previous experience. The synthetic organic chemist can prepare new substances much faster than they can possibly be tested,"[14] is the fear expressed by Director of Research of the Glasgow Royal Cancer Hospital, R. Peacock. Such an admission by a member of the scientific community characterizes another area fraught with concern—technological agriculture.

Our awareness of the danger of new materials used by modern agriculture is reflected in the explosion of the natural foods industry, which employs the rallying cries of "organic," "100 percent natural," or "no additives" as an extremely effective selling device. It appears that the price tags of many such products carry a premium for the organic label and the familiar mono- and disyllabic ingredients that we can all identify. But high prices of a number of carefully produced natural food items, such as organic fruits, vegetables, and meat, reflect a more important economic fact of life. The technology of mainstream agriculture is required to produce the national output that fills our stomachs at prices we can afford.

A prime example of the importance of agricultural technology can be found in the cattle farming industry. As in automobile manufacturing, the emphasis in cattle farming is on economies of scale, with the animal becoming very much an assembly line object. Typically, feedlots have grown in size—a trend that has reduced costs. In one comparison by *Feedstuffs* magazine, large cattle lots incurred costs 30 percent below those that they classified as small.

An integral part of the assembly line process for cattle is the use of chemicals. Animals are confined to small spaces, limiting problems of feeding, watering, and cleaning. Confinement also reduces the animal's expenditure of energy, resulting in faster weight gain per unit of feed. The end result is a need for tranquilizers and, more important, antibiotics to prevent infectious diseases that might overrun animals living at such close quarters.

Increasingly the new methods of technological agriculture are being challenged by consumer activist groups. *The Chemical Feast,* authored by James Turner and produced by a group established by Ralph Nader, warned that "the potential hazards from chemicals in the environment are staggering."

Of late, concern has spread well beyond the domain of organized groups. According to Ross Hume Hall, whose book *Food for Nought, The Decline in Nutrition* serves up a hefty attack against today's food industry, the reaction against such use of technology is growing. "In the last few years the general public has become aware of the effects of technology. One response to this awareness has been the creation of citizen's groups to assess, to question, and even to block innovations and new technologies."

Hall thinks that consciousness must move beyond efforts to block tangible innovation and technology to attack a more subtle danger—hidden technology. "The technologies that the public have reacted to have been visible ones—a dam, a highway, a pesticide. However, society also contains numerous technologies that are completely hidden, and their influence on our life-style and the future of society can be more profound than any visible highway or dam."

During the late 1950s and 1960s Americans were treated to large doses of such a hidden technology, which stirred deep concern and raised the general level of consciousness. Diethylstilbestrol, or DES as it became known, was fed to cattle as a growth stimulant. It was the first synthetic compound employed in this way, and it was highly effective. According to some estimates weight gain on cattle was hastened by as much as 15 percent, resulting in a 10 percent decline in feed requirements. Spurred by good results, the industry's use of DES became the rule rather than the exception. Then, in the 1970s, DES, which was also used as a drug to prevent miscarriages in pregnant women, was linked to cases of cancer in the daughters of women who received such treatment. Public debate ensued about its use in meat production, pitting cattlemen and the chemical industry against vigilant members of Congress and consumer groups. Subsequently, the Delany Amendment of the Federal Food and Drug Act was invoked—a section that outlaws the use of additives deemed carcinogenic. This move did not please everyone. "Careful analysis indicates that strict enforcement [of the Delaney Amendment] would be catastrophic," objected D. M. Graham of the University of Missouri Agricultural Department. "Considerations of quality and risk-benefit ratios are not allowed for in judging the safety of such materials."[15]

Catastrophe did not strike the cattle industry, contrary to Graham's prediction. Restricted use of DES was subsequently allowed as a result of a court ruling, but the use of other chemical substitutes such as Synovex eased the situation for cattlemen.

It is often difficult to conclusively test a chemical for carcinogenic properties. The reason for this underlies much of the debate surrounding technological agriculture: adequate tests that will totally eliminate doubt cannot always be devised. Small doses of toxic substances may not appear harmful in tests involving a limited animal sample. However, when sustained over a human population, even in the most minute dosage, the end result may be different. Unwieldy large samples must be exposed over sustained periods to approach a proper risk assessment.

Despite these problems, some authorities favor taking safety consciousness to the full degree. One such group was the Ad Hoc

Committee on the Evaluation of Low Levels of Environmental Chemical Carcinogens, a group formed by the National Cancer Institute. This committee delivered the following testimony before hearings of the U.S. Senate:

> Because the latent period in human carcinogenisis is so long, epidemiologic evidence develops only over periods of 15 to 20 years. Timely decisions to exclude materials from uses involving exposure to man, therefore, must be based solely on adequately conducted animal bioassays. Retrospective human evidence of risk must not be allowed to show itself before controlling action. Chemicals should be subjected to scientific scrutiny rather than given individual "rights."[16]

The Committee emphasized its message with this word play on the principles of jurisprudence: "they [potentially carcinogenic chemicals] must be considered potentially guilty unless and until proven innocent."

Zero-risk decision rules such as this come as a result of the growing concern about the incidence of cancer in society. It has climbed from the eighth leading cause of death in the United States in 1900 to the second today. Only heart disease kills more people. On the basis of wide agreement among scientists that environmental factors are primarily responsible for the majority of cancer cases, public pressure for some greater measure of safety is being felt. "Environmental and occupational cancer are now becoming prime topics of national concern. Their underlying political and economic determinants are at last becoming appreciated," says Samuel Epstein, who, in his well-researched account *The Politics of Cancer,* contributes to that concern. Efforts such as those of Epstein, an activist physician-researcher in the field of carcinogenesis, are beginning to arouse the American consciousness with their emphasis on what is thought to be a prime environmental cause of cancer: the widespread use of chemicals to which the human body cannot successfully adapt.

The debate about the extent of harm resulting from chemical use in production of the nation's food and other goods bears some similarity to the nuclear power controversy. It is characterized by growing doubt about the extent of scientific understanding of the phenomenon. Says Epstein, *"There is no known method for measuring or predicting a 'safe' level of exposure to any known carcinogen below which cancer will not result in any individual or population group.* That is, there is no basis for the threshold hypothesis which claims that exposure to relatively low levels of carcinogens is safe and therefore justifiable."

Other scientists share Epstein's concern about our inability to limit risk from carcinogenic substances. The National Cancer Institute, in a report to the U.S. Surgeon General, states that the major difference between the exposure of tissues to carcinogens as opposed to other toxins is that in the former case, they don't return to a normal state. In other words, exposure of tissue to carcinogens may have a cumulative effect. Determining safe levels of a new carcinogenic substance becomes problematic when the negative effect of exposure to others remains for a long time.

Concern is not limited to activists in the scientific community. "Indeed, since the 1960's, members of society have looked upon themselves not only as mere consumers of goods and services but also as persons entitled to certain rights attachable to the process through which goods and services are made available"[17] is the way Gerald Gall, law professor at the University of Alberta, sums up the growing consumer safety consciousness.

These concerns, which have raised the consumer's guard against chemical uses in production, have had a marked impact in the political arena. According to Gall, the Canadian Parliament has enacted no fewer than eighteen pieces of legislation that attempt to guarantee consumer rights in the consumption of food and durable goods. They are: the Food and Drug Act, the Narcotics Control Act, the Department of Consumer and Corporate Affairs Act, the Canada Agricultural Products Standards Act, the Fruits and Vegetables and Honey Act, the Pesticide Residue Compensation Act, the Canadian Dairy Commission Act, the Cold Storage Act, the Livestock and Livestock Products Act, the Maple and Canned Foods Act, the Meat Inspection Act, the Canada Dairy Products Act, the Hazardous Product Act, the Humane Slaughter of Food Animals Act, the Seeds Act, the Fish Inspection Act, the Milk Test Act, and, finally, the Consumer Packaging and Labelling Act.

A similar situation exists in the United States. The concern about carcinogens, chemicals, and safety is expressed by an uneasy alliance of government officials and regulatory authorities, public interest groups and labor unions. Largely under the impetus of labor and public pressure, legislation has been passed that provides regulatory authorities with the power to restrict the use of pesticides, herbicides, growth hormones, and petrochemicals used in production of the nation's food and other goods.

The federal government has seen fit to enact a number of laws that are designed, at least in part, to deal with the carcinogenic threat. This reflects the balkanized jurisdictional responsibility in Congress for dealing with these matters. For example, one Congressional committee passes laws covering the production of pesticides but another is concerned with pesticide residues in food. The diffuse jurisdiction evident in the creation of the laws is mirrored in the many agencies responsible for their enforcement. The Occupation Health and Safety Act, which, among other things, controls hazardous substances in the workplace, is administered by Occupational Safety and Health Administration (OSHA). The Consumer Product Safety Act, designed to protect citizens as "consumers," is administered by the Consumer Product Safety Commission, which also administers the Federal Hazardous Substances Act. The EPA administers five acts that deal with carcinogens in one way or another.

All together there are nine pieces of legislation that attempt, with widely varying degrees of success and dedication, to protect the American population from cancer. The strictest and most straightforward example was the 1958 Delaney Amendment to the federal Food, Drug and Cosmetic Act, which categorically states: "No additive shall be claimed to be safe if it is found to induce cancer when ingested by man or animal, or if it is found after tests which are appropriate for the evaluation of safety of food additives to induce cancer in man or animal."[18]

The Delaney Amendment is the only piece of legislation dealing with carcinogenesis that, in an attempt to reduce risk, ignores the consideration of economic benefit derived from the substances being regulated. Another more recent act of Congress is the Toxic Substances Act, which provides, according to Epstein, "for the first time . . . the opportunity of controlling industrial chemicals and anticipating carcinogenic and other adverse effects." Essentially, the law gives the EPA the power to ban the use of chemicals it considers hazardous to public health. It mandates that the EPA provide detailed examination of any new chemicals or chemicals used in new contexts.

"Not many people are worried about what the possible effects of pesticides will be 10 or 20 years from now," says Douglas Costle, present Administrator of the EPA, which has been given such broad regulatory authority, "but if there are enough chemical time bombs ticking away out there we're going to see the public demand action." The action to which Costle alludes will likely come through U.S. regulatory authorities. Until now, their record in ensuring human and environmental safety from chemical damage has been spotty, at least according to Epstein: "Of the few regulatory actions that have been undertaken against carcinogens in the past few years, virtually all have been initiated or instigated by public interest or labor groups."

One major use of regulatory power came in the case of a well-known input in high-technologic agriculture—DDT, the granddaddy of pesticides. It was ultimately the EPA that, under pressure from environmental groups, concluded that DDT's secondary effects—its movement through the ecosystem without breakdown—posed too great a threat to allow its continued use. Originally, however, it was the DDT breakthrough in technological agriculture that introduced growers to the notion that they could do something on a large scale to control pests. It became a vital link in the defense of crops rendered highly vulnerable by the acres and acres of single cropping that characterize modern agriculture.

The defense of the fruit, vegetable, and grain growing system is now aided by the multitude of pesticides that have filled and expanded the role left vacant by DDT. In fact there are some 1400 active chemical ingredients being used in nearly 40,000 different pesticide products. The use of such chemicals has come under increasing attack as they too purportedly fail to break down rapidly enough, persisting for long periods within the environment.

Proponents of chemical use argue that this lasting effect is an inescapable result of the very function of pesticides. They decry the regulation of pesticides that is enabled by legislation such as the Toxic Substances Act. What is needed, they claim, are substances "persistent enough to break the life cycle [of pests] so that you can go in and make, say, one treatment and be pretty well assured that we've got 90% or 95% control. And we are simply losing the tools that we had to break the life cycle,"[19] maintains John Stackhouse, Agricultural Director of Ohio.

It is not possible to quantify the precise contribution to production made by pesticides or herbicides, asbestos, benzene, growth hormones, vinyl chloride, or a number of other contentious chemicals and materials. But some claim that this is not even relevant to the debate that surrounds the use of chemicals. "Safety considerations override whatever costs are involved," says one regulator, Gerald Barkdoll, Assistant Commissioner of the Food and Drug Administration (FDA), "Carcinogenic properties override everything else."[20]

Rules as pure as this are about as uncommon as the purity of the food that they are designed to ensure. Regulatory authorities such as the FDA are most frequently forced to walk a fine line in the conflict between production efficiency and concern for our future health and safety.

That narrow line is defined by the pressure of public interest groups, which are aroused by the increasing incidence of cancer, and industry officials and lobbyists, concerned about the growth of regulation. The latter includes the American Industrial Health Council, which is supported by large chemical firms. According to the Council: "Even in an emotional context such as cancer, sound public policy must take into account the inevitability of some risk."[21] The suggestion that society should accept some risk arouses an angry reaction from Peggy Seminario, an industrial hygienist with the AFL-CIO. "Socially acceptable risk to whom decided by whom?" she asks. "The question becomes how many workers' lives we are willing to sacrifice for benefits to society; how many workers can we get away with killing by not controlling a substance so we can make more money."[22]

Certainly in this context all but a zero-risk level is indefensible. But the adoption of such a policy will severely hamper our productive system. As tests for the carcinogenic properties of chemicals and substances used in industry are lengthy and often inconclusive, testing and not production will become a preoccupation of industry.

For other activists however, this prospect is a red herring. Epstein, for example, says, "It is not as if there is any necessary conflict between long-term industrial growth and the prevention of cancer. Many carcinogens are used for purposes that are trivial, or under conditions where they can be replaced by non-carcinogenic substitutes." Furthermore, as Epstein correctly contends, cancer exacts large costs on society that stand to be reduced by careful regulation and testing of potentially noxious chemicals.

A high level of government regulation over chemical substances is necessary if society is ultimately to succeed in reducing the incidence of cancer and other disorders. However, regulation will be costly. One prime cost will be in the reduced level of technological innovation in the chemical industry. Consider the following from a *Business Week* special report.

> The major petrochemical producers—Union Carbide, Du Pont, Dow, and Monsanto—concede that the prime focus of their capital spending today is no longer basically market anticipation. Other things have grown in importance. "Just a few years ago, we were spending about 6% of our total annual capital investments on environmental control equipment" says Edward G. Jefferson, senior vice president of Du Pont. "Today it's on the order of 12% to 15%, and through the next decade, the average would approach 30% if changes are not made in federal environmental rules."[23]

Although projections such as these are open to question, there is little doubt that our concern over chemicals and human health has had a marked impact on industry. For example, when Eli Lilly and Company asked the FDA to approve a new drug for arthritis, its applications ran to 120,000 pages—enough to fill two light-duty trucks. One study, cited by the Research Vice President of Bell Telephone Laboratories N. Bruce Hanney points to the dramatic change in regulation affecting the chemical industry. An application in 1938 to the FDA for adrenaline in oil was accomplished in twenty-seven pages. An application in 1958 for treatment of pin-worms took 439 pages. An application in 1972 for a skeletal muscle relaxant took 456 volumes, weighing 1 ton.

Industry is not responding passively to the advent of regulatory controls. One response, the flight of productive industry abroad, is creating concern even among industry critics such as Epstein, who says, " 'Runaway' shops were created in lesser developed countries such as Brazil or Taiwan, where there are virtually no regulatory controls and where cheap and unorganized labor is amply available. More surprising, however, is the increasing flight of segments of the chemical industry to runaway shops in eastern Europe, where regulatory controls and opportunities for public protest are minimal compared to the United States."

One particular example of flight from regulation involves the asbestos industry, which has been subject to increasingly stringent OSHA standards as to allowable fiber content in the workplace. The strong fire-resistant qualities of asbestos fiber have been used in cement, asphalt, wallboard pipes, textiles, and in the food and beverage industry, among many others. However, its apparent effect on the incidence of lung cancer and respiratory disease among those working with the substance has brought about an increasing level of government regulation. According to Epstein, this regulation has had the following effect: "The greatest flight is seen in the asbestos textile industries, which are increasingly located in Mexican border towns and in Taiwan and South Korea. There are also indications that other asbestos manufacturers, particularly of friction products such as brake linings and disc pads will follow this course. Other flights involve arsenic-producing copper smelters and the plastics, benzidine dye and pesticide industries."

In addition to the flight of industries and their production capacity to countries with a lower level of safety consciousness, regulation of the chemical industry's new products will also reduce the level of spending on chemical research and development. This impact of regulation upon R&D spending has been discussed earlier in this book.

Safety consciousness and widespread concern for the future extends as well to forms of soft technology. The ability to lay pipe across barren regions in inhospitable climates is one such technology, of which the Alaska oil pipeline is the most striking example. But the vast social and ecological consequences of that effort served to derail another—the well-funded and planned MacKenzie Valley Pipeline, which was proposed to transport Alaskan and Canadian gas from Arctic regions. "It is all too easy to be over-confident of our ability to act as social engineers and to suppose—quite wrongly—that all problems can be foreseen and resolved,"[24] wrote Justice Thomas Berger in his well-reasoned "Berger Commission Report," which succeeded in crippling the pipeline in Canada. "The nature of human affairs often defies the planners," he added.

Berger was quite specific in discussing some of the prospective social mishaps, as well as the more commonly discussed physical consequences:

> I am not prepared to accept that, in the case of an enormous project like the pipeline, there can be any real control over how much people will drink and over what the abuse of alcohol will do to their lives. There can be no control over how many families will break up, how many children will become delinquent and have criminal records, how many communities will see their young people drifting towards the larger urban centers, and how many people may be driven from a way of life they know to one they do not understand and in which they have no real places.

Such words were instrumental in the subsequent negative verdict handed down in the pipeline decision by the government of Canada. It laid to rest volumes of exhibits that comprised the work of the Canadian Arctic Gas Consortium—a group that purports to have spent some $130 million in planning for the gas transport system.

We can see that our safety consciousness is inhibiting outward movement of the production frontier, which has been expanded so often by technology in the past. Whether it be in the production of our food or our energy, in soft technology or hard, our concern for the effects on the future is impinging on our willingness to try the advances provided by modern science. The effect of that unwillingness will undoubtedly have an impact on our standard of material comfort. We need only consider the research of MIT economist Robert Solow, who found that more than half the increase in American productivity has come from technological change. Solow included within this both scientific and engineering advances, as well as improvement in managerial techniques and labor training. Indeed, the same conclusion was reached in a 1977 Commerce Department study, which stated that technological innovation was responsible for 45 percent of the nation's economic growth from 1929 to 1969.

Today we are confronted with an ongoing debate about science and technology, a debate that threatens innovation. One reason for the division between proponents of technology and industry and those with a high level of safety consciousness is summarized by the well-known mathematician and educator Jacob Bronowski:

> All these divisions, I believe, derive from one gap at the center: the distance between the new view ossified in vernacular speech and thought. Between the personal discovery and the public use of a mechanism, a principal, or a concept, there must be a translation of thought; and the years since 1900 have opened a gap across which, at present, translation is almost impossible. The laboratory language and the everyday have, for the time being, no bridging metaphors in common. The public still pictures nature as the first scientific revolution did, as an engine; and there is no way of putting into this picture the algebra of nature which the laboratory now conceives. The translation is as false at bottom, as one of Shakespeare's Sonnets into Chinese ideographs: the two languages do not have the same structure, nor an imagery to flash and a fire to spark from one into the other. Today the scientist's language shares no imagery with the vernacular, and is as private and imprisoned as the modern poet's or the modern painter's. The public is at a loss; and afraid of them all.[25]

This fear is translating itself through regulation into an inability to maintain a high rate of scientific implementation and innovation. As a result we are bound to see a drop in labor productivity and growth. This is assured by constraints on the use of raw materials and machines and by a drop in human effort, which stem from our broad and developing consciousness.

chapter 8

Working for More Output

"Shortly after his purchase of the Sunday Times *in 1959, the late Lord Thomson of Fleet paid a visit to the paper's London office to meet the staff. Among their ranks was a top union official from the printing floor.*

'How do you do?' said the genial proprietor. 'I'm Roy Thomson, the owner of this paper.'

'You may own it,' replied the man, 'but I run it.' "[1]
—Newspaper account by M. Thompson-Noel.

Almost twenty years after this exchange took place, presses at the *Times of London* fell silent. The power of the union man who ran the shop was proved. In November 1978, after failing to come to an agreement with the typesetters union, the management of the Times Newspapers (owner of the *Times* and *Sunday Times*) locked out its employees. The key issue was a management proposal to install computerized typesetting to be operated by the *Times*'s journalists and clerical staff. "Direct inputting" was vetoed by the typesetters union, which saw it as an effort to wrest power away from union leaders and introduce lower manning levels on the printing press floor. It was not until one year later that the papers resumed publication. It may be considerably longer before modern technology is finally adopted.

In the simplest terms, the dispute that shut down the *Times of London* was about technology versus jobs. It was the result of job consciousness. This consciousness will become an increasing part of our own labor-management scene as the attempt is made to install technology to boost the output of the American worker. Our economy is poised at new thresholds of innovation in economic sectors, particularly electronics and communications, that remain relatively unconstrained. Crossing these thresholds, however, will raise the level of concern about jobs. As that concern slows or delays our employment of new technology, our ability to combat slowth will recede. Job consciousness will work in this way, as an added force alongside concerns for our environment, safety, and our fellows, in reducing the rate of growth of available output. It is yet another form of consciousness that makes slowth inevitable.

The issue of technology versus jobs has been felt by the newspaper industry on both sides of the Atlantic. It stopped the presses also at *The New York Times* and the other New York dailies just as it did in London. The labor history of the New York papers has been turbulent for years. Over the past two decades, thirty separate disputes have blacked out one New York newspaper or another. One strike in 1962 closed the city's four major papers for 114 days. The strike created hardship for retailers who relied in selling their wares on the near addiction of New Yorkers to their daily newspapers. Automation and jobs have been a central feature of a number of these strikes and disputes. It was not until 1974 that an agreement was reached between the dailies and the International Typographical Union (ITU) permitting installations of an automatic typesetting process. That agreement allowed the papers to do away with the manual preparation of plates used in printing, under the proviso that no layoffs occurred.

At *The New York Times,* the major installation of automated printing came in 1979 with the abandonment of hot metal typesetting, a process the paper had used since the nineteenth century. *"The Times* Enters a New Era of Electronic Printing," heralded the paper's first cold type issue.[2] Predictably, the paper's typesetters were less enthusiastic, as indicated by one piece of graffito chalked on a casting machine: "Hot Lead Is Dead—but We're Not Rooters for Computers."[3] Typesetters of the paper had cause for concern: the new process spelled the death of their craft. At the time of the changeover, the composing room that once employed 1000 linotype operators was down to 600. Reporters and editors had begun to type their pieces onto video machines for storage, editing, and composition. Five automatic typesetting units were installed, each of which composed 1000 newspaper lines per minute. Clearly, the job of manual typesetter was gone.

The mere fact that such a technology was installed—in contrast to the case of the *Times of London* newspapers—means that the typesetters unions eventually cooperated. Linotype operators of the New York papers chose retraining and lifetime job security in preference to an entrenched opposition to technology. But this settlement did not come easily. Only one month after *The Times* changeover to electronic typesetting, peace in the industry was ruptured again. This time the strike was ignited by the efforts of the New York papers to reduce printing-press staffing levels. Again, the dispute was emotionally charged—automation of the printing process had eliminated the need for some 700 positions at *The Times* alone. As with the typesetters union, the printers union settled for job guarantees, making reduction of staffing levels possible only through attrition.

Perhaps the story of innovation on these two newspapers, the *Times of London* and *The New York Times,* is also a part of the economic tale of the two nations. In England, union opposition to innovation has been steadfast and successful in its obstruction. With *The New York Times* and its fellow American dailies, technology prevailed. But this distinction blurs when one considers that the New York newspapers were slow to adopt the new technology. *The Times* was among the last of the nation's 1700 journals to adopt the cold type process. Furthermore, this was accomplished only with some sacrifice of output through both prolonged strikes and minor slowdowns, as well as implementation of agreements that ensured the continuation of some unnecessary jobs. Retaining workers in jobs with no productive use results in the loss of their output in productive positions. Although these losses may be small in the case of the newspaper and printing industries, other examples show that the precedence of jobs over technological innovation is costly. As these cases are tallied across the entire economy, they do indeed contribute to slowth.

Job consciousness is a spinoff of technological innovation. It is a concern for the threat that technology poses not to our future safety and the environment but to job security and the quality of the work experience. Yet, like the safety-oriented resistance to new technologies, this consciousness threatens the future growth of output.

The demand for job security is not new. The history of industrial relations documents many such disputes, from the one that accompanied the introduction of the diesel locomotive and eliminated the need for a man to stoke the coal-fired engine to the disputes that have plagued the newspaper industry. What is relevant in the 1980s, however, is the role that job consciousness will play in interacting with other concerns to exacerbate slowth. In prior times the concern for jobs may have indeed slowed introduction of technology or led to the retention of workers in unproductive positions. Yet it was only one obstacle to growth. Today it is one among many newer constraints, and it promises to grow worse over time.

From the standpoint of output, jobs are irrelevant. The number of people employed is a distinctly different economic consideration from the standard of living we enjoy as a nation. This will prove incomprehensible to anyone who has suffered the self-doubt and insecurity of unemployment. It is not a notion that will find great acceptance among those who realize how intertwined work is with self-esteem and human development. Yet the creation of jobs forms an entirely separate and at times conflicting goal to that of improving our living standards.

From the standpoint of living standards, what really matters to us as a nation is not the number of jobs we create, but that those who hold jobs are as productive as possible in providing what we consume. If we as individuals could enjoy the same output of goods and services by working fewer hours, we would be better off. Indeed, the more we could be golfing, sailing, reading, gardening, or enjoying other leisure activities while still enjoying the same outputs, the better off we would be. The fewer hours we need to work to consume the same basket of goods and services, the better.

But is a person better off who is fulfilled materially, but without a job? In the narrow economic sense we can say yes, although at risk in such a case is the vital substance of human dignity and identity. "Nothing is more degrading to a man than unemployment," is the way Louis Goldblatt, coauthor of *Men and Machines,* expresses it. "It robs a man of dignity, destroys his place at the head of the family and deprives him of the essential feeling of usefulness as a human being." Perhaps because of the undeniable social good entailed, perhaps because of the politics involved, we have pursued the noble goal of attempting to maximize employment. The Employment Act of 1946, which still serves as the statement of national economic purpose, singles out the goals of "maximum employment, production and purchasing power." The potential conflict inherent in maximum employment and purchasing power is a subject that has received wide attention. The conflict between employment and output, which exists in certain cases, has been comparatively ignored.

We need output, not jobs. The fact that these can conflict poses a dilemma. For those faced with unemployment, there is no dilemma, only the need for work. Enforced idleness is debilitating and soul-destroying, and the reasons for job consciousness are real and just. Yet this should not mean that we lose sight of the inimical effects that an enforced consciousness can have on output. There are powerful ways that this job consciousness adds to slowth. Its major effect comes in slowing or preventing productivity gains that result from the introduction of labor-saving technology.

Technology is like a pipeline that provides enhanced production. It is particularly crucial in view of constraints we place on material, human, and machine inputs. A continual flow of new innovation is required to maintain growth of output, a continuity that is embodied in the language of new technological developments that often carry labels of sequential generations. For example, a "second generation" of industrial robots is now being readied by a growing U.S. robot-making industry. About 5000 first-generation robots are already in industrial use today and about 150 of these are used by General Motors. At GM they perform a fixed series of tasks that are unsafe or generally unappealing to human workers, like welding and spray painting. These first-generation machines are useful only in a static environment, as the right part must be at the right place, at fixed intervals. Otherwise, those blind first-generation robots will weld or paint thin air.

The second-generation robots now being built can adapt to a dynamic environment—one where position and speed of parts in the production line can change. They are being anthropomorphized, endowed with human qualities such as "vision." The metallic worker being prepared for GM will have camera eyes with vision fields divided into 100 rows and columns, which are distinguished by light-sensitive elements. This supersensitive camera will be supplemented by vision programs that interpret signals from these elements to locate a part's position.

With the aid of such devices, automobile manufacturers like GM will be transforming the workplace. The Society of Manufacturing Engineers predicts that by 1985 half of the direct labor component in assembly of the final automobile will be automated. Even a portion of inspection work will be done by machines. But automation in the automobile industry is by no means a recent event. Installation of the first materials-handling machines created a great scare among auto workers. The fear of massive unemployment, however, proved unwarranted. "The companies have played it very intelligently," says a former staff member of the United Auto Workers (UAW), Anthony W. Connole. "They've introduced [technology] gradually with no immediate layoffs."[4] This gradual introduction of new technology was supplemented by union-automaker agreements that provided for a spreading of work through more paid time off. Until now the job reduction resulting from new technology in the auto industry has been limited to the rate of retirement of auto workers.

According to some observers, labor's relative willingness to accept new production methods may be changing. The pressure exerted by competition with foreign imports and the need to retool for smaller cars are leading American automakers to attempt to speed up the innovation process. This pressure to improve productivity is creating a renewed concern for automakers' jobs. "Perhaps we've heard 'wolf' cried too frequently in the past, when we were really in an evolutionary stage," says Robert T. Lund, Senior Research Associate at the Massachusetts Institute of Technology Center for Policy Alternatives.[5] In a report on automation undertaken for GM, Lund says that substantial unemployment may be created by a stepped-up rate of technological innovation. "We may still be [in] an evolutionary stage, but the capability to move ahead rapidly is now here." In response to renewed concern about the prospect of job loss from technology, job security has again become a UAW issue. The four-day workweek—one response to maintaining job levels—is becoming a key demand of union officials.

In other industries job consciousness has for a time prevailed in holding technology at bay. One industry with opportunity for rapid technological advance is shipping. In looking to the future, a Finnish company has developed an automation system that will allow a single person to unload an entire ship. By means of an overhead movable crane, this person can lift giant containers used to transport the ship's entire cargo. Can such labor-saving technology actually be utilized? Given the general response of the longshore worker to innovation in the past, this is highly questionable.

Containerization of cargo has been the key innovation in the shipping industry. The use of giant boxes that can be loaded on and off a ship's hold and transported in and around the harbor affords the potential for substantial reduction of human effort. A container ship holding 6500 tons in almost 300 containers requires 850 worker hours to unload. That same cargo in a conventional operation would require more than 11,000 hours. A container ship can be turned around in four hours. A conventional operation takes five and a half days. Yet the use of containers was delayed in many ports because of the concern for job security.

The fear that machines would cut into job levels was widespread among certain longshore union locals on the West Coast, even though many jobs lost in unloading ships were merely shifted to the "destuffing" of containers. Nevertheless, the fear persisted. "Machines when they came appeared as merciless monsters, more deadly by far than slack times, because jobs swallowed never came back, as one could hope would happen when slack times eased,"[6] was the way the situation was viewed by Harry Bridges, President of the International Longshoremen's Warehousemen's Union (ILWU) at the time the use of containers was first being sought by management. As a result of this fear, adoption of containerization was held up all along the West Coast for a number of years while the much-heralded Mechanization and Modernization (M&M) Agreement was being hammered out. Output in the industry was constrained and business was lost. It wasn't until the M&M Agreement was finally concluded that the use of containers was implemented.

The automation development feared by people like Bridges has not been justified for the most part. Unions have generally achieved job security through "natural" attrition and a reduction in working hours. But will the working person continue to have a benign attitude toward labor-saving innovation?

A new chapter may be required in the history of jobs and technology, one characterized by a much stronger concern about job security and the quality of life at work. The background of that chapter would show that the history of automation in manufacturing has not been an entirely happy event. Machines take the sting out of strenuous, dangerous, and repetitive tasks, but they replace them with a sometimes noisier and more quickly paced work in which isolation and alienation are not uncommon. Automation substitutes nervous fatigue for that of the more physical variety. This has been graphically described by Louis Kaufman, former President of Local 500 of the ILWU, in his description of life on the modern waterfront:

> In the longshore industry a man is taken from a gang and placed three stories in the air atop a straddle carrier which makes more noise than a tractor, handed a radio which he must listen to and answer, sit sideways to drive this $200,000 machine turning his head front to back constantly, and drive down narrow channels of concrete between rows of containers valued at between $3,000 for the smallest empty to $30,000 for a packed 40 footer filled with color T.V.'s. He must pick up the container by dropping 4 or 6 pins precisely on target into the container top, then maneuver the whole apparatus either over a rail car or truck, or up to a line to destuff. Speed and accuracy are extremely important, otherwise the whole thing loses its value. I'm tired just telling you about it; imagine the nervous fatigue the strad driver has.

One prominent critic of the automated workplace is Volvo President Peter Gyllenhammer. He speaks for a company that seriously questions the value of the assembly line and has substituted in its Kalmar plant techniques of a more human scale. "We invent machines to eliminate some of the physical stresses of work," says Gyllenhammer, "and then we find that psychological tensions cause even more health and behavior problems. People don't want to be subservient to machines and systems. They react to inhuman conditions in very human ways: by job-hopping, absenteeism, apathetic attitudes, antagonism, and even malicious mischief."[7]

Working with machines can also destroy human communication on the job. Those who work in crews have the opportunity to help each other and perhaps to become friends; at least they can communicate. As the machine replaces the crew, that opportunity is lost to the worker who remains on the job. Again, according to Gyllenhammer, "There is an antisocial atmosphere built into the production line. People want to have some social contact, a chance to look at each others' faces now and then. But in an assembly line, people are physically isolated from each other." In an article written for *Harvard Business Review,* Gyllenhammer goes on to imply that today's better-educated young work force will not accept assembly line conditions.

As automation in manufacturing continues, workers, both young and old, educated and educable, have been switching to services to earn their living. Many of these service workers today occupy jobs that were unknown to their parents. Business consultants, agricultural extension agents, speech therapists, and industrial hygienists are just a few of the many job havens for people who in generations past would have found work producing goods. "Society always manages one way or the other to create activities which can be called jobs. That is the way society works,"[8] says Abraham Jaffe of Columbia University's Graduate School of Business. Statistics bear this out. In the face of automation, the composition of the workplace has shifted dramatically. The number of nonmanufacturing and government jobs has doubled since 1955, whereas the number of people producing goods is up only 30 percent. The growth of the service sector has accounted for a large part of the over 11 million additional jobs that have appeared during the past three and a half years. The ranks of those who are busy taking out another's laundry have swelled enormously.

Technological innovation now threatens jobs in the service-sector haven. In the process, job consciousness may be stirred to the point where the use of technology is severely restricted. Indeed, concern is already growing among the ranks of organized labor. Ron Lang, an official of the powerful Canadian Labor Congress, sums it up this way: "The labor movement in Canada has not opposed technological change because it has viewed it as necessary to increased productivity and Canada's ability to compete in the markets of the world. . . . The labor movement has also accepted the argument that, although jobs are lost in one sector, the spinoff effect would maintain the balance of jobs in other areas such as the tertiary and secondary manufacturing sectors. However, this traditional assumption about the overall net increase of jobs from technological change is now being seriously re-examined."[9]

There is good reason for concern among Lang and his colleagues in the Canadian and American labor movements. The service sector—including banking, insurance, retail trade, and government—is a massive employer of people. It is, in the language of economics, a highly labor-intensive sector. It employs mostly people, not machines, many of whom are producing and distributing information and ideas. This process of manipulating information is now the great frontier of American technology. Computers employing silicon chip technology, which provides unbelievable powers of manipulation and memory, are being tied into a telecommunications technology that is developing rapidly. The results will have a striking effect on the shape of the offices where so many of us work. "The intention is ultimately for offices to be equipped and reorganized as were factories during the first half of the century, to greatly increase efficiency and reduce the cost of creating and processing the main product of an office—Information," says businessman P. de Cavaignic in *Data Management*.[10]

The office will be vastly different from what it is now. As with the factory, the first manual tasks to succumb to technology are those entailing drudgery and repetition. Word processors, machines that permit easy storage and manipulation of the typed word, make the retyping of office copy unnecessary. Increasingly sophisticated photocopy machines make copying and collating tasks insignificant. Manipulation of all kinds of data is now largely a task for computers. Yet rapid change in the microelectronics industry will have effects that go far beyond what we have seen. Information may be stored, manipulated, or transmitted, based on the spoken word. Integrated systems will make it possible to store and process data in an expedient way, doing away with paper and files. Model offices that are run without paper already exist. The wastepaper basket may become a thing of the past. Communications hookups will enable jobs to be performed at home, decentralizing the office and helping to reduce the need for conventional energy sources used up in transportation.

A major implication of the automated office is that managers will have immediate access to information without having to rely on secretaries or other clerical staff. Implicitly, secretarial jobs will be lost. This was a major concern of those at a 1978 European conference sponsored by the International Federation of Commercial, Clerical and Technical Employment (FIET). It was their estimate that almost 25 percent or 5 million, of the secretaries in western Europe could lose their jobs over the next ten years. A separate estimate, the *Nora Report* written for the French government, speculated that 30 percent of the employees in the French banking and insurance industries would lose their jobs to data processing equipment and automatic tellers. A number of other studies are underway in other countries, including one by the U.S. Office of Technological Assessment. Whatever numbers are derived by future studies, the effect of automation on the size of the office clerical staff can be expected to be massive.

Wholesale technological innovation in services would help boost output in that sector dramatically. Yet the potential may be partly lost if these new labor-saving technologies violate our job consciousness. Innovation in the service sector will put our willingness to accept technology to the test. At least initially it would not be surprising to see job consciousness prevail.

The impact of an expanded role for computers will not be confined to those doing clerical work. More and more managerial functions are being accomplished with the aid of electronics. We can cite as examples cost accounting, auditing, general administration, purchasing and sales, operations research, and inventory management. Nor is the computer confined to business. Computer-aided design is common in the European and North American engineering industry. So far, this use has been confined to "noncreative" areas such as drawing and the listing of parts and manufacturing specifications. Yet the growing ability of engineers and other technicians to interact with a computer is changing the role of the professional as well.

Automation of the service sector raises the question of where displaced workers will find jobs. This is the major concern of those who observe the growing level of office automation, including those at the FIET conference in Europe: "Unlike the industrial revolution of the 19th century in Europe where steam power replaced manpower, but was associated with such an expansion of demand and markets that there was an increase in the demand for labor to tend the machines, in the new industrial 'revolution' no significant employment effect is likely to be felt," is the note summing up the *FIET Conference on Computers and Work.*"[11] Inherent in this statement is the fact that the manufacturing end of the communications and data processing industry is not at all labor intensive. Furthermore, tasks that involve the most labor are being done in South Korea, Taiwan, Singapore, or other nations where labor is less expensive. Although we have automated the manufacturing process without an overall sacrifice of jobs, it is not at all clear how this can be accomplished should technology come to dominate the service sector. If many jobs are lost, job consciousness could surely slow the pace of technological advance and output growth.

Automation in the service industry will also have a dramatic effect on the type of jobs and skills that are demanded. Office innovations threaten to create a workplace that is divided up between the superskilled and the unskilled. "Short-term unemployment trends are likely," says consultant Philip Dorn. "But far more critical are the long-term changes of drastic population bipolarization. This would appear to generate a small minority of technologically oriented elitists against a vast majority of unskilled, nearly unemployable workers."[12] Union officials are concerned that this polarization is already occurring in the office. They point to a phenomenon known as "deskilling"—reduction in the skills required of workers.

According to Christian Defour, staff member of the International Labor Office, "The fact that young graduates are finding it more and more difficult to obtain direct access to jobs that match their qualifications has led many people to speak of the 'deskilling' of the labor force. They argue that product standardization, mechanization and work organization methods are tending to create a whole host of unskilled jobs and only a few supervisory posts."[13] Dufour claims that whereas the educational level of the American work force has risen, the skill requirements of jobs have not.

The "deskilling" concern is certainly valid if Bruce Hasenyager, Citibank Vice President, is correct. Hasenyager, in charge of the massive effort to computerize the flow of information in and among Citibank's many offices around the world, suggests that secretarial qualifications ultimately may be redefined. The prerequisite he suggests is a master's degree in business administration as secretarial duties become entry-level positions for those with management aspirations.

Job loss, a polarization of the work force, and a change in the work environment are potential by-products of technological innovation. They are taken very seriously in Europe where white-collar unions are stronger than in America. In Norway and Sweden unions have been offered a voice in the introduction of computers into the workplace. Although such veto power over computers is difficult to envision occurring in the United States, a growing concern among affected workers is inevitable. Ultimately, the threat posed by innovation may increase the ranks and power of white-collar unions. Yet whatever the form of expression, the reaction to technology as it is applied to services is bound to be strong. Innovation, radical in the ways it could boost output, is just as likely to stir opposition to its use. Although technology holds the only remaining key to improving productivity and eventually averting slowth, its use is bound to release a tempest in the American workplace. It may ultimately fall victim to a well-entrenched job consciousness, despite the negative impact such an occurrence would have on output. Two examples can illustrate the point that the creation of jobs does not mean more output.

We have deemed it necessary to retire people at a certain age to create jobs for younger workers. Young people, it has been maintained, deserve jobs and career advancement despite the fact that they may lack the experience and productivity of those people being retired. One product of this job concern was the recently amended Age Discrimination in Employment Act of 1967, which prescribed mandatory retirement in the private sector for those aged 65. The Social Security system was designed to accomplish the same thing. "The condition that first led to fixing the age eligibility for Social Security benefits at age 65 and subsequently to encouraging even younger workforce withdrawals was one of a seeming excess of workers," observed former U.S. Commerce Secretary Juanita Kreps. "Unemployment was massive when the act was passed and quite severe when the decision was made to allow men to retire at age 62 with a reduced benefit."[14] Legislative efforts to push the aging worker out the revolving employment door have often been supplemented by the "blue plate special." These are inducements to older employees to move up and out of their jobs. The lure is enhanced pensions or retirement relocation assistance to Florida or some other sunny climate.

The "wisdom" of enforcing retirement has evolved in the total absence of indications that older workers are less productive. If anything, conclusions of studies would lead to the opposite belief. At least one such study by the Federal Bureau of Labor Statistics surveyed 6000 federal office employees. Differences in output found among hourly wage groups were insignificant. Older workers, in fact, were found to be marginally more productive. It makes good sense that a number of jobs are better filled by people with greater experience. Yet until recently we have retired our citizens who are over 65, claiming that they denied jobs to those with the qualification of relative youth.

The first sign of change came in 1978, with an amendment to the Age Discrimination in Employment Act, which extended the mandatory retirement age to 70. Congress did this with mixed motivations. In some ways it is part of a broader trend toward providing job and life rights. More important, though, it is an acknowledgment that pensions are being eroded and that their recipients are beginning through sheer numbers to constitute an effective political force.

Today there are seven times the number of people aged 65 and over than there were in 1900, whereas the labor participation rate for those over 65 has fallen from 67 to 22 percent over approximately the same period. It is hard for Congress to ignore the reality of charts that trace the baby boom population bulge into middle and older age. This reality means that as the work force ages, the economy will need the efforts of those who choose a longer working life.

With an aging of the population and the work force, the urge by government to retire the old to "create" jobs will no doubt fade. It will not go away easily, however. Mandatory retirement in the private sector is still on the books, though now at age 70. "What's magic about age 70?" Dave Trezice, Vice President of Personnel of Westinghouse Corporation, is quoted as asking in an *Industry Week* article, "Aging Workers." "What's threatening about the fact that we need all the creative, talented and productive people we can get for as long as we can get them?"[15] Sears Roebuck and Co. does not agree. It sued the government, as part of a broader case, seeking among other things an overturning of the higher retirement ceiling. Sears claimed in Congressional testimony that if the retirement age was increased, the attrition rate of those employed by its firm would slow and prevent the introduction of new employees.

We are approaching an important transition in our attitude toward older workers as we enable them to produce at an older age if they so desire. We can help by allowing shorter working hours and seasonal shifts, although reasonable tests of productive ability would be required. The level of production would undoubtedly benefit from the more experienced work force. Yet the urge to open up jobs to the young by retiring the old may endure as long as the pressure of unemployment remains.

The focus on jobs rather than on output diverts our attention away from improving the level of skill of the work force. A lengthy retirement also is worrying older citizens, causing them to demand a pension that is indexed against inflation. Cost-of-living allowances in pensions are now in increasing demand. Unions are seeking them as part of wage contracts, and pensioners, who are a growing political force, are demanding benefits that keep pace with rising prices. Although protection of the retired person from inflation is a noble cause, indexed pensions cannot possibly achieve what they set out to do. Money in pension funds means nothing without the availability of future goods and services on which the money can be spent. Without striking gains in productivity and output, an older population that is increasingly dominated by the elderly who are denied work will be unable to provide the goods. Indexed pensions will be doomed by rising living costs that will drive down the buying power of all money, including that in enlarged pension funds.

Older workers are needed to help produce the goods for themselves. We must abandon our efforts at creating job openings by pushing older workers out of the work force and instead provide them with a working environment in which they can productively remain. Unless we do this, security for the old will be nothing more than a bankrupt ideal. We must turn our attention toward output, not jobs.

Protectionism, in all its strange and creative guises, provides another example of the job consciousness fallacy. This comes in a variety of forms—tariffs, quotas, and the increasingly popular form known as the nontariff barrier to trade. This is often an exclusionary product standard set by "concerned" governments, guarding the safety and welfare of its citizens from "harmful" products made abroad. Protectionism has one main justification—protection of local industry and jobs. Yet it keeps us from adding to the available supply of goods and holds down our standard of living.

Take the following absurd but illustrative example. Suppose the government of Canada decided in its wisdom to stimulate domestic employment by creating a local industry to grow bananas. It could proceed by throwing up tariffs or quotas on the imported fruit. If sufficient demand could endure in the face of the outrageous price, a local industry would develop. Hothouses would be built in the sometimes frozen countryside to produce bananas in defiance of nature. Jobs would be created for those who construct the hothouses and those who grow the fruit. But who would benefit? The answer is no one. Those who could no longer afford to buy bananas or pay the outrageous price would be the obvious losers, along with the foreign producer. Yet this perversity could be justified for the sake of creating jobs. Restrictions on the importation of foreign footwear or televisions, although less perverse, will have the same effect. The entire world benefits from a focus on boosting output rather than creating jobs. Protectionism, in whatever form it arises, is oriented toward the wrong goal. If other nations produce televisions and stereos more cheaply than we can, we should consume theirs. In return, we should provide them with the goods we produce efficiently.

This discussion should illustrate the perverse nature of the job consciousness that is strongly entrenched. It shows how the concern for preserving and creating jobs can stand in the way of output and a higher living standard. If this chapter shows anything, it shows how consciousness will hamper technological innovation that threatens job security. In this dampening of technology, job consciousness can contribute to blocking the last remaining path that can lead us away from slowth.

chapter 9

The Productivity Puzzle

Nobel Prize-winning economist Milton Friedman relates the story of a man who is seen one night intensely searching the sidewalk beneath the illuminating rays of a street lamp.

"What have you lost?" asked a passerby.

"My key," replied the man.

"If you had lost it here, surely you would be able to see it," the observer reasoned.

"But I lost it over there," protested the gentleman, "a few yards away."

"Then why are you looking around the lamp?" asked the confused passerby.

"Because it's dark over there," came the reply.

At the outset of this book we admit that the problem with providing an explanation for slowth is in the size of the area that must be searched. The causes of our current economic dilemma cannot be illuminated by a narrowly focused light that renders everything clear and amenable to simple proof. Instead we have had to grope in a wide dark area in search of a less clearly established reality.

Up to this point our emphasis has been on the variety of consciousness-led constraints on production. It might therefore still be possible for a few readers to remain unconvinced about the reasons for slowth and for some others to perhaps even doubt its existence. Indeed, by presenting our work in the vein of a hypothesis, we are open to the charge that our efforts represent groping in darkness in search of a key that does not exist. To remedy this we present in the following two chapters evidence to support the fact that the key *is* lost and that we are looking in the right place.

The existence of slow economic growth can be demonstrated not only by the statistics on slow growth that we provide earlier, but also by virtue of the fact that our economy is currently plagued by the very problems we would expect to result from slowth. In fact, the existence of slowth, accompanied by a failure to recognize it for what it is, provides a simple and direct means of explaining many of our current economic problems. Conventional economic wisdom cannot explain them in a consistent way. Some of the problems it cannot explain at all.

We can easily show that the factors causing slowth are the very ones behind the dismal performance in the rate of growth of American productivity. The productivity of labor, as an output per person, is just another side of average real income. It is only an additional step, after showing how our constraints on inputs of materials, labor, and machines, as well as technology contribute to disappointing productivity figures, to show that the existence of slowth and the misunderstanding of its cause can explain other problems. Slowth and economists' and politicians' faulty diagnosis of it lead to inflation, currency crises, mushrooming balance of payments deficits, excessive government economic tinkering, stagflation, and the taxpayer revolt. It is important that an explanation of slowth can also shed light on the many other current economic problems that have caused confusion and disarray among many economists. These problems are clearly linked and have a common route—in slowth.

Economists, politicians, and the financial press have focused with increasing bewilderment on what may be termed the productivity puzzle. We quote *Business Week*'s comments on a 1978 report of the body of economic advisors to the President: "This week's report of the Council of Economic Advisors shows that the President's economists are deeply concerned that persistent low growth rates of productivity may prevent the economy from growing at that pace [4½–5%] for an extended period. . . . What is at stake is nothing less than the future of economic growth."¹ It is no surprise that in its *Midyear Report of 1979,* the U.S. Joint Economic Committee dubbed lagging productivity the "Linchpin of the Eighties" and that in a major collection of studies compiled by William Fellner, which examine contemporary economic problems, the first five studies are devoted to the productivity problem.

Compared with other nations, our productivity performance has been abysmal indeed. Over the decade of 1967–1977 productivity increased at an average annual rate of 6.8 percent in Japan, 6.6 percent in Denmark, 5.3 percent in Germany, and 5.3 percent in Italy—all well ahead of the 2.3 percent U.S. growth rate. From 1973 the growth rate of productivity for the remainder of the 1970s has averaged only about 0.5 percent, and there are numerous periods when productivity actually declined. Apart from revealing a glaring comparative weakness in the U.S. economic performance relative to other industrial nations, the slow growth of productivity casts doubt on the ability of the United States to achieve substantial real economic growth. The headline of the *Wall Street Journal* that greeted the announcement of the dismal productivity growth figure for 1978 puts the matter in perspective: "Figures Add to Fears That Standard of Living Gains Will Decrease Markedly."² This headline is not unduly alarmist: it merely reflects the fact that growth in our standard of living is dependent on our ability to produce more efficiently the goods and services that are demanded.

The cost of stagnant productivity is by no means a mere statistic. According to Jackson Carlson, an economist at the U.S. Chamber of Commerce, the real income of the average household would have been $3700 higher in 1978 if the productivity over the previous decade had continued to grow at the old rates. And that is real income, which means income adjusted for inflation. Just imagine an extra $3700 dollars for the family budget each and every year. That would be no mere statistic when translated into holidays, furniture, and other goods.

Despite the widespread concern about productivity, few explanations of its cause have gained wide acceptance. At the same time, this productivity performance has challenged traditional economic wisdom, one element of which is named Okun's Law after the former head of the President's Council of Economic Advisors, Arthur M. Okun. It used to be believed that real gross national product (GNP) would grow by three percentage points for every 1 percent fall in unemployment. The additional gain in output in excess of the growth in employment has been attributed to increases in the length of the workweek, the rate of labor force participation, and the rise in productivity that accompanies more efficient use of labor during economic expansions.

"A real shocker came in the first quarter of this year [1978], when the number of jobs rose by one million although there was no real growth in GNP. . . . Okun's Law wasn't working at all,"[3] was the way *Newsweek* expressed its surprise. *Newsweek* commented, "Okun's Law has been repealed—or at least suspended. In recent months, employment has been growing and layoffs falling even while the real gross national product actually declined."[4] The 1979 *Economic Report of the President* summarizes the anomaly between the recent performance of the economy and Okun's Law. "The use of this relationship and previous estimates of potential GNP produced substantial overestimates of the unemployment rate in 1977 and 1978."[5]

How is it possible for employment to be growing and for the output of this larger number of producers to actually decline? The answer may be found by unraveling the productivity puzzle. A decline in output, given more workers, can occur only if the output per worker, meaning productivity, falls. But Okun's Law fails even when output per worker is on the rise. As long as productivity moves up by less than enough to raise output by three times the growth in employment, the artifact called Okun's Law will at least have to be revised. It is here, in the issue of productivity, where we can find the reasons why Okun's Law has become outdated. The slowdown in productivity growth is the main factor that breaks the link between employment and the rate of economic growth.

The consciousness explosion of the 1960s provides the key to explaining the poor productivity showing and the consequent suspension of Okun's Law. The statistics of low productivity growth are a direct reflection of the combined effect of input constraints. Growth in the output of working people is reduced as we slow the growth in supply of materials they convert, as they apply less effort, as we give them fewer new machines, and as we constrain the technology we allow them to use. Because we have been doing all these things, it should come as no surprise that productivity is failing to grow as fast as it grew in the past.

Although few economists or government officials view the productivity problem as traceable to restrictions on all inputs, the Council of Economic Advisors points correctly to at least part of the problem. They admit:

> Increased economic and social regulation has aggravated the productivity slowdown in a number of ways. Productivity is a measure of output produced per unit of resources used in production. Economic regulation, as in transportation, precludes labor and capital from flowing to those uses that have a relatively high value. The effects of social regulations are more complicated. The gains from social regulation—in such forms as reduced pollution and greater safety—are generally not included in measured output. When an increasing fraction of society's labor and capital resources is diverted to producing these gains, measured productivity growth is reduced.[6]

As we are attempting to show, this is an accurate but limited account of the productivity puzzle. Not only are our nation's labor and capital resources being "diverted" to produce the trappings of a higher quality life, but the total level of human and capital input is also being eroded. Furthermore, the rise of consciousness and its enactment through regulation and other means such as job and life rights are also threatening vital determinants of production such as resource input and the use of technology.

Other economists and officials take an even narrower view than the council in examining the productivity puzzle. John Kendrick of George Washington University attributes the productivity decline partly to a rise in the proportion of less skilled workers in the labor force, as well as to drugs, crime, and antiestablishment behavior. These views are echoed by Harvard University sociologist David Riesman, who blames the imposition of counterculture attitudes and sentiments onto the workplace. He holds that the drive, discipline, and energy displayed on the job and the devotion to it have all suffered from this change of view within the American labor force. Herbert Stein, the Chairman of the Council of Economic Advisors to both Presidents Richard Nixon and Gerald Ford also found life-style and social trends to be at the root of the productivity slowdown. Stein sees the "me generation" attitude as a culprit. All such explanations are accurate, but narrow in their focus on the human input into the production process.

Sanford Rose, in a *Fortune* story entitled "The Global Slowdown Won't Last Forever," puts the bulk of the blame on the higher price of oil. "It takes energy to run machinery, so high energy prices favor greater use of labor rather than greater use of machines. Accordingly, high energy prices tend to depress demand for capital goods and slow the growth of productivity."[7] Although it holds some truth, this argument attributes the decline of productivity growth to a single input, energy, and excludes consideration of materials, labor, machines, or technology.

In an article entitled "The Shrinking Standard of Living," *Business Week* also blames the price of oil. In a cover story devoted to the standard of living (rather than declining productivity), it plainly states that "high priced oil lies at the heart of the shrinking U.S. standard of living."[8] As Sanford Rose claimed in *Fortune, Business Week* argues that higher oil prices decrease capital-intensity in production and thereby production efficiency and output. But *Business Week* goes further. Having recognized that higher oil prices mean poorer consumers and richer producers and are causing a mere flow of national dollars from one group to the other, the article looks toward the Organization of Petroleum Exporting Countries (OPEC). "In this inflation, the people on the receiving end are the Arab sheiks," says *Business Week*. But we should not allow ourselves to confuse this balance of payments effect with the matter of national income that we are discussing. It is our failure to produce not only oil but everything else that has contributed to slowth. It is true that in consuming more oil than we ourselves produce we send dollars abroad that are used to buy up other parts of our national output. This means that less of this output is available and that we must make do without the items bought with these petrodollars. But it is the shortage in the growth of output that is the fundamental cause of slowth in national income. If we produced more, there would be growth even after the expenditure of petrodollars for fossil fuels from the Middle East. Countries such as Japan and members of the European Economic Community (EEC) have paid for their oil out of greater domestic production, even in cases where some of these countries rely entirely on imported oil.

But the Council of Economic Advisors casts some doubt about the power of the oil price increase to explain low productivity growth: "Some suggest that the oil embargo of 1973–74 and the subsequent quadrupling of oil prices had an adverse impact on productivity growth. However, it is difficult to find a mechanism by which an oil crisis could have such an immediate and severe effect on the economy. . . . Actually, adjustment to the new oil prices has been extremely slow. Moreover, other countries in which energy prices rose more than in the United States did not show such large productivity declines."[9] Edward Denison is the expert on productivity studies, the man who has concentrated on this important issue of supply when so many of his fellow economists sought output explanations in demand. In his studies, "Where Has Productivity Gone" and "The Puzzling Drop in Productivity,"[10] he has reached the same conclusion about the limited power of energy prices to explain declining productive growth. Denison attributes a mere 0.2 percent of productivity losses during the important period of 1972–1976 to the higher energy prices. Others like John Tatom of the Federal Reserve Bank of St. Louis would attach a higher value. But as Tatom's extensive research of numerous factors demonstrates, others who offer the oil price explanation for slow productivity growth are confined in their search to one well-lit corner.

There is a great deal of additional carefully produced evidence that would portray oil, and even energy in general, as only part of the picture of declining growth in output and productivity. Such evidence was provided in the almost 800 page study entitled *Energy in Transition,* published in January 1980. This study, commissioned by a group that was then named the Energy Research and Development Administration, involved the work of more than 250 professionals from economics, science, engineering, and industry. Although the purpose of the study was not to explain declining economic performance in the past, it did draw conclusions about how energy production slowdowns would affect output in the early 1980s. The study, cochaired by Harvey Brooks of Harvard and Edward Ginzton, the Chairman of Varian Associates, a Palo Alto (California) electronics firm, showed that by conserving available energy we do not have to experience an economic slowdown as a result of energy shortages alone. Half the energy we presently use could provide the same standard of living if the right technologies were applied, the study argued. But the slowth we have described has much more widespread roots than can be found in any individual input, even oil or energy.

Just as we should not blame our failure to grow on one *material* input such as oil, we should not trace slowing productivity and economic growth to the rise in crime, an antiestablishment attitude, or the entry of less skilled individuals into the work force. Such a focus is far too narrow. It centers solely around the labor force as the determinate of productivity. The same is true of a study that has received wide attention in the financial press, *Britains' Economic Problem: Too Few Producers.* In this book the authors, Robert Bacon and Walter Eltis, pin the problem solely on the labor input, arguing, to use the summarizing words of *Fortune,* that "the supporting cast includes too many extras." This is a euphemistic condemnation of Britain's burgeoning bureaucracy. Bacon and Eltis decry the trend they perceive toward the involvement of fewer and fewer workers in what the authors consider to be productive endeavor.

Michael Blumenthal, the former Treasury Secretary, also focuses in public statements on a single nonmaterial determinant of productivity. He attributes the slowdown in productivity growth to haphazard growth of federal regulations that reduce investment and thereby limit the quantity and quality of machines with which we must work. Although our national consciousness has indeed led to the erection of regulations with large detrimental effects, we must not overlook the fact that this is still only one *part* of the problem. Regulation inhibits investment in capital equipment but machines remain as only one input into the production process. It is the limitations of *all* the inputs, imposed by the full range of national consciousness, that strikes out against our production capabilities.

The productivity puzzle has left politicians and the public alike mistrustful of economists, who are chastised in a number of statements made to *Fortune* for viewing circumstances in light of old and irrelevant theory. "I don't trust any economists today," is the way U.S. Senate Budget Committee member Peter Domenici of New Mexico puts it. "Their theories are out of date." Lyle Gramley, a respected member of the Council of Economic Advisors, was forced to admit that "our old rules of thumb no longer work. And we haven't been able to develop new ones." According to another economist on the staff of the council, "something strange has been going on out there. We have taken the numbers apart, but we still can't tell what's the matter." Blumenthal adds, "I think the economics profession is close to bankruptcy in understanding the present situation—before or after the fact." This lack of understanding has thrown policy into disarray. "Governments have lost confidence in their ability to manage their economies and have no long-term prospectives," says Oxford University economist Peter Oppenheimer. "They have no strategy, and as a result are reduced to ad hockery, tinkering and drift."[11]

Any account that traces the shift in national values away from a pure production orientation will shed considerable light on the malaise of the economics profession, the suspension of Okun's Law, and the factors that lie behind the productivity puzzle. This has been recognized by others. Juan Cameron, for example, writing in *Fortune* comes close to the mark; "the explanation of the confusion in economics probably lies outside economics. While established laws have not been repealed, the political and social context in which they function has changed momentously over the past decade or so."[12]

It will not be surprising in the years ahead to find that an increasing number of those economists and policy-makers who shed light on the problem of slow growth in productivity and therefore in output do so by referring to the shift in national values that has taken place. In so doing, as we shortly show, they will find the basic explanation for a variety of other phenomena including currency crises, balance of payments deficits, excessive government tinkering, stagflation, and the taxpayer revolt, all of which find their roots in slowth and the accompanying failure to admit its presence. Understanding the existence and cause of slowth can illuminate many problems and thereby provide a valuable key to the solution of some of the troubles of our times.

chapter 10

The Slowth Backlash

American values are changing. They are shifting toward a more sensitive and compassionate existence with a growing emphasis on the less tangible qualities of life. Although our movement along this path may on occasion waver, the general direction is clear. But like the cause, the effect of this shift should also be clear: our living standards will improve more slowly.

The choice we are making may not be a bad bargain in itself. A higher quality of life is an unquestionably desirable goal. And more goods and services can be traded by an already affluent society for a greater degree of freedom from economic insecurity, pollution, on-the-job mishaps, or a technologically induced Armageddon. But the tradeoff is not so simple, especially if it is misunderstood by those who have to live with it.

The potential ill effects of slowth can be far more serious than a slowing in the growth of living standards. Unrecognized or unaccepted as it is today, slowth stands to produce turmoil in our economic and political circumstances as our national frustration and anxiety induce an angry backlash from normally peaceful citizens and misdirected action from a dazed and confused government. These reactions reflect a total misunderstanding of an economy forced into lower gear by the drive toward a higher quality existence.

STAGFLATION AND GOVERNMENT TINKERING

Government tinkering with the economy predates the advent of slowth. The most rapid spurts of intervention followed upon the theories of John Maynard Keynes and were enacted during the economically activist administrations of post-Depression America. The hallmark of this activism has been the effort by government to provide economic demand whenever the national product falls short of its full employment level. This has led to a perplexing variety of tax rebates, spending programs, transfer schemes, incentive subsidies, and other esoteric devices, all of which invariably increase the size of the federal budget deficit.

Over time, the confidence in the government's ability to control the economy grew along with the government's propensity for deficit spending. During the 1970s these deficits amounted to more than $300 billion. They are the product of more than one determinant. Efforts to stimulate the economy during periods of slow growth have combined with a growing demand for government services and transfer payments to support expanded "entitlements." Over time, the spending has become intractable. The constituency of government spending programs—an enlarged civil service and an ever greater army of recipients—provides a cohesive political base that mitigates against any large-scale reversal of our path down this one-way street.

Transfer payments, for one, account for an increasingly large share of the GNP and government spending. The cost of programs administered by federal, state, and local agencies has grown from 7 percent of the gross national product (GNP), or $55 billion, in 1966 to 12 percent, or $266 billion, in 1977. Social Security, Medicare, and various public assistance and insurance programs support not only the recipients, but also those who administer the programs. Indeed the growth of such programs continues to ratchet upward the ranks of the civil service in a seemingly limitless spiral.

Transfer payments, along with expanded efforts to regulate and administer "temporary" schemes designed to stimulate a sluggish economy, tend to become institutionalized. This ratchet, whereby civil servants are added more easily than they are later displaced, appears inevitable without the axe that government is so reluctant to wield on the ranks of civil service employment.

The questionable record of government in achieving its ever widening goals has been overshadowed by the advent of stagflation—periods during which the economy is besieged by both high inflation and slow growth. Traditional theories of aggregate demand management have been challenged by this persistence of slow growth alongside huge budget deficits. Stagflation has had a devastating effect on our confidence in the efforts of government to control the economy. The credibility of government and private economists has been questioned by many.

The failure of the economy of the 1970s to return to the growth rates of the 1950s and 1960s, despite growing deficits and monetary tinkering, is explained by the nature of slowth. Demand-oriented fiscal policies have simply nothing to do with the basic cause of slow growth. They have no positive impact on the slower rate of productivity growth that results from a fundamental shift in public objectives. Monetary or fiscal policy has no effect on the values that drive our economy. They cannot call forth a stepped-up rate of production if the requisite inputs fail to grow sufficiently fast. Demand-stimulation policy has little relevance to an economy constrained by slow growth in the potential rate of supply. No rule of nature brings forth steady growth in potential supply, however carefully engineered the effort to stimulate demand.

If stimulative policies were merely ineffective, that would not be too bad. Unfortunately, though, these policies do have a powerful effect. Futile efforts to generate production by continuing to bolster the level of demand can only result in an alarming increase in prices, accentuating the inflationary disease. This is particularly true if demand stimulation takes the form of an irresponsible expansion of the money supply. The virulent inflation, which is the inevitable result, will coexist alongside slow growth.

The ill effects of stimulative policy have not been confined to our own experience in the United States. Futile attempts to use demand-stimulation measures have been responsible for a large portion of Britain's economic ills over the past several years. This is the reluctant conclusion drawn by former Prime Minister James

Callahan, who bravely admitted in 1977, "We used to think that you could just spend your way out of a recession and increase employment by cutting taxes and boosting government spending. I tell you, in all candor, that the option no longer exists, and that insofar as it ever did exist, it only worked by injecting bigger doses of inflation into the economy, followed by higher levels of unemployment as the next step."[1]

Confronted with the need to reduce inflation, any vote-sensitive government that hopes to be reelected is confined by its central role within the American economy to mere proclamations of austerity and promises of reduced spending. Bloated both by past stimulative policy and rising "entitlements," real government spending will not be easy to reduce. Economist Milton Friedman tells us why: "The Federal government is the engine of inflation—the only one there is. But it has been the engine of inflation at the behest of the American public, which wants the government to spend more but not to raise taxes—so encouraging resort to the hidden tax of inflation."[2] In the face of intractable government spending and an expanding money stock, even a deepening recession does not slow inflation. Says Arthur Okun, "You get so little deflation from recessions now that it's like burning down your house to bake a loaf of bread."[3]

Faced with the errors of past-demand-oriented ways, a reexamination of our economic policy and potential appears to be underway. Jimmy Carter, in his 1979 *Economic Report of the President,* echoes the realization of Callahan and admits the economic straitjacket in which his policy options are confined: "Twice in the past decade inflation has accelerated and a recession has followed, but each recession brought only limited relief from inflation. The underlying pressures behind rising prices and costs continued to be strong, and inflation eventually accelerated again when recovery began. Stop and go policies do not work."

The Carter Administration also shows signs of recognizing the reality of slowth. As part of the same economic report, the economic council advising the President recaps the fact that in 1977 it revised its estimate of potential GNP growth downward in reaction to poor productivity performance, about which the council writes, "It no longer seems reasonable to assume that the exceedingly poor productivity growth in 1973–74 and 1977–78 represented statistical aberrations or one-time events, implying no reduction in the long-term trend. Downward revisions of our estimate of long-term productivity growth and of potential GNP are clearly necessary."

Although the likelihood of slow economic growth is overtly recognized by the council, it is less clear whether this awareness will translate into a serious change in policies. So long as the government and general public misunderstand the nature of our plight, little can be done. Discussion of the dilemma will remain confined to the election-time rhetoric of politicians seeking public office. An administration that advocates the recognition and acceptance of slow improvements in living standards runs the risk of being painted "un-American" by its political adversaries. "We must reject the doctrine which says that our destiny is limited to the sharing of scarcity," is the way politician John Connally was quoted in an article by *Fortune.* "It is unthinkable that we Americans will turn our backs on the American dream of opportunity and upward mobility. It is common sense that we all prosper only as the pie gets bigger."[4] Connally's "common sense" rejection of a stagnant American economy is typical of the criticism aspiring politicians will level at those officeholders who see slowth for what it is and accept it. Pressure to maintain growth rates of the past will be generated by politicians making their lunge for high office. The result will be increasingly exotic forms of tinkering, subtle perhaps, but futile in their efforts to force the economy onto a higher growth track.

There is great confusion caused by the failure of government tinkering. The following account from *Fortune,* provides an example:

Congress has come to feel that the White House doesn't know what it's doing. Many members, uncertain whether to step on the gas or the brakes, are turning to radical proposals. Some are urging that a new form of wage and price control, so-called TIP, or Tax-Based Incomes Policy, be given a try. Senator William Roth of Delaware and Representative Jack Kemp of New York have gathered wide support for their proposal to cut federal taxes by 33 percent, or more than $100 billion, over a span of three years without corresponding cuts in federal spending. Some conservative members want to put on a clenched teeth demonstration of fiscal and monetary restraint to break inflation.[5]

No major inroads in fighting inflation and the bureaucratic tangle can come until slowth is seen for what it is. Nothing short of a widespread awareness of the limits placed on our production potential will keep authorities from attempting to pull us out of what they see as a recession by excessively increasing the money supply, tinkering more, and creating larger government deficits. A misreading or lack of acceptance of the state of our economy will lead only to greater inflation caused by growth in the supply of money and expansion of the federal bureaucracy as tinkering and deficit spending continue. This inflation will not hide the true fact of economic life that is responsible for bringing it about—a slow moving growth in the standard of economic life. The inflation that we see is the mechanism through which we experience slowth, but the true problem is slowth itself and not inflation that serves as its veil. The symptom is inflation; the illness is slowth. Slowth is what makes it difficult for all of us to obtain what we think we deserve as high prices simply ration out the limited amount we produce.

PROTECTIONISM

"Foreign trade," says the late and long-time AFL-CIO boss George Meany, "is the guerilla war of economics, and right now the U.S. is being ambushed." Such protectionist sentiment does not come as a surprise from a leader of American labor. What is noteworthy are the increasing number of shots being fired across the bow of the free trade movement during a number of recent skirmishes. Threatened is U.S. participation in this thirty-year-old movement aimed at liberalizing the world trade and payments system.

Although this movement continues to make gains, as it has done with the completion of the latest General Agreement on Tariffs and Trade (GATT) negotiations, these will be increasingly harder to maintain in the face of slowth. Slow growth erodes the determination of nations to strip barriers to trade, particularly those protecting troubled industries. *The Economist* maintains that achievement of freer trade is largely a matter of confidence on the part of government leaders. "That confidence has been shaken by five years of slower growth and once-unthinkable unemployment levels. Not so badly that governments are ready to undo 25 years of trade liberalization—but enough to cast shadows over the future."[6]

In the United States those shadows are now being cast by efforts to protect the beleaguered steel industry. It is an industry hard pressed by foreign competition and one in which jobs are increasingly threatened. Competition from foreign steel manufacturers, especially Japanese companies, expanded during 1976–1977 as a result of relatively sluggish demand outside the United States. American imports of steel grew rapidly, leading the domestic industry to call for protection against the dumping of Japanese steel. The Carter Administration has thus far resisted these calls for import restrictions, setting in its place an assistance program for workers whose jobs are under siege. Nevertheless, the administration was also forced to set up a trigger price mechanism that would monitor steel imports. It also extracted export restraint agreements from Hong Kong, Japan, and Korea.

Steel is not the only U.S. industry to exert pressure for protectionism. In 1976 the United States imported an incredible 400 million pairs of shoes, an average of two pairs for each person. Half of these came from Taiwan and South Korea. In mid-1977 the United States induced these two countries to cut back shipments by almost one-fourth of their 1976 levels. Meanwhile, efforts have been made to revitalize the footwear industry by means of a three-year $56 million federal program. Restraint agreements have also been negotiated with Japan to force a reduction in her exports of color televisions to the United States.

Despite its apparent dedication to the cause of free trade, the American government is up against substantial pressures that result from the decline in manufacturing productivity. Part of the cause of this situation was summed up by the late Nelson Rockefeller in discussing prospects for American industry. "The costs of meeting environmental standards and adjusting to changing regulations have increased the total price of a product to the point where it is not competitive." In the steel industry he cites examples of foundries that were closed because of an inability to meet the cost of controls. "In other nations," says Rockefeller, "foundries are being established that would not have met earlier American standards much less current ones."

The void of environmental concern that provides a competitive advantage for other nations is only part of the picture. We are witnessing today the economic emergence of nations that, in many respects, exhibit the same dedication to production that forged the present industrialized world ahead so rapidly in the past. These are nations without extensive pollution controls, job and life right entitlements, or detailed deliberations about the impact of social and technological change. Nations like Singapore (in which real GNP growth between 1970 and 1975 averaged 7.3 percent), Hong Kong (4.2 percent), Brazil (6.2 percent), Turkey (4.9 percent), Malaysia (5.3 percent), and South Korea (8.2 percent) have placed economic growth in the forefront of their priorities. Over this same period real growth in the quality-of-life-conscious United States averaged a meager 1.6 percent.

The dedication of other nations to production has been matched by the United States only in our dedication to consumption, which has brought about a marked increase in U.S. imports. In 1977 the volume of imports into the United States rose by 13 percent, compared to a mere 3.5 percent in both Japan and Germany. Although this is partly due to the slower recoveries of these two nations from the deep slump of the mid-1970s, the growth in U.S. imports is still shocking. Imports from Japan, for example, grew from over $15 billion in 1975 to over $24 billion in 1978. The result of this has been enormous U.S. balance of payments deficits, running well over $20 billion in 1977 and 1978. In the end it may be this, rather than organized protectionist lobbies, that undermines U.S. dedication to free trade. With demand growing unrestrainedly, and our own aggregate supply checked by an entrenched consciousness, the deficiency can be met in only one way. The gap must be filled with the products of other nations. The balance of trade deficit that results *is* the difference between our consumption and production. We have been satisfying this difference with deficits of 1 to 2 percent of our aggregate demand. This is the meaning of a more than $20 billion deficit in a $2 trillion national economy. We are burdened with this deficit simply because we fail to add to our supply but nevertheless refuse to trim our demand. With demand unlikely to be checked effectively, the trade deficit and consequent flirtation with protectionism can only be controlled by freeing the production process from some of the constraints imposed by our consciousness.

The case of the trans-Alaska oil pipeline provides a direct example of how consciousness can reduce the available domestic product, thereby wrecking the balance of payments through the importation of what we do not produce. If we consume anything at a rate exceeding our own domestic production, it must come from abroad. One of the companies reporting to the Business Roundtable Study observed that payments for imported oil (oil that could otherwise have been provided from the North Slope fields of Alaska) during the regulatory delay were $20 billion. This sum is almost as large as one of the larger trade deficits for any year in the late 1970s—a very sizable sum indeed. It is clear that if we encumber production without trimming demands, a trade deficit is the obvious result.

In the face of our inability to restrict imports or improve productivity, the value of the U.S. dollar will continue to plunge. In the year ending August 1978, the dollar declined by over 50 percent against the Swiss franc, 44 percent against the Japanese yen, 19 percent against the German mark, and 13 percent against the British pound. For most nations this rapid decline in the value of the currency would, of itself, provide import protection by rendering foreign goods more expensive. Any greater protection in the form of renewed depreciation, however, may be foreshortened by political pressure. Americans are becoming conscious of the effect that a declining dollar has on their purchasing power and the international value of their income and wealth. Domestic pressure for measures to arrest a further decline will be supplemented by protests from those abroad who hold dollars, particularly the oil producing nations that have a vested interest in the stability of the dollar. Thus the temptation may grow for the U.S. government to attempt to stem import consumption and provide continuous support for the dollar on the world money markets. At the same time it might seek to score domestic political points by building protective cocoons around endangered industries.

The continued depreciation of the foreign-exchange value of the dollar serves as a clear and politically embarrassing reminder of the slow growth in our living standards relative to that of other nations. It has very real consequences and directly reflects the economic reality of slowth in both an absolute and relative sense. It is useful to examine why this is so. We have made the case that the deficit in the American balance of payments is the result of unchecked expansion of our desire to consume, accompanied by a well-checked ability to produce. The consequent shortfall of production has been overcome by running a deficit on the merchandise component of the international balance, the balance of trade. This has worked to create a relative glut of our currency and to bring down the international value of the U.S. dollar. But this is tantamount to having a cut in the growth of our living standards.

As we have become all too painfully aware, a fall in the value of our currency relative to that of the countries with which we trade serves to raise the U.S. dollar price of the imported goods we buy. We see this on the price tags of imported goods. These higher prices for the goods we crave reduces the value of the incomes we earn, shrinking the growth we experience in our absolute standards of living.

On the other face of our falling dollar is the rising value of the currencies for which it is exchanged. As the prices of our imports rise, import prices in countries with appreciating currencies will fall. In other words, the foreign buying power of these currencies will rise, and as it does so the buying power of foreign incomes go up, with the result that we become poorer and those nations with rising currency values make an absolute and relative gain. The flood to our continent of hard-monied tourists from Europe and Japan, a complete reversal of the patterns of decades before, is evidence of the income gains of these people relative to ourselves.

This process can be seen in another way. When comparing standards of living prevailing in different nations, dollars cannot be compared with the German mark, the yen, or any other currency. A conversion must be made and these comparisons are then made in terms of dollars. As the dollar is translated into fewer marks, yen, or any of the number of other currencies against which it has depreciated, those foreign incomes will be relatively greater in number of dollars. This relative worsening of our living standards is a direct outcome of the failure of production to keep pace with consumption because of the shackles we have placed on the production process.

According to the World Bank, even before the major 1978 fall in the value of the U.S. dollar, income of the average American ranked fourth in the world. When the new results become available, we expect this position to be even lower because slowth, which results from holding down production, has forced a dramatic relative decline in the income of Americans. Indeed, by 1979 the prestigious twenty-four nation Organization for Economic Cooperation and Development (OECD) had the United States ranked fifth among its members. It placed Switzerland first with an average per capita income of $9580, Sweden next with $9480, Denmark at $9040, Norway $8800, and Iceland with $8680. Americans with their $8670 per year were scarcely ahead of Canadians at $8590, West Germans at $8410, and Belgians with $8060.

Some economists, including the members of the team led by Irving B. Kravis of the University of Pennsylvania, question the validity of the ranking statistics once complex adjustments have been made for the various costs of living and for services provided through different governments. But even these economists cannot dispute that the United States is losing in comparison with other countries.

Protectionism may be the way U.S. officials seek to arrest the decline in the value of the dollar while preserving domestic employment. But it would have nothing to do with the real problem of slow growth in production and would be a sad reaction to the advent of slowth in America. It would erase the benefit of trade that has been largely responsible for the high living standards achieved by the industrialized world. But it is a possible and perhaps likely outcome of the decline in the U.S. growth in productivity relative to that of other nations. The alternative, continued erosion of the buying power of the U.S. dollar through depreciation on the foreign-exchange markets, is one that political realities may not allow. Nor, as we show, would a depreciated dollar value arrest a decline in our living standards. One way or another we as individuals pay the price of our consciousness in the shrinking amount of what we can afford.

THE TAX REVOLT

Howard Jarvis, the mentor of tax revolt, is characteristically blunt about the movement he helped so much to create. "We're not going to permit the people to go broke while the government gets rich. It's them or us, and we're for us. We're not playing with feather dusters. We're playing with machetes."[7]

The object of anger is the enlarged bureaucracy and the growth in government spending. But in a sense this is not the basic cause. Even rising taxes resulting from the bloating of the tax base by inflation is merely a symptom. It is true that property tax as well as income tax bites have risen markedly, a trend that seems unfair to those who may live in the same home and consume the same amount as before. There is, however, a more fundamental force behind the taxpayer's anger. The problem is that real living standards are just not going up as quickly these days as the rate to which we have become accustomed. With slowly growing incomes, rising taxes to finance government spending are a far greater irritant than they would be in times of rapid real income growth.

When both the effects of inflation and federal income taxes are stripped away, the average American's buying power between 1965 and 1977 has grown, according to the federal Bureau of Labor Statistics, by less than 3 percent. This is a gain over a twelve-year period, not an average gain per year. Although we must be careful in interpreting this statistic, it comes as a rude shock to the citizenry of a nation that has seen the same measure rise by more than 36 percent between 1947 and 1965. These figures represent efforts by the Bureau of Labor Statistics to track real purchasing power after taxes—the amount of goods and services that the average worker's take-home pay can acquire. They lie behind the national income figures given previously and reflect the hard times we are experiencing in our efforts to get ahead.

The average worker's ability to acquire goods and services has risen more slowly because we are not turning them out at the same rate. Inflation is the smokescreen behind which this real reason for taxpayer discontent is hidden. It distorts the near stagnant living standards and distracts attention from the real essentials of our economic dilemma: slow growth in our output of goods and services. Indeed, in the long run we cannot enjoy more goods and services than we collectively produce. Inflation simply helps spread the limited amount around.

Some Americans have responded to their condition by attempting to reduce one determinant of disposable income over which there is some control, taxes. In doing so they will have very dramatic effects on public services and the way we go about the business of government. It is true that the Proposition 13 electoral victory in California and its aftereffects have thus far provided supporters with cause for celebration. Whereas machetes have succeeded in chopping local property taxes, the cut into public services has resembled more the work of a paring knife. State officials came to the aid of local governments with a redistribution of a large chunk of the enormous $6.6 billion surplus. The result, at least for 1978, was small local spending cuts averaging 10 percent.

Other states now playing with the machetes are unlikely to be so fortunate. Enactments approved by voters in other states are likely to result in a more severe curtailment of services by governments with coffers leaner than those of California. And it is not even clear whether this backlash will curtail the size of the bureaucracy. Public officials unwilling to wield the hatchet on portions of its bureaucracy not providing valued service may simply respond to tax cuts by reducing the level of public pass-through of funds. Ultimately, services may be the only thing to be cut.

The hazards of the slowth backlash may go farther still. The revolt against taxes is surfacing over a wider front. As part of their contribution to the national revolt against taxes, a majority of states have passed resolutions calling for a constitutional amendment prohibiting federal deficit spending. Advocated by an amalgam of presidential hopefuls, supporters of a group called the National Taxpayers Union, and just plain folks who don't like taxes, these proposals offer the prospect of an extreme limitation on the discretion of our elected officials. It arises out of the general mistrust of their ability to govern. The effect would be to curtail the ability of our leaders to deal with changing circumstances and to cast in stone the distraught mood of the present populace as a legacy for future generations. In so doing, the machete approach could go well beyond the need for the ordering of public priorities and a systematic paring of government.

The approach of the tax revolt is to slash away above the roots of taxpayer dissatisfaction with slower living standard improvements. Unless the productive process is freed from major encumbrances, unless the popularly mandated acts of consciousness are repealed or somehow subverted, slowth and the frustration of Americans will prove intractable, and taxpayer resistance will stiffen.

chapter 11

Learning from Land

"Buy real estate," Mark Twain counseled. "I understand they're not making it anymore." Those who heeded this advice have of late come to recognize its wisdom. Many of those who did not are now forced to deal with the consequence: skyrocketing housing prices are now threatening to eclipse the ambition of owning one's home.

Housing prices in recent times have grown well in excess of personal incomes or measures of inflation. The U.S. Department of Housing and Urban Development (HUD) estimated that in 1970 half the people in the United States could have afforded to buy a medium-priced home. That measure of affordability means that no more than 25 percent of pretax income would be spent on mortgage payments. Today, only one decade later, HUD estimates that only 13 percent of the population can afford to own a new home. In 1970, the median price for a house was over $23,000; in May 1979 it was almost $63,000. At the rate some housing prices have increased, it can be measured in terms of dollars per hour, twenty-four hours a day, seven days a week.

It is the rising cost of the land on which we build that, over the past half decade, has been the prime contributor to this housing price explosion. And although land is not included in our national product, the shortage of land available for building is traceable to the same expanding consciousness that lies behind slowth. Therefore, within the explosion of land prices is a vivid lesson and illustration of the economic cost of our consciousness.

Who among us can explain the phenomenon of rising land prices? Some theories point to the evil hand of speculation or cite baby-boom demographic statistics—both factors that influence demand. Yet there is a more fundamental cause—the limitations on land supply. To a large extent, these limitations are not the natural ones that Mark Twain had in mind. They result from our own actions and are prompted by a genuine concern over the nature of our urban life-styles. Our expanding consciousness has, to a striking degree, begun to conflict with the comfort and security of owning our own homes. And although the housing shortage is not reflected in the statistics of slow economic growth, it is an excellent illustration of the way our nonmaterial concerns extract a heavy price on growth in the standard of material life.

Urban consciousness is an awareness of the destruction wreaked by urban sprawl. It is an appreciation of the parks and open space that grace our cities. And it is a distaste for the height and density of buildings that, despite their efficient use of confined urban spaces, violate the human scale and dwarf our home and working lives. The result of this new consciousness is the spate of no and slow growth movements that dictate the way we use our land.

"Dulcus est urbs sub urbe," "sweet is the city beyond the city," wrote the Roman poet Horace. The effort to escape the trials of urban life is at least 2000 years old. Many in our society, like those in ancient Rome, have instead sought the more restful suburban life. Indeed, the pressures of our urban existence have made it urgent for some people to escape. The result, urban sprawl, has become a fact of American life.

It is the highway that has made possible both suburbs and the consequent urban sprawl. Its arteries are both sculptor and prime feature of the American landscape. Yet today there are abundant signs of the disfavor into which highways have fallen. Their choked arteries, noise, and foul air have earned the highways a number of enemies. In San Francisco, for example, freeway building is at a standstill and talk of tearing down the unsightly overhead structures has received widespread support. In Vancouver, British Columbia, plans for a "third crossing" of the Burrard Inlet were defeated after long debate, despite and because it would provide access to more suburban land. More than one expressway in the United States stands unfinished, perched in mid-air, as a monument to the concern over the sequence of events set in motion by highway expansion.

Today, just as in ancient Greece and Rome, the commerce and culture of our society remain within the more crowded inner urban spaces. Those who flee to the sweetness of life outside the city still depend for both work and amusement on the business remaining in the core. City businesses in turn rely on those from outside for a pool of labor and a source of demand for what they provide. And so the pressure develops for expressway links between these vitally dependent groups.

Yet, with an almost eerie precision, the solution to one problem becomes a problem of its own. The easier it becomes to move along the superwide corridors that were built to satisfy those who first moved farther afield, the more readily large numbers of people find it practical to share the placidness on the edge of town. The highways rapidly become overloaded, so more and larger ones are built. More move and the process continues, *ad nauseam*. The result is the death of the inner city. More middle-class families with much money to spend flee with an ever greater urgency from the decay of the once grand neighborhoods in town. Stores move; offices follow. Minority groups and the poor remain, forming a tax base that is too slim to support high-quality city services.

"It may be better not to build a highway if it is only likely to induce more sprawl,"[1] observes Russell Train, former Chairman of the Council of Environmental Quality. The population drift resulting from such sprawl is dramatically revealed in the numbers of the U.S. Census Bureau. They show that in cities that constitute their sample, growth has been one quarter that of surrounding areas during the past two decades. In fact between 1970 and 1974 U.S. cities have recorded a net loss of 1.7 million people. Eight cities with a population of over 2 million—New York, Chicago, Los Angeles, Philadelphia, Detroit, St. Louis, Pittsburgh, and Newark—recorded a loss of population since 1970.

Those fleeing the cities, by virtue of their sheer numbers, carry with them the usual urban problems. Jammed expressways extend what might have once been a short commute. Automobile exhaust and industrial emissions spread out along the ribbons of highway. Schools and sewage systems overload. Wetlands are subverted, disturbing a delicate ecological balance. This is the legacy that we bequeath to our land; these are the causes of concern about our sprawling urbanized environment.

Americans have responded to the threat of creeping urbanization in a variety of striking ways. Over the past half decade a rising level of consciousness has sought ways of placing limits on our urban growth. A look at the methods used to enact that consciousness, all of which date since the early and mid-1970s, demonstrates the extensive nature of no and slow growth urban movements. The existence of such pressures within almost every community makes it easier to understand the reason for the massive increase in the price of developable land.

Former Oregon Governor Tom McCall was one of the first elected officials in the United States to plead for "undevelopment." But he was reflecting more than his own view. He sensed the expanding awareness of fellow Oregonians who were fearful of the explosive growth they witnessed to the immediate south. "Do not Californicate Oregon," read one expressive bumper sticker. But even San Jose, California, whose growth and virtues have been heralded on the pop charts of 1960s America, has decided since 1978 to limit residential construction to 5000 new units each year.

Whereas effective measures may limit population in one area, they will merely serve to increase population in another. "It's like pressure underneath a bubble," remarked a planner for San Francisco's Association of Bay Area Governments (ABAG). "Counter pressure will make it disappear, but it will surface somewhere else."[2] If it had its way, ABAG would suppress the Bay Area's growing population bubble to far outside the entire region. In an effort to export its population problem, the association adopted a policy to limit the number of residents to 5.5 million by 1980, only a million more than 1973 when the policy was adopted.

Sentiment against growth has not been confined to western communities. Boca Raton, just north of Miami, Florida, was the first municipality to place a direct ceiling on population growth.

Even newly arrived residents became dismayed at the congestion that other newcomers had wrought. After growing in population from 990 in 1950 to 38,000 in 1973, the residents of Boca Raton moved to close the city gates. They voted an amendment to the city charter, limiting the number of dwelling units to 40,000.

Where explicit population limits have not been adopted, frequently because effectiveness cannot be guaranteed without means of implementation, a less direct route has been taken. Many municipalities have resorted to zoning to limit density. In fact, such density restrictions, alleged to be efforts at preserving the racial or economic homogeneity of those living in the communities, have with increasing frequency wound up in the nation's courts. An effort at more restrictive zoning was made by the town of New Canaan, among many others. This New York City suburb has one of the highest per capita income levels of any U.S. town, village, or city. The suburb's efforts to raise its zoning ordinances to 4-acre minimum lots was upheld by that state's Supreme Court. Challenges to these ordinances are often mounted with the contention that large lot zoning is not merely an effort at environmental preservation but a move to wall out the nonwhite and less wealthy.

Sanbornton, New Hampshire, is a town that established a "forest conservation district" in which buildings could be constructed only on lots of 6 acres or more. Its efforts were challenged, and reluctantly sustained, in the courts. The federal circuit court was most disturbed by the offhand manner in which this was attempted without prior study. In its decision the judges summed up the matter of urban growth restriction in this statement: "Where there is natural population growth it has to go somewhere, unwelcome as it might be, and in that case we do not think it should be channeled by the happenstance of what town gets its veto in first."[3]

Undaunted by the risk of being labeled (at best) elitist, those uniting under the banner for the preservation of urban space have pressed on. In doing so, they have resorted to a variety of new techniques that are much subtler than large lot zoning. In Boulder, Colorado, a completely different tack has been taken. To keep sprawling development from usurping the scenic mountain backdrop, citizens approved a greenbelt program. Part of this consists of raising tax revenues to purchase valuable open space. This supplemented a 1958 "Blue Line" amendment to the city charter that prohibited the piping of city water above a certain elevation on the surrounding mountains.

Few cities enjoy the mountainous splendor of Boulder, but a number of communities have moved to preserve their heritage of valuable farmland. There is a clear indication that the subdivision of farmland for housing and industrial use is a critical trend. By 1971, according to the Environmental Protection Agency, the United States was losing 4000 acres of agricultural land each day to nonagricultural uses. This adds up to 1.5 million acres each year. At such a preposterous rate, a third of the current stock of agricultural land would be lost in the next century. Although the rate will slow, it is a problem of which many Americans have become acutely aware. In January 1978 the California Poll revealed that 84 percent of Californians viewed the protection of farmland as more important than the expansion of suburbs.

Marin County, California, in response to these concerns, placed two-thirds of its 300,000 acres into agricultural preserve. Land in the preserve was downzoned to allow a dwelling for every 60, rather than every 3 acres, which had been the previous limit. In British Columbia all designated prime agricultural land has been frozen in its current use. The hotly debated "Bill 42" made it past the bitter protests of landowners to become enacted into law. Lot prices in communities bordering on the agricultural reserve jumped noticeably.

Efforts to preserve agricultural land have not been confined to the West. One Midwestern state has adopted a measure that relies on tax incentives to guarantee that acreage will remain as farmland. Michigan's Farmland and Open Space Preservation Act has led to an enrollment of over 225,000 acres of agricultural land for periods as long as forty years.

The concern for our land also extends to our scenic and fragile coasts. The Connecticut legislature added 7000 acres of shorelands to those already eligible for protection under existing state agencies. In California voters approved a coastline initiative to control the nature of development along the coastline proper. Virginia has enacted the Wetlands Protection Law that permits localities to set up zoning boards to determine the use of wetlands within their jurisdiction. Washington voters, choosing from among three shoreline protection measures in the 1972 election, approved a law that gave local governments the authority to curb shoreline activity, including offshore drilling for oil. All these activities have a common cause and a common effect. They are reactions to the sprawling outward movement of our cities and towns, which they seek to contain, and they put wild price pressures on what remains for development.

One of the more creative and increasingly popular tools of the no and slow growth movements is the resort to community service restrictions. California municipalities initiated such measures as sewer, utility, and water moratoria. Areas of western Marin County, for example, resorted to the last in 1972 and suffered the consequences during the drought of 1976. Among the most elaborate schemes aimed at slowing and controlling development was the one employed by the residents of Ramapo, New York. In 1969 the town amended the zoning law to incorporate a number of controls on the timing and sequence of development. Approval for housing development was made to hinge on the availability of a variety of public facilities, which included sewers, drainage facilities, adequate parklands, good roads, and proximity to fire protection services. Although similar measures have since become more common in planning large housing developments, they can be used to restrict the influx of population in towns that employ them.

Whatever the system, the move is on to halt the advance of urban sprawl. All plans have in common the preservation of environmental quality. In a number of cases the plans are also schemes to promote self-interest, enacted by those already owning property. But all fail to consider the national picture in which an estimated additional 54 million people will need living space by the century's end. The Rockefeller Task Force on Land Use and Urban Growth, which derived these estimates, goes on to exclaim, "Stop growth here and it will pop up there; slow it down over there and it will speed up somewhere else, because people are not going to go away."[4]

The move to halt urban sprawl is now beginning to take on a more positive note. Long commutes and long gas lines have rekindled interest in living in our downtown centers. Older neighborhoods in San Francisco and New York are being renovated, gaining life not only from the efforts of individuals but from families as well. Governments in locales such as Kansas City, Denver, and Minneapolis are rejuvenating their downtown cores by block development schemes involving residential units, often at subsidized rates. Should these prove successful, other urban neighborhoods like New York's South Bronx, Chicago's Hyde Park, and Washington, D.C.'s Capital Hill will be the site of new residential development. Blighted neighborhoods such as these are an available, if limited, outlet for urban growth.

Such outlets are necessary as even with zero population growth urban and suburban populations will continue to grow. Migrations from rural to urban areas and from city core to suburb will not stop. The President's Citizens Advisory Committee on Environmental Quality estimates that by the year 2000, five-sixths of Americans will live in urban centers. With the potential for sprawl limited by our urban consciousness, where will these people live if our cities can't grow outward?

Certainly there will not be enough room for them in the city itself. Inner city parks and greenbelts have become sacrosanct. Indeed, the push is on for more of these to help ease the confined feeling that is so hard to avoid in busy urban life. In 1972 Congress set a precedent in laying aside large open spaces within two major urban metropolises. In its creation of the Golden Gate National Recreation Area near San Francisco and the Gateway National Recreation Area near New York City, Congress departed from the practice of confining such land set-asides to rural areas. Its political justification was that such measures, however costly, provide low-income families lacking in financial resources with the opportunity to enjoy open-space recreation. Typifying this trend is the existence of an organized body, the National Recreation and Park Association, which sets ideal standards for minimum park space.

Calgary, Alberta, exemplifies the problems of urban growth. Boosted by its eminent position as the oil capital of Canada, Calgary has enjoyed one of the fastest population growth rates in North America. But prices of housing have grown as well, creating a concern that has led to a high-level public agency study, which concluded that "the lack of developable land in a high demand situation has been the major factor in the dramatic increase in housing costs."[5]

This statement is borne out by the jump in raw land prices in Calgary from an average of $6000 per acre in 1971 to $40,000 per acre in 1977. The agency was outspoken about the factors causing the shortage of developable land. It cited delays in urban annexation, foot-dragging in water and sewage installations, and slow planner response to increased housing demand. Included among its prime targets were bylaws requiring "larger than necessary" lot sizes, density restrictions on land use, and bylaws setting aside "excessive" parkland. Further study shows one source of the agency's findings about parkland. In the seven years beginning in 1970, the number of acres of park space in Calgary nearly doubled, recording an increase of almost 50 percent in the number of acres available per thousand residents. And this took place in a city with an explosive boom-town atmosphere and an almost religious devotion to growth!

Upward growth of our cities and towns is no longer an entirely open option either. More than one community has slapped on height ceiling restraints of one sort or another. San Diego has imposed a limit on building height along its shoreline. In Boulder a 55-foot height limit was placed on downtown buildings. A heavily populated residential section of Vancouver, British Columbia, is yet another North American city neighborhood to have a height zoning restriction. In this case, a four-story height limit was imposed. Even in a section of dense New York City, the reaction against highrise development can be seen. Blocks of crowded tenements in the lower Manhattan section known as Little Italy have recently been rezoned to prevent the building of high rise structures.

It is clear that the squeeze for urban land is on. As the object of growing demand, our urban land is also the source of rising concern. That concern, when expressed through the growing body of restrictions on the use of urban land, poses a direct threat to all new housing development, particularly the single-family home. The common dream is not merely that of an apartment or a condominium; it is for a house. Moreover, it is for a house with a strip of land in front and back, a tree or two, and, of course, a driveway down the side. "We've built in standards of living we can't afford," says Alan R. Talbot, Executive Director of the Citizens Housing and Planning Council. "In the next ten to twenty years the problem will be to determine what housing combinations best minimize both capital and operating expenses. We must determine not what is desirable but what is necessary. Standards will go lower,"[6] Evidence of the truth of this statement exists in any neighborhood in which single-family houses are replaced with the increasingly visible multiplex homes. And although the hard costs of labor and materials have surely risen, it is the price of land that has put the single-family home out of the reach of many. Those who do not own a home know this situation only too well. Yet how many of them still push for more space, which further limits the supply of land on which to build?

At least one academic institute has documented the deterioration in American housing standards. Our society, according to the Joint Center for Urban Studies of the Massachusetts Institute of Technology and Harvard University in its 1977 report, is characterized by a great many instances of "housing deprivation." "If the trends from 1971 to 1976 continue for another five years," the report says, "typical new homes in 1981 would sell for $78,000 and only the most affluent groups would be able to afford them."[7] The rising price trends that the authors cite hold for existing houses, the median price of which rose over the five years by 65 percent, as well as new homes, which rose by 89 percent. Over the study period, 1970–1976, the Consumer Price Index rose much less, by 46 percent.

Factors such as population shifts and demographic trends share the responsibility for rising land prices. Contributing in no small way to this trend, however, are the barriers to developing our communities that we ourselves have erected. All over the United States citizens are acting to preserve the quality of their land and living environment. The effect of these efforts is becoming evident to professional planners and economists, if not to members of the general public. "The growth constraints are forcing quantum jumps in new housing prices as prices for developable land double and triple due to scarcity,"[8] state Donald Priest and J. Thomas Black of the Urban Land Institute.

Land scarcity, resulting from restrictions on the use of developable lots, is not the only cause of higher housing prices. Regulation to protect the quality of the land and the environment is also built directly into the price of housing. This is the conclusion of an examination by business economist Murray Weidenbaum, who has attempted to compute the overall costs of a range of governmental regulations. While giving credit to the beneficial aspects of regulation on the living environment, he concludes, "Government regulation can increase the cost of new homes in many ways, driving up land and development costs, increasing the number of expensive building code features to be incorporated, raising overhead expenses of real estate and financial institutions, and increasing financing costs because of project delays."[9] Weidenbaum cites a number of studies that show this cost to be highly consequential. One such study covering twenty-one residential projects in New Jersey from 1972–1975 estimated that an average single-family home cost $1600 more because of thirty-eight separate permits required by the communities to regulate the quality of development.

Land is an obvious necessity. As with the natural resources discussed earlier, we have consumed a large portion of what is best. We have used the land on the coast and bordering the park, land with quick and ready access to urban centers and that which affords scenic pleasure or a measure of peace. As continued building has threatened to produce an unpleasant urban environment through encroaching development and sprawl, people with vested concern have acted to protect what they have. The fact that their actions have translated into high prices for those who do not yet own a home is a vivid example of the costs of consciousness.

The preservation of whatever is good about the quality of our communities, in light of the diminishing resource of attractive land, is desirable but comes at great expense. Unlike the cost of the other forms of consciousness, which inhibits the production process, the expense of our urban consciousness is not difficult to see. It is visible in the classified ads, clearly exhibiting to those without a home the price of their fading dream.

chapter 12

Slowth and the Growth Debate

The economic growth debate, a topic of discourse so fashionable in the 1960s and 1970s, is dead. In its livelier moments it pitted those who viewed growth as both possible and desirable against those who saw disaster as its unavoidable result. Since the late 1970s, a new reality has caused the shift of that debate away from an examination of the merits and physical limits of growth and toward a frantic search for a cure for the maladies plaguing our economy. That reality is slowth.

The slow growth that we have begun to observe is not a vindication of those growth critics whose rallying cry, "We can't grow on like this," now seems satisfied. Rather, as demonstrated throughout this book, the limitations to growth we now experience are mostly self-imposed. Furthermore, they are being imposed in an unwitting back-door fashion and not through any conviction that growth is unsustainable or bad. We are limiting growth simply by placing priorities of consciousness before those of production, thereby limiting the inputs into the production process that continued growth demands.

The growth debate took place during a period of shifting values that subtly affected many of its participants. As an example, take the case of Jerry, an avid canoeist and backpacker, who thinks that his father has peculiar tastes. "He likes to live near oil refineries," says Jerry. To his father, the pipes, lights, and the ever present flare bear the promise of improved living standards. To Jerry, the site can be nothing but ugly—the source of pollution and industrial blight.

But the shift in attitude is not necessarily an intergenerational one; and it is not confined to Jerry and his dad. Says C. M. Mc-Coy, former President of the DuPont Chemical Company, "We used to have a mural in the DuPont auditorium which showed our smokestacks belching smoke, and we took that as a symbol of industrial prosperity. But now we have had to erase that picture from our wall."[1]

McCoy and DuPont have taken their signals from a marked change in attitude by the American public. Environmental consciousness has grown dramatically since the mid-1960s. In 1965 an Opinion Research Corporation survey concluded that only 28 percent of those questioned considered air pollution a "very or somewhat serious problem." By 1970 that proportion had grown to 69 percent. A similar shift took place in concerns about water pollution, with those considering it to be "serious" growing from 35 to 75 percent within the same period. These numbers are presumably more the result of an expanded environmental consciousness than of any deterioration in air and water quality within that short five-year period.

The shifts in social and individual values are not limited to concerns about pollution. We are worried about technological risk and depletion of resources. But that is not all. The newly enacted social concerns for our fellows has created a veritable revolution, not only in social welfare spending, but also in what sociologist Daniel Bells calls a "revolution of rising entitlements."

This revolution, according to Bell, "has taken the form—a basic shift in the values of society—that what was once considered to be an individual effort is now a claim on the government, a claim for protection against social hazards and, in effect, an entitlement, something that a person is entitled to by virtue of being a citizen of that society."[2] One of those claims, through the social welfare system, is to receive income without work. This entitlement reduces the human input of effort and, along with other forms of input-restricting consciousness, leads to slowth.

Slowth has begun to put a damper on the debate about whether growth is good, bad, or even physically possible. This slowth has resulted from neither the "immutable limits" that formed the centerpiece of such debate nor the belief that a higher standard of living is bad. Very few of even the most ardent critics of growth have worried about larger real incomes for each of us to enjoy, but rather about the limited ability of the Earth to sustain the absolute growth in sheer numbers of people and their ensuing production of waste. Slowth has come from barriers to real growth that are primarily self-imposed through restrictions on each of the inputs into production. Slowth does not herald the victory of the growth critics. It is not a tribute to their predictive insight. Instead it is a propaganda victory of well-motivated souls, who have unconsciously ushered in the era of slowth.

THE CONCEPT OF PHYSICAL LIMITS

The hallmark of the belief in natural limits is the view that rigid biological and physical ceilings are destined to constrain economic and population growth. Its prime proponents are Donella Meadows and the other authors of *Limits to Growth,* a computer simulation study that predicts a critical excess of population and pollution, and shortages of raw materials and sources of energy. Their ideas bear a striking resemblance to those of the Reverend Thomas Malthus, whose eighteenth-century writings thrust him into the role of the darkest of the dismal scientists. In referring to *Limits to Growth,* consultant Robert Theobald remarked, "Malthus has been updated and placed in modern dress using computers."[3] This reference to Malthus arises from his projection that population must eventually outgrow the means of subsistence, resulting in mass starvation.

Limits to Growth, in its insistence on physical limits of a different sort, has been discredited. The noisy debate that surrounded publication of the study has long since died down. In retrospect it is recognized that some of the persuasion of the study was provided by the Arab Oil Embargo and the energy crisis, which followed on the heels of the study's release. The main contribution of the work, however, was its emphasis on the idea of physical limits. This is a theme that has been picked up by a new wave of critics who emphasize physical limits, among them Herman Daly, who states, "The difficulty is twofold. First, we will run out of terrestrial resources eventually. Second, even if we never ran out we would still face problems of ecological breakdown caused by a growing throughput of matter energy."[4]

Daly's second point, which refers to the problems in using fossil and nuclear energy, is also a theme of *Limits to Growth*. Together, they raise the idea of another physical limit: the potential of growing levels of pollution. It is a view that the Earth is small and limited not only in resources but also in its ability to absorb wastes at levels associated with high rates of growth. As a remedy Daly offers a recipe for an economy of the steady state, one which is bound to be unpalatable to all who lack refined and unusual taste: "constant stocks of people and artifacts maintained at chosen levels that are sufficient for a good life and sustainable for a long future, by the lowest rate of throughput."[5] A forerunner of 1984? Perhaps.

But time has proven Malthus wrong and it is unlikely to be any kinder to the modern-day advocates of a similar futuristic fare. Physical limits are not the binding constraint facing us today. Rather, it is our *perception* of limits, coupled with our willingness to respond to them, that contributes to a self-imposed slowdown in our economic growth rates. This understanding of the problem relegates the notion of actual physical limits to a more distant and abstract realm.

Sometimes our perceptions bear little resemblance to reality. For example, estimates of crude oil recoverable in the United States differed, at one time, by 900 percent. According to one 1944 estimate in another resource area, the United States should now have exhausted its reserves of tin, nickel, lead, zinc, and seventeen other minerals. The fact is that new deposits were found. Indeed, according to a large study conducted by Interfutures (Organization for Economic Cooperation and Development, OECD), the proven reserves of all major minerals are now higher than they were back in 1950. In terms of the number of years of known reserves, according to current annual usage we have 194 years of iron, 300 years of chromium, 54 years of copper, 42 years of tin and 29 years of lead. And these exclude seabed reserves that could much more than double these amounts.

Whether perceptions of limits are correct or faulty, it is our willingness to act on them that helps determine our rate of growth. We have not yet directly limited resource use but instead have sought to protect the environment, thereby imposing a back-door limitation on the resources we allow ourselves to use. The effect is the same: the enactment of restrictions that decrease resource inputs and thereby contribute to slowth.

Resource inputs constitute only a part of the inputs into the production process. In limiting their concerns to physical resources, modern-day "Malthusians" disregard the other factors of production, all of which affect the rate of economic growth. The decline in the growth of human and capital inputs we have traced also contributes greatly to slowth. The same is true of the barriers to developing and adopting new technology.

PROPONENTS OF THE TECHNOLOGICAL FIX

The futurologists Herman Kahn, William Brown, and Leon Martel, in their book *The Next 200 Years: A Scenario for America and the World,* fly optimism in the face of those predictors of economic gloom. In an upbeat fashion Kahn and his colleagues at the Hudson Institute in New York herald the arrival of an era of opportunity and "relative peace and prosperity for nearly everyone." They see as plausible the view that technology "which caused problems can also solve them—it only requires mankind's attention and desire." Their scenario for "growth and technology," which they claim is more accurate than the theory of physical limits, is rooted in the belief that resources of capital, technology, and educated people are in ever greater supply, thereby offering hope for continued growth.

In offering this cure to Malthusian-like stagnation embodied in their miracle of the technological fix, Kahn and his coauthors are not unique. Numerous commentators have alleged that those forecasting physical barriers to rising living standards fail to recognize a vital factor that boosted post-World War II growth: production know-how. Kahn and his group, however, go even farther by offering the hope of a *deus ex machina*. They suggest that technology may open up an entirely new frontier of land and resources—the world beyond planet Earth.

Often those rejecting the idea of relevant physical limits are a great deal less ethereal. They point to the vastly different ways goods and services are provided now in contrast to years past. Such an argument is advanced by Bell. "The crucial point is that economic development, while it does depend upon technology, has a wide range of alternative methods, each one characterized by a different mix of capital, labor and resource inputs."[6] Unfortunately, we no longer have these wide-ranging alternatives. We can no longer reasonably expect technology or any of these inputs to boost our rate of growth. Our well-motivated consciousness has erected too many production barriers that mitigate against continued rapid growth.

Our economy is moving away from the influence of technology. A study by Edward Denison reveals that during the 1950s and 1960s advances in technology accounted for well over one-third of the average annual growth in national income. This estimate is close to that of Robert Solow whom we mentioned earlier. Technology was far and away the most important growth factor, exceeding the combined effects of increases in capital stocks, labor inputs, or improvements in the allocation of resources. But in years to come, technology, rather than acting as a dynamic engine driving the economy to new levels of prosperity, will, along with the other inputs, be subject to numerous obstructions.

These obstructions are becoming increasingly visible. Our unwillingness to take technological risks keeps us busy devising tighter safety controls and checks on the application of new methods, machines, and chemicals. Widening public concern about nuclear power, the use of pesticides and herbicides, and potential disbenefits arising from economically important projects have precipitated a mushrooming of regulation and civil litigation. These enactments and lawsuits limit the extent to which technology can improve the prospects for growth. Not only do they directly slow the application of known technology, but they also discourage investment in research and development and reduce long-term prospects for technologically led growth.

Our potential benefit from technology will be a great deal less than what Kahn and his coauthors anticipate. Yet their book is interesting because of the number of other controversial scenarios it develops. Their view is very much a global one in which they foresee mankind at some kind of growth inflection point that will mark a "gradual slowing" of the rate of economic growth. Their reasons are vastly different from those presented in this book. They state, "We believe that because of the flexibility of modern economies and the huge surplus of land, energy and resources available, the limitations set by scarcity should not normally prove dominant. We emphasize instead the *demand* side of the equation" (emphasis our own).

In contrast to these views we expect slowth to be induced by factors that limit *supply*. It is the limitations placed on the very flexibility emphasized by Kahn, Brown, and Martel that will cause a slowing in the rate of growth of production. The emphasis we place on supply as distinct from demand stems from the barriers to greater production. We are moving away from market-determined values toward national values of "fairness" arising from our consciousness.

The distinction between a demand-induced slowdown and one caused by a diminished rate of growth of supply is an important one to make. Kahn, Brown, and Martel are optimistic in their reasons for expecting a slowing of demand. They expect some people to begin to want less; "There is likely to be a diminution in the marginal utility of wealth and production. With insurance, social security and welfare for all, there will be protection against most of the vagaries of life and this should produce a shift in priorities and values."

Kahn and his colleagues also point to a number of "vested interests," or well-to-do individuals who oppose growth and its accompanying changes. The end result, they feel, will be an economy of the "steady state"—oddly enough the same state advocated by Daly and other growth critics—as a result of the decline in goods and services demanded by society.

The path to some steady economic state will be by no means

as smooth as Kahn, Brown, and Martel assert. Economic growth is not slowing because less is being demanded of the system. There is little indication that even the most affluent Americans are forsaking their economic demands, satiated with a rich variety of goods and services. Rather, while demand fails to decline, the willingness of society or individuals to ensure the fulfillment of these demands is on the wane. Instead we insist that consciousness be satisfied alongside production, apparently unaware of the tight limit we impose on the growth in supply of desirable goods and services.

The shortfall in economic production in satisfying our demands carries with it great potential for anxiety, frustration, and stress. There is also the risk of social conflict. The adjustment to living with less will be a difficult one as a dynamic factor that shapes our lives will be gone. "In the American Dream," says sociologist Robert Merton, "there is no final stopping point. At each income level, Americans want just about 25% more."[7] Slowth stems from our failure to supply the trappings of the American Dream and not, as Kahn and his colleagues suggest, from a decline in our expectations and wants.

In direct opposition to the *Limits to Growth*, Kahn, Brown, and Martel predict a slowing in the rate of population growth. They maintain that we are in a "demographic transition" that will result in a slowing of both birth and death rates. They attribute this to economic growth. It is a transition that will be accelerated, they feel, by the spread of economic well-being to developing nations. But slowth does not depend on the rate of population growth. Whether one subscribes to the notion that we are headed toward some overpopulated Armageddon or a world of zero population growth, slowth is becoming a fact of life. It refers to the output *per person*. Due to the consciousness-rooted constraints on production, less will be supplied by each of us for each of us. Hence growth of the average standard of economic life will slow whatever the demographic trends we face.

Predictions of some golden era, free of economic want, is by no means unique to Kahn and his colleagues. John Maynard Keynes had such a vision more than thirty years ago. As he wrote in his essay, "Economics for Our Grandchildren," however, Keynes seemed to view the elimination of scarcity as a problem in itself:

> Suppose that a hundred years hence we are all of us . . . eight times better off . . . than we are today. . . . Assuming no important wars and no important increase in population, the economic problem may be solved. . . . This means that the economic problem is not—if we look into the future—the permanent problem of the human race.

> Why, you may ask, is this so startling? It is startling because—if instead of looking into the future, we look into the past—we find that the economic problem, the struggle for subsistence, always has been hitherto the primary, most pressing problem of the human race—not only of the human race, but of the whole biological kingdom from the beginnings of life in its most primitive forms.

> Thus we have been expressly evolved by nature—with all our impulses and deepest instincts—for the purpose of solving the economic problem. If the economic problem is solved, mankind will be deprived of its traditional purpose. . . . I think with dread of the readjustment of the habits and instincts of the ordinary man, bred into him for countless generations, which he may be asked to discard within a few decades.[8]

An era free of economic scarcity seems even more remote today than it did at the time Keynes wrote. And we have not reached the affluent society of John Kenneth Galbraith. "The economic problem" to which Keynes alludes is now undergoing metamorphosis from one of managing continued production and growth to one of striking a tolerable balance between production and the quality of life.

DEFENDERS OF THE QUALITY OF LIFE

Noted British economist Ezra Mishan fired the opening rounds of the growth debate. He was among the first economists to question whether the standard of living was synonymous with the quality of life. He both asked and answered what he called the vital question of economic priorities, "whether further economic growth in the already prosperous countries of the world is more likely or not to improve the human condition."

No, answered Mishan in *The Cost of Economic Growth,* one of a string of well-written books and essays in which he carried the cudgel of the antigrowth movement. Mishan felt that economists during the late 1960s, when he picked up the theme, as well as the lay individual today

> will dare to wonder whether it is really worth it: whether economic progress over the last couple of centuries has succeeded only in making life increasingly complex, frantic and wearing. The speed of travel grows from year to year, and from year to year more time is devoted in moving from one place to another. Physically, however, we are more idle and our lives more sedentary than our fathers'. We know the world's business from minute to minute, and practically nothing of the people who live in the neighborhood. Far removed from the forces of nature, denizens of the new subtopia, we are degenerating into a breed of passenger-spectators whose first impulse on awakening is to reach for a switch.

Mishan was joined in his sentiments by other critics, among them Ernst F. Schumacher. His work, *Small is Beautiful,* supplemented Mishan's by contributing in terms of circulation whatever it lacked in eloquence or focused thought. Schumacher seemed to advocate "a new life-style, with new methods of production and new patterns of consumption: a life-style designed for permanence." Schumacher's protest against the "inhuman" organization of production and technology no doubt struck a responsive chord with his readers.

It is difficult to dispute the contention of these two men that economic growth, as defined by a society's output of goods and services, is a narrow goal. An improved quality of human existence with compassion, a concern for the preservation of environmental quality, and the safety of future generations are undeniably noble goals. Yet they are not included in the conventionally measured national product that is still very much in demand.

We can express this in another way. How many of us would be satisfied with an unchanging real buying power on the grounds that we have cleaner air, better cared-for elderly people, or more stringent regulations saving us from technological mishap? Very few of us. We measure our own success from the same sort of narrow measuring rod as is used in computing the gross national product. We do not value improvements in the quality of life as part of the fruits of our own effort. How often have you walked outside and been proud of yourself for your part in contributing to cleaner air, better homes for the aged, and agencies that reduce technological risk? We are no more likely to thank ourselves for these than we would blame ourselves for air pollution or an accident at a nuclear power plant, even though it is through our own demands that we suffer these. This reflection should only confirm what we already know. Improvements in our society are the responsibility of government and of someone else. Improvements in our own lives are what we individually effect. We can be proud and show off our new car but not the cleaner air or nuclear safety agencies. Yet we pay for these attributes of the quality of life as much as we pay for an automobile. Only the form of payment is different—it is slow growth in our material standard of living.

Schumacher went a great deal further in his criticism of growth by suggesting the need for a freshly reordered set of national values. His 1973 book advocated "development of a life-style which accords to material things their proper legitimate place, which is secondary not primary." Themes of this sort seemed to give voice to the consciousness that was advancing so rapidly at the time his book was published.

Today we are living with the legacy of the rising consciousness. The American economic landscape has been radically altered since the writing of *Small is Beautiful*. Its present features of low economic growth, high inflation, enormous deficits in the American balance of payments, and a sinking dollar make Schumacher's prescriptions seem irrelevant. To continue to subscribe to the view that we need to reexamine our material values is to avoid recognizing the fact that economic growth has slowed markedly since the early 1970s. Slowth is now a fact of life. The real question now is how do we live with it.

A more objective examination of our failure to grow will help. It must go beyond the catchy phrases and quick explanations that characterized the hardened positions of the growth debate. In the preceding pages we have presented a diagnosis that can be summarized as one of the subversion of our will to produce by an admirable yet costly burgeoning national consciousness. Unless we understand this reason for the presence of slowth, we will not be able to choose a rational path for the future.

Advocates emphasizing the quality of life have failed to come to grips with the strain that slowth imposes on a great many Americans and their institutions of government. They might view the strain we face in making ends meet as a small price to pay for our consciousness and a higher quality of life. Yet for the people who suffer from inflation or slowth, this would come as meager consolation. To these people, slow growth entails disappointment—the frustration of failing to meet material aspirations that are extrapolated from a prosperous past. For many people this disappointment overshadows the less tangible improvements in the quality of life.

It is against the yardstick of aspiration that many of us measure our economic accomplishments, rather than against some absolute level of "enoughness." By this measure the past few years have brought failure to many who seek to advance their standards of living. Many of us will have to adapt. This means living with the disappointment of having less. For some it will also require coping with a hampered ability to make ends meet and a general feeling of relative deprivation. These may indeed prove as stressful as the growing pains that formed the targets of the critics of economic growth.

chapter 13

The Inevitable State of Slowth

"Ten years ago 'modern capitalism seemed to be on the verge of producing the permanently affluent society' [economist] George Stigler announced 'economics is finally at the threshold of its Golden Age—nay, we already have one foot through the door.' Today few would express such euphoria."[1]

—Time.

Where is this Golden Age we were approaching? How can we explain the chronic inflation and slow growth that we are now experiencing? What happened to us at the threshold of permanent affluence?

We have maintained throughout that a growing consciousness has diverted us from the path of high growth and greater economic prosperity. It is the origin of that consciousness that now merits closer scrutiny. As we argue, it is the very approach of our economy up to the threshold of the Golden Age of affluence that has engendered these nonmaterial values. The high living standard many of us now enjoy is *itself* a barrier to further high growth because we now demand, and can afford, an improvement in the quality of life. In short, material economic progress, in an almost dialectical fashion, has contained the seeds of its own destruction.

The United States is a mature industrial nation. It has proven capable of the most sophisticated modes of mass production and of satisfying an enormously broad range of consumer demands. That maturity, however, is translated not only into productive capability but also into a new focus for large sectors of its populace. A high standard of living, which grows out of expanding productive capability, creates the impetus and the means for a shift in awareness and concern. That new awareness or consciousness, although entirely compatible with high living standards, is inherently antithetical to the continued *growth* of those standards.

Environmentalism, the so-called Vietnam of the middle class, followed closely on the heels of that unpopular war. As a political issue, environmentalism exploded as we entered the 1970s. Its appearance might well have been more gradual through the 1960s were it not for the pressing concerns of the Asian war. Environmentalism was an issue that arose with, and because of, prosperity. High living standards meant that we felt we could *afford* to pay the price of cleaner air and waterways. A poor people cannot afford the luxury of environmental progress. It should be no surprise that as one of the richer nations of the world, the United States would undertake one of the more ambitious environmental wars.

As our living standards have made environmentalism affordable, it has also helped to make it desirable. A key component of economic growth has been an expansion in the leisure time that growth has made possible. As the workweek shrank to fewer than forty hours, and two-day weekends became the norm, Americans found the time and the means to enjoy the environment. The quality of the air, water, and our environs in general became something that a growing number of Americans experienced more often.

The attainment of a high living standard has played yet another role in raising the level of environmental consciousness. The modern information and communications networks—surely one of the hallmarks of our affluent society—have increased the level of consciousness. Television and the press have brought environmental and technological issues home to Americans in much the same manner as they brought home scenes from the Vietnam War. The drama of an event such as the Three Mile Island nuclear accident can be followed in all its horrific detail, as can the inevitable local news story about the dumping of chemicals or the latest in scientific probes for the carcinogenic properties of one chemical or another. "The American public has just sustained perhaps the largest single dose of nuclear information since the dropping of the first atomic bomb," declared *The Economist* after the events at Three Mile Island. The incident "provided a crash course in accident management and made every television viewer an armchair expert on the weak spots in reactor safety systems."[2] The message of protest demonstrations or the actions of regulatory agencies also receive dramatic and widespread dissemination. In 1950, a rally of 200 persons at a power plant or a polluted lake would have gone relatively unnoticed. Today it is brought into millions of living rooms to be seen in color on television.

Mass communication, especially television, has allowed almost every American to witness potential threats to health, safety, or the environment. A resident of Los Angeles can be alarmed about a power plant in New Hampshire. People in Portland, Oregon, become aware of the shrinking Florida Everglades. Never before have so many been exposed to so much information so quickly. This has no doubt been a catalyst for our environmental concern and has reduced the first productive input that we have mentioned—raw materials. "On the news broadcast we were lectured on the evils of atomic energy plants," says Carl Beck, a Canadian writer, "the crime of atomic energy plants; the crime of storing spent material from these plants in a deserted island in the Pacific Ocean, the ruin of Ontario's lakes by acid rain; the wiping out of whales by overkilling. This was an exceptional day, but a stranger from outer space, listening to our news, could easily believe that our chief concern is our environment; all other problems are insignificant."[3]

The effects of widespread education and the revolution in communication have had an impact well beyond the creation of concern about the physical environment. Both have combined to heighten awareness of the risk inherent in much of technology as well. Education and communication have provided the two essential ingredients that combine to create the concern about technology: the public has been educated to evaluate its dangers, and those dangers have been impressed upon them through the mass communications media. It is clear that these ingredients are a part of the high living standards fostered by economic growth and that they constrain growth through the important route of restricting technological advance.

The key by-product of the concern for the environment and technology has been government regulation of business activity. This has raised the cost and risk of doing business, as we have discussed, and thereby reduced the important input of new capital. It is important to recognize that these regulations are a result of environmental and technological safety consciousness, which has in turn resulted from improved education and communications derived from economic growth. In this almost circular manner, it is evident that economic growth, which renders a nation mature in its stage of industrial development, also weakens the props of continued rapid growth. Economic growth affords a people the ability to enjoy a high-quality and safe environment. It also creates an awareness of the threat to such an environment. The controls that are subsequently demanded undermine capital formation by reducing the returns and increasing the risk of investment. All this leads to forces that undermine the very growth that has brought about these high living standards. This same circular pattern is as true of the remaining input, human effort, as of raw materials, technology, and new capital.

Growth in our general standard of living affords greater human independence. In poorer economic times a stable family unit was required for the security and protection it afforded. The varying fortunes of the individuals that formed this unit were balanced against the rest so that those without incomes were not deprived of the necessities of life. Today the opportunity for larger personal incomes has allowed individual members of the family to pursue their own goals and often to move away from home. It is not uncommon for young people to cross the country in search of a job or a different life-style. As part of this process the cohesiveness and sense of responsibility of family members for one another has waned.

The increasing dispersion of the family unit, enabled by a generally improved living standard, has decreased the security of the family's vulnerable members. Those who at one time or another become unable to provide for themselves by virtue of unemployment, sickness, or old age still require assistance. Yet the weakness of the family unit brought about by geographic or social distance, means that a portion of this help must now come from the public domain. The state, to an ever larger extent, is supplanting the protective and supportive function of the family. A George Washington University Family Impact Seminar held in 1976 identified 331 domestic assistance programs, accounting for $247 billion in direct or indirect aid to families.

A high living standard is at the root of social trends that are redefining the role of the family. It has induced other changes that also propel the state into the active role of providing security for its citizens. Modern medicine, which has advanced alongside living standards, unwittingly contributes by preserving the lives of those enfeebled by sickness or age, some of whom rely on the graces of the state.

Job and life rights directly result from this leap of the state into the social breach. It is these job and life rights that erode human effort in the manner we have shown. To finance these large-scale social expenditures, a higher tax burden has been required. The carrying of this burden is proving a trying experience for American taxpayers and a real test of the social consciousness of each of us. It has reduced the effort that some people apply at work. "Why work harder when it all disappears as taxes?" they may ask.

One source of difficulty the taxpayer has in accepting this social burden is that the state is now the nominal donor of welfare funds. Although its role is supposed to be that of a conduit, its function makes it harder for each of us to be generous. Payments by a donor are no longer received by his or her own family members, neighbors, or friends. Rather, the go-between role provided by the state makes the recipient totally anonymous and makes it seem as if no one benefits at all from our tax payments. Without seeing where the money goes, it becomes easier to assume that it is wasted. Formerly the benefits were obvious; they went to help those we knew and loved. This generosity within family, church, or community groups was undoubtedly help of a much easier kind. When money is provided by way of the state, not only is the donor ignorant of where it goes, the recipient also does not know who provided the assistance. If such assistance came through family or friends, it might temper the demand. But when the donor is the state, restraint in receiving seems out of the question.

The state as a conduit makes generosity less satisfying because donors do not associate their tax payments with specific individuals. They certainly receive no thanks. The increased impersonality of the process contributes to the resentment toward government that characterizes the tax revolt. More important, the resentment about paying taxes reduces human incentive and input. It is easier to work in part to help support someone else when that person is close and in obvious need. Many of us willingly work to provide for a parent or less fortunate family member who is ill. But when the funds go to someone of the same need, who is hidden on the other side of the transfer agency that is the state, it becomes tougher. And as the state replaces the family, human input is threatened.

Hovering above these other checks on human effort that accompany economic progress is what Nobel Prize-winning economist Paul Samuelson calls "a weakening of the hungriness motives." Certainly, the level of saturation of human desires has not been reached, as we have expanded our needs as fast as our means to fill them. But today's living standards place many Americans in a relatively luxurious state. With ample food and access to the luxuries of life, the struggle to survive can hardly be called desperate. Yet even with the decline of effort from the low levels of hungriness in the majority of us, our desire to enjoy more shows no signs of letting up.

Accompanying high living standards, as we see, are elements that themselves work to restrict the growth of all inputs. The slowdown in growth that results might therefore be regarded as an inevitable stage in the development of a mature economy. The development and pursuit of values that include a better physical environment, more care in the use and adoption of technology, and greater independence of life-styles are just a part of the maturation process.

We began this chapter by asking what went wrong. But in reality we might claim that nothing went wrong. The threshold of the Golden Age of affluence has brought unquestionably valuable alternate goals. Improved environmental quality and safety and a compassionate social system, although not easily compared with material standards, are undeniably important human objectives. The appropriate concern in the 1980s is how we can go about achieving a mix between traditional material values and the more broadly defined quality of life. Expressed differently, concern about the slowdown in economic growth might be dispelled if we had a comprehensive measure of "output" that included not only the production of goods and services, but also a measure of the more abstract quality of life. Unfortunately, however, our measure of economic performance, which is provided by real per capita gross national product, does not include much of the nonmaterial dimension of performance. The establishment of a measure of changes in our economic state that included cleaner air, a less pressured workplace, more freedom from fear of technological mishap and loss of livelihood would present a Herculian task. It would require a dollar assessment of values that do not generally enter the marketplace. It would also require that improvements be measured as gains over and above what would have occurred without our effort. Bad air quality, for example, would require a positive value if without our effort it would have been even worse. Indeed, a comprehensive measure of performance is not within our grasp. And so governments and individuals continue to measure progress against traditional material measures. We now see the dangers of this.

chapter 14

The Looming Battle

Suppose that a staunch champion of unfettered economic development emerged to lead the nation in the 1980s. What would he do? Certainly he would repeal the acts of consciousness. He would start by allowing trees to be freely cut and other resources to be extracted without care for the environment. Factories would be assisted in producing at the lowest cost regardless of what happens to our air and water. The hatchet could be wielded to thin the ranks of the civil service. He would ignore social consciousness and make welfare and unemployment benefits well-nigh impossible to achieve. Effort and output would rise as unemployment would become unaffordable. Such a champion of the economy would allow the latest technology to be used, and he would accept the risks this might pose. Regulations would be trimmed, giving business a freer hand in operating their shops. Investment would rise and so would productivity. Goods and services would be turned out at a faster rate.

But will we see this kind of reaction in the 1980s? Will Americans invest any government with the mandate to sweep aside the deeds of the past decades, adopting the kind of unanimity reserved for war? No, America today lacks the consensus required to recant its newly found consciousness. The roots of this consciousness are too deeply buried in the expectations of the kind of society we have come to value. Even the most right-wing politician will not attempt to unearth them.

The steps taken to satisfy growing American consciousness have been large and deliberate ones. Says economist Burkhard Strumpel of the University of Michigan Survey Research Center, "The dominant issues of the sixties—aid to poor nations, racial inequality, domestic poverty, urban problems, pollution, war and peace—focused on ideological rather than economic considerations."[1] Today it appears that our society is preoccupied once again with economics. Yet there is no indication that we are embarked on an abandonment of the steps of the 1960s. In interpreting data gathered by the National Opinion Research Center, political scientist Everett Carl Ladd, Jr., noted that "ninety percent or more of those who insist that federal taxes are too high want to maintain or increase public spending to clean up the environment, to improve the nation's health, and to strengthen the educational system. . . . Among those who think their taxes are too high, for example, 70 percent or more favor high spending to solve urban problems and to improve the situation of black Americans." Conservatives, Ladd continues, have continually failed to "appreciate the depth of the popular commitment to the service state."[2]

Even as matters of the pocketbook become the leading issues, it will not be possible for our political leaders to attempt to scrap the fabric designed to enhance fairness and the quality of life. For example, despite the uproar about regulation, it will not be simple to alter even this visible cause of slowth. Currently over 100 pieces of legislation to reduce the level of government bureaucracy are kicking about in Congress. Regulators are also being asked to police themselves. A regulatory council has been established that is composed of the heads of thirty-five agencies that issue regulations. Its objective, according to its Chairman Douglas Costle of the Environmental Protection Agency (EPA), is to "prune the undergrowth of regulation that has sprung up over the years." The council has undertaken some ambitious projects, including the development of a cancer policy to be administered jointly by the EPA, the Occupational Safety and Health Administration, the Agriculture Department, and the Food and Drug Administration.

The Jimmy Carter Administration is also considering introducing legislation that would require regulatory agencies to evaluate the cost and effectiveness of new regulation. Is this more than a pruning effort, perhaps a move to cut regulation by chopping it off at the roots? Although there may be growing sympathy for such action, the mechanics of deregulation will require politicians to cut their way through a maze erected to protect vested interests, jobs, and public concerns. A *Wall Street Journal* editorial sums it up in an accurate if callous manner. "Regulatory bureaucrats and their 'constituencies' (as they fondly call them) can always subvert rules that attempt to force them to balance costs and benefits, or weed out inanities or end special privileges. Subversion of edicts from on high has developed into a multidimensional art form in Washington."[3]

Despite the journalistic and political wrath they have inspired, regulations, along with all the other factors contributing to slowth, are much more than forms of art without function. They are in place because they satisfy a constituency far broader than the civil servants who administer them or the journalists or businessmen who indict them. Take an issue of *Newsweek,* featuring the story "Innovation—Has America Lost Its Edge." Quotations and cartoon characters are used to drive home the story of the enervating effect regulation has on research and development. Nevertheless, the magazine suggests there is hope for the future embodied in two key innovations, one of which is genetic engineering. Yet if there is a form of new technology with potentially frightening consequences for those who unwittingly face exposure, it is the splicing of genes to alter the characteristics of living organisms. *Newsweek* writers point to the beneficial potential of such research but warn that "a host of rules will have to be drawn up to make sure that it will not—literally—create a monster."[4] The prospect of humans seizing control of the biological process may be required to invoke the fear of technology in some individuals; others become concerned about relatively "minor" matters such as nuclear power plant safety, chemical pollution of the atmosphere, or the soundness of children's toys. These concerns, spread over a broad constituency, provide the origin of regulation. Reliance on government to ensure public welfare and safety is not likely to disappear no matter how much anger is directed at its side effects.

"If society reckons that consumers need protection," says *The Economist*, "it must reckon too that armies of lawyers, ranging from public servants to private rogues, will busy themselves providing it."[5] The consciousness of the 1960s and 1970s that invoked the protection and social programs will not shrink in the face of slowth. We shall not turn away from environmental consciousness, even if there are challenges to specific issues that give rise to political disputes. As Gladwin Hill states in a *New York Times* article summing up the 1970s, "The tocsin that sounded for the environment a decade ago is 'a bell that cannot be unrung.' "[6] Even so, as Hill clearly appreciates, the very unwillingness of many in our society to give up their lofty environmental goals will lead to a series of skirmishes. "The original wave of zeal is giving way to an era of hard-fought case-by-case tradeoffs," notes Hill.

Politicians who fail to attempt these tradeoffs skillfully will be spurned. Our leaders must now walk a fine line between clearing the way for economic growth and not appearing callous. President Carter was aware of this when he submitted the 1979 *Economic Report of the President,* in which he bemoaned inflation and the low growth of productivity. "Ours is a compassionate Nation," he intones on the first page as if these were words intended for a metal plaque, "dedicated to a sense of fairness."

America moves into the 1980s, as Carter must surely know, as both a compassionate and an angry nation. This is the paradox facing today's political leaders. They must appeal to both the idealism and the materialism in the goals of the American citizenry, a citizenry that harbors the belief that both are attainable if only government would become more efficient.

As we have tried to show, the evolution of the present consciousness has economic consequences that far outweigh the matter of government efficiency. It imposes very powerful constraints on our productive system. Although acts of consciousness can be attempted in a more efficient manner, thereby reducing their cost, that cost cannot be eliminated. The idea, according to anti-inflation chief Alfred Kahn, is "to figure out where one can get the biggest environmental and safety bang for society's environmental buck."[7] But some price must still be paid in a slower growth of production and standard of living. Each of us must pay.

What course of action is open to our political leaders in the decade ahead? The most courageous and least harmful course is, as always, to admit and deal with the truth. This would mean working toward recognition of the tradeoffs. Slowth would be acknowledged as the cost of a higher quality life. Pressure for government to fire up the stimulative growth machine to reach unattainable real targets would be resisted. The citizenry would be encouraged to lower their material aspirations to a level more in line with what is attainable. At the same time, any further expansion of consciousness would be scrutinized carefully to ensure minimum additional constraints on growth unless the purpose was clearly worth the price.

Unfortunately, this has not been done. The American government and people have not been realistic about national goals. The results have been persistent inflation, expanding balance of payments deficits, a plummeting national currency, and a rise in protectionism. By far the most harmful outcomes, however, are the disillusionment with government and the feeling that it cannot deliver. This is evident from the proliferation of voter referenda and initiatives, such as California's Proposition 13 and the move toward constitutional prohibition on deficit spending. This swelling of dissatisfaction is also expressed in public opinion polls. One ongoing survey by Louis Harris is typical in that it shows a marked decline in confidence in government leadership since the 1960s. That decline stems partly from the suspicion that government in its ad hoc opportunistic economic policies has contributed to stagflation.

This disillusionment with government will set the stage for the slowth skirmishes. Some of these clashes will be between those who want to reduce the social welfare and regulatory role of government and those who want this role preserved or even enlarged. There will always be people and causes in need. Herein lies a classical American confrontation. But the slowth skirmishes will also be fought over specific and local issues in which questions of economic welfare are pitted against matters of consciousness. These confrontations will be accompanied by a marked sense of urgency, as the need to curtail the growth of consciousness becomes a recognized requirement for maintaining our economic success. As the issue-by-issue conflicts of purpose become more visible, we shall witness more confrontations of the type that took place in the San Francisco Bay Area on April 19, 1977. On that day a convoy of logging trucks tied up commuter traffic on their way to work. Shouting "No more parks, no more parks,"[8] the group of angry loggers were protesting a proposed addition of 74,000 redwood timber acres to the nine-year-old Redwood National Park. The proposed expansion had been adopted as a result of the conservationist view that the surrounding acreage was needed to save the park from erosion damage resulting from logging operations. The loggers, along with pulp mill workers and their families, were concerned about their livelihood. In 1978, after a series of hearings and much heated debate, the extension was granted and 48,000 acres belonging to private companies were appropriated to form part of the park.

Confrontations between environmentalists and those concerned about jobs are not new to California. But against the background of slowth and inflation, events such as these will become more heated and widespread. The debate will include arguments for and against the use of chemicals in agriculture, nuclear power stations, maintenance of welfare and unemployment benefits, the building of new pipelines, and major projects not yet even conceived.

Sometimes it does not even require an organized group to create a skirmish between those who value growth and those who attempt to preserve the level of consciousness and quality of life. Californian Mark Dubois managed a skirmish all on his own. Dubois, an avid outdoorsman and mountaineer, had developed a strong feeling for the environment of the Stanislaus River Canyon of California.

The Army Corps of Engineers had been given the task of building and filling the New Melones Reservoir that fed hydrogenerators to produce electricity. This had been opposed by environmental groups including the Friends of the River, directed by Dubois. As their opposition failed in its objective, Dubois took up the task on his own. He chained himself to a rock inside the canyon and had the key hidden well out of reach. The water level, as it was raised, threatened his life.

Successive search parties using helicopters and planes failed to

locate Dubois, who received visitors from the press just to prove
he had done what he had threatened. As days passed, the Army
Corps of Engineers was eventually forced to stop raising the water
level of the dam. His protest had gone to the top. The Governor of
California, Jerry Brown, wrote to President Carter. "I urge you to
instruct the U.S. Army Corps of Engineers to halt the filling of the
New Melones Reservoir at the Parrots Ferry Bridge. The beauty
of the Stanislaus River and the life of Mark Dubois demand your
personal intervention."[9]

It is unlikely that Dubois could receive blame from Californians for the lights that might fail to come on when the switches
are flicked. Yet he is an effective part of the forces that can darken
many more lights than the ones used by him and his supporters.

To counter the rising consciousness forces, new movements
and groups will grow and add to organized labor and business in
promoting growth. The National Taxpayers Union is one such
group, as is the Fusion Energy Foundation, a New York based
lobby for nuclear power. The Fusion Energy Foundation is an odd
coalition of people from organized labor, academia, and engineering, all thrown together in their effort to achieve "a strong nuclear
based domestic energy program combined with incentives for nuclear exports."[10]

Nuclear power is a prime theater for the clash of values. Debates for and against it, with an urgency accented by the Three
Mile Island affair, seem to be a weekly feature on television news
programs. The nuclear issue is no longer solely the subject of rational forum and intellectual debate. It has moved into the streets,
accompanied by heated rhetoric. "Mr. President," warned Dennis
Banks of the American Indian Movement before a San Francisco
antinuclear rally, "you should know that we'll go back to the
streets to stop nuclear production in this country."[11] Ralph Nader
suggested at the same rally that the antinuclear movement will be
joined by "those who never had an opinion on nuclear power before. You will see young and old, Republican and Democrat, liberals and conservatives. Plutonium doesn't discriminate according
to race, color, creed or sex."[12]

Although the prospects of large-scale protest activity may make
the juices flow among the still committed political activists of the

1960s, they should be prepared for a far different struggle in the "technological Vietnam" envisioned by Nader. Those who are on the other side of this struggle will not ultimately be the government, the business establishment, or a member of the reactionary right. Those who will ultimately be polarized into a position in support of nuclear power and all the other growth issues, will be the young and old, Republicans and Democrats, liberals and conservatives who do not want to see their own living standards sacrificed by those espousing a set of less tangible, nonmaterial values.

These debates have a long history in the United States. But one facet of slowth will underline their intensity. The closer our economic state approaches to a no growth condition, the more the unfettered aspirations of one individual or interest group will be realized at the expense of others. As growth slows, standard of living gains of the type to which many Americans currently aspire have to come from sources other than growth. Some can make gains only by lowering the living standards of fellow citizens.

Such conditions provide a fertile breeding ground for conflict. This conflict need not directly involve matters of consciousness versus growth but will surface because of it. These skirmishes will take place over the subject of equity and will involve hardened interest groups that perceive that they are being deprived. Government programs that are seen to transfer income, or wage agreements that affect the well-being of one group relative to another, will be particularly contentious. They will produce more conflict between various minority groups, between labor and management, between those working and those retired. "Almost everybody thinks he has the short end of the stick and is sure that someone else has the longer end," said Arthur Okun of Brookings Institution. "But when you look at the data, it becomes clear that the great new product of this era is a stick with two short ends."[13] It is our view that the slowth skirmishes will not let up until the average citizen has learned that we all hold the short end of a shorter and leaner stick.

The conflicts can be even between different levels of government, such as those that have occurred between the federal government and certain states. Picking the opportune moment provided by growing gas lines in U.S. cities, Alaska launched advertisements in the early summer of 1979, attacking the policies of Washington, D.C. The state claimed that it could offer fuel for the United States for twenty centuries if only the federal government would allow it to do what it wanted. "Alaska Wants America to Declare a New Independence Day," was the headline in full-page advertisements in *The New York Times,* the *Daily News,* and the *New York Post.*

"Alaska has the potential to help eliminate the lines at American gas stations," read the ads. "Last year we supplied nearly one-sixth of the nation's oil production—a fraction of the potential that may yet be discovered in the 49th state. We have already discovered trillions of cubic feet of natural gas. Our coal could fuel America for 20 centuries." Skirmishes like the one over Alaskan lands will serve as a major indication of who has the upper hand— the slowthers or the growthers. With the exception of nuclear power, no other issue before the public today reflects more clearly the debate about slowth than the debate over land. At stake are large portions of America's remaining oil, natural gas, timber, and uranium reserves. Much of these lie on rugged, scenic terrain that constitutes much of the 760 million acres owned by the federal government. This is one-third the nation's land mass.

Government policy that evolved over the years allowed private interests to capture the resources on these lands. Indeed, of the oil produced in the United States in 1978, 50 percent was drawn from land leased by the federal government. Since the 1960s, environmental groups have achieved some success in getting Congress to withdraw portions of these lands from use in providing resources. The case of Alaska and the stands of national forest timber in the Northwest are two examples. However, a much greater bounty is at stake in the review currently being conducted of lands owned by the Bureau of Land Management. The review will establish which of the bureau's 400 million acres are to be designated as wilderness, placing them out of bounds for resource extraction.

Although this issue will be decided in the national political arena, its implications extend down to the smallest communities. The debate over federal lands will multiply, resembling the kind of heated exchange that took place in California over land for Redwood National Park. "A price must be paid for wilderness, often in terms of severe impacts on local communities; effects on the price and availability of energy fuels, hardrock minerals, lumber and paper products, and lost opportunities for developed recreation," says George S. Dibble, Vice President of Husky Oil Company. "Few Americans recognize the trade-offs—economic and social—involved in wilderness set-asides."[14] The skirmishes over such set-asides will be a pronounced feature of the 1980s. Because they are so basic and broad in scope, they represent an issue that will act as an indicator of prevailing public sentiment.

According to the view of William Keegan of the *London Observer,* we might be lucky if the only conflict is between governments within the same country. In his column in June 1979, Keegan writes that "there has begun an uneasy transitional phase during which aspirations for unlimited economic growth are giving way to a desperate struggle for maintenance of living standards. . . . The result is, potentially, extremely nasty. The West German head of government, Helmut Schmidt, has publicly voiced what many privately fear—that wars could be set off by the mad mercantilist scramble for oil now taking place."[15] We run the danger that slow economic performance on a wide front can have the same effect as oil shortages, as countries scramble to maintain their economic standard of living.

Amid an increasing number of political skirmishes entailing a growing and more esoteric variety of combatants, a truce will, it is hoped, be erected. Its terms will be ones more sensitive to the consciousness versus growth tradeoff than the attitudes that fostered the remarkably high rates of postwar growth or those that now threaten to extinguish it. But the inevitable outcome will be a slower rate of growth.

Ultimately, a large part of the adjustment to slowth will have to come through a reduction of our economic aspirations. To avoid an escalation of slowth skirmishes, this is the only means left if we are unwilling to abandon our checks on supply. But although this holds true for the nation as a whole, the options open to us as individuals are far broader.

chapter 15

Slowth and the American Way of Life

"Thinking rosy futures is as biological as sexual fantasy." Those are words that could be chosen from anthropologist Lionel Tiger's book *Optimism: The Biology of Hope* to summarize its central theme. In this sentence, Tiger's theory of the existence of a firm biological basis for optimism takes on very concrete meaning. Optimism, which Tiger defines as a "mode or attitude associated with an expectation about the social or material future," has also been a driving force behind economic growth. The promise of a materially better, even if not rosy, future lies behind the portrait of America as the land of opportunity and the home of Horatio Alger. It is hope, analyzed in the much broader sense by Tiger, that underlies the powerful economic forces of investment and risk-taking, hard work, and the striving for production skills and material advancement.

Optimism, to which Tiger attaches such extreme importance, will be threatened during the period of slow growth by an ever widening satisfaction gap—the difference between slower improvements in living standards and higher aspirations that are products of experience. Slowth is the key to this gap. It is the force that dictates that consumption aspirations will grow beyond what our incomes will attain. At first, *personal* aspirations will be untouched by bleak national economic trends. Even now Americans view their personal fates as separate from the whole of society. Rose-colored personal expectations clash with the more somber tones characterizing the common view of national prospects, a trend noted by sociologist Amitai Etzioni and documented by more than one public opinion poll. Says Etzioni, "The private self and public self in the American persons have split off from each other. . . . Privately, many people feel quite self-confident, optimistic about their future, able to cope, satisfied, even happy. But when they view their public life, as members of a national community, they are quite pessimistic."[1] The major factor that explains this incongruity is our innate optimism. It explains why we believe we shall be spared the brunt of bleak economic and social trends foreseen for the nation as a whole.

Is this innate sense of optimism a positive and highly individual response to any current reality, including the decline of economic prospects? The role of rose-colored perspectives as they affect at least psychological well-being is today the subject of debate. Among some psychologists, there seems to be little support for self-deception as a way of dealing with a dark reality. But it takes time to grasp reality, and even then what we grasp may bear little resemblance to reality. "Life is ambiguous," says psychologist Richard Lazarus. "Many of the beliefs we have about the world around us—about justice, about our integrity, about the attitudes of those around us, about our own future—are based on, at best ambiguous information. One can maintain illusions about those that have a positive aura without necessarily distorting reality. Such illusions are not pathological, hope is not the same as denial."

Rose-colored perspectives, at least as far as our economic prospects are concerned, may be positive illusions now, but as this decade proceeds they will be transformed into a form of denial. Slowth in the 1980s will be less an ambiguous trend and more a reality to be faced squarely. But even in the face of unambiguous reality, we have a choice about the way we react to it. As Lazarus puts it, "Here's where one difference between a threat and a challenge counts. Threat is a state in which the person feels oppressed, blocked, reduced. Coping is poor. But challenge actually facilitates functioning. When a person is challenged, he's more apt to be loose, to use skills effectively." Our job in facing the reality of slowth is to maintain this sense of challenge. That challenge will come in adapting to an economic environment far less conducive to the achievement of material goals. Or, in the parlance of Tiger, we shall now be forced to translate innate optimism into action, which propels thoughts of personal betterment out of the realm of mere fantasy.

The need to adjust our life-styles is the inevitable consequence of slowth. Americans are afflicted by a desire to consume in excess of their personal incomes, a phenomenon we shall label the "satisfaction gap." This is true both for our society and for many of us as individuals. Adjustment requires that we effect a better balance between income and consumption. This can be done by either *boosting income* or *cutting consumption*. To the extent that economics influences the way we conduct our lives, major and even dramatic life-style changes will follow.

A new era is underway. This is certainly the case for the majority of the population whose awareness of the Great Depression now comes only through the history book or by word of mouth. This will be an era during which control over personal economic affairs will be critical. We can gain a large degree of that control by consuming more efficiently. We can also attempt to increase our incomes faster than do others in the nation. These are the two responses to slowth by which we can increase personal satisfaction. But the reality of slowth means that the income growth approach will not be available to all of us. In fact, the very meaning of slowth is that income advancements in the nation as a whole will fall short of collective aspirations. Many of us, therefore, will remain unable to close the satisfaction gap in this way. The only way of dealing with slowth for the nation as a whole is to pull back on what we consume.

During the decades of the 1950s and 1960s we did not need personal control of our economic lives. We could achieve the fulfillment allowed by a rising standard of living by running with a strong wind at our backs. Today the wind of economic growth is dying and any forward movement we make toward achieving economic satisfaction will come solely from our personal power. In noting the life-style adjustments that result from slowth, we are not suggesting that change is universal. Adaptability of individuals is no more a uniform trait in the economic sphere than it is in the realm of biology. For some of us there is no acceptable alternative to economic progress; for others new difficulties represent a form of challenge. In the words of historian Oscar Handlin, "The idea of progress can be a kind of narcotic, or it can be a sense of possibility which means you've got to struggle."[2] The ways we adapt will vary markedly owing to the breadth of human personalities and values. In this glimpse into life-style changes, we suggest only that one or more of these measures is a logical way to respond to slowth and its inevitable widening of the satisfaction gap.

The more dynamic life-style adjustments are made by those who are attempting to cut consumption. "Reduce your wants and supply your needs," warned former Indian leader Mahatma Gandhi in very practical advice to his impoverished nation. "Our needs make us vulnerable enough. Why increase our vulnerability?"[3] Americans in greater numbers will be realizing that this advice is well worth personal consideration. One means to reduce wants and satisfy needs entails a reversal of the trend toward becoming a specialized member of the economy. The long-term trend has meant that we perform a single specific role in work to earn the means to satisfy all our wide and varied needs. The economic reality of slowth will reverse this trend. It will provide an incentive to diversify our human energies, reduce consumption from the marketplace, and instead provide directly for ourselves. Increasingly, some of us will be developing economic skills outside work to satisfy our own needs from our own production.

One example, already well ingrained in American households, is the trend toward "do-it-yourself." The wealth of alternative possibilities captured in this label shows the breadth of skills that people have developed beyond their line of work. Those who enjoy gardening, home improvement, or carpentry might well have begun these pursuits as an enjoyable way of spending leisure time.

Now their efforts have expanded into other activities that are not necessarily fun, such as plumbing and auto repair. Ultimately, the economic reality of slowth will force even more consumers to abandon the marketplace as too costly a source for what they can provide themselves. A growth industry will be created for those who provide the means for people to do things themselves. Enterprises renting tools and facilities will benefit by providing the hardware for a growing market. Adult education courses, do-it-yourself books, and television instruction will help develop the wherewithal. Opportunities will be created for those who market do-it-yourself products and information. In the process, do-it-yourself activities will become one major means for exerting greater personal control. As a result of this shift, the time spent in home decorating and repair, auto maintenance, plumbing, carpentry, and growing food will mean more than filling leisure time. For some of us they will become a major means of reducing consumption and reliance on the marketplace.

The need to cut consumption will bring out the consumer in us. In increasing numbers we shall attempt to achieve greater efficiency in buying. This requires that we make a sharper distinction between our wants and needs, with the expansion of the former becoming part of the burdensome baggage of unfettered material aspirations. Condominiums with houseplants will become a small family substitute for the traditional home and garden. The grass and open spaces of public parks will have to replace the backyard of the large lot home. Cluster and multiplex housing will subvert the single-family detached house as affordability becomes the key issue. Consumption efficiency, as part of an effort at overall economy of consumption, will boost the popularity of less costly recreation. Bicycling, hiking, camping, and just plain staying at home will prevail more frequently over trips to Europe or Disneyland. We shall witness greater care in buying. An emphasis on the value, quality, and durability of consumer goods will shift demand away from goods whose sole appeal is based on convenience or a twitch of advertising-induced recognition.

Consumerism is more than frugality. The wisdom of buying well-crafted items—houses carefully constructed and built to last over a century, cars for which style takes a backseat to durability—is apparent in the context of slowth. The consumer who has chosen goods that last is in a better position to reduce the level consumed over this next decade. Goods that continue to provide satisfaction better insulate the consumer against the slowdown in production than goods that continually need replacing.

In a story about how middle- and upper-class Americans are learning this lesson, *Time* surveyed retailers of consumer goods and concluded, "Americans are beginning to behave like Europeans. With a new attitude of less can be more, they are buying fewer but better goods than in earlier years. . . . This trend may well result from the new conservative ethic. Because resources are scarce and goods are costly, there is a fresh appreciation for their value. Waste is gauche; goods should last—and that requires moving up to quality."[4] This move to quality is no mere fad, and it will not be confined to the wealthy. It is the way many discerning buyers will adapt to the state of slow growth in real incomes.

Quite apart from any trend in consumerism, a great American characteristic—waste—will also fall victim to the need to cut consumption. More than a few families will be driving older cars, walking or bicycling to the store, turning off electric lights and appliances when they are not in use, and widening the comfort range on their thermostats.

Another method of reducing consumption, and thereby narrowing the satisfaction gap, is to improve the way we use our leisure time. We can derive more satisfaction from leisure by applying more skill and effort in employing the time at hand. The use of leisure, however, is a consumption skill that is still badly neglected by many of us. Leisure activity has come to mean prodigious spending that will become increasingly harder to maintain. One challenge of slowth will come as we try to improve the quality of leisure time without expanding the associated expense.

Economist Tibor Scitovsky is a highly articulate critic of what he feels is the low level of economic satisfaction derived by those living in this time of "the joyless economy" (which is also the title of his book). He attributes this state of affairs in part to the failure of Americans to develop their skill in using leisure time enjoyably. Says Scitovsky, "We have access to more sports, more games, more pastimes than others, and to many more places to see and visit, but we lack the skills and knowledge needed fully to enjoy them and we even seem to lack the inclination to acquire such competence. It is as though we preferred unskilled consumption, trying everything once or twice, or in three easy lessons if necessary, but often remaining dilettantes and seldom aspiring to the more enjoyable higher reaches of consumer expertise."

Although Scitovsky's indictment of our society may seem harsh, it is fair to say that the contraction of the average workweek has caused more than a few of us to grope for better ways to spend our leisure. As a result of slowth, we cannot allow massive doses of income to be channeled into leisure activities. We shall require the will to expand our level of leisure-related skills. This is an apt way to mitigate the negative impact of slowth. Slowth will bring a greater frustration of the economic progress we are able to achieve in work, creating a void of satisfaction. More creative use of leisure time will help fill that void. It will also reduce growth in the amount we feel we must spend to enjoy ourselves.

Such newly gained skills would offer great relief to people as they become older. As Scitovsky observes, "When people retire they are suddenly deprived of the stimulus satisfaction their work has given them, and naturally they try to fall back on the other sources of stimulation accessible to them. If they are unskilled consumers, they soon find their sources of stimulation inadequate; the result is the heartrending spectacle of elderly people trying desperately to keep themselves busy and amused but not knowing how to do so."

Even for the younger set, the rewarding disposition of leisure represents an exciting challenge. In the years ahead it will present an opportunity to supplement the declining doses of material gains that accompany slowth. This demands the development and cultivation of interests outside work. Some of these interests will continue to be the expensive activities that exploded onto the consumer scene during times of growing incomes and leisure, like scuba diving, motor home travel, and alpine skiing. Yet less costly interests are slowly taking their place. The activities gaining in popularity involve skill and effort and perhaps no more equipment than the human body and mind.

One such activity is skill-oriented education. Leisure time

courses in handicrafts, furniture making, art, gardening, personal development, acting, and music are among an enormous assortment of courses that will experience growing demand. California Governor Jerry Brown has been quick to try to capitalize on the value of these activities to the state's University of California employees. "Their ready access to doses of 'psychic income,' " he suggested, "should act as a good substitute for higher salaries."[5] The effort to enrich our own lives by utilizing this "psychic income" will be spurred by the slowing of economic growth and our frustrations in trying to close the material satisfaction gap.

Cultural interests will represent a more sizable part of leisure time development. Some slowth victims will emphasize reading, appreciation of music and art, and the lessons of history or rudiments of dance. All these activities have in common the need for, as Scitovsky puts it, a certain level of "knowledge which provides the redundancy needed to render stimulation enjoyable." That knowledge will be in great demand in the period of slowth.

Physical fitness is among the more fulfilling and less costly uses of leisure. The wild popularity of jogging, even if its recent growth cannot be sustained, shows how readily we can adopt a new challenge and interest. As a result of slowth even more people will partake in a wide range of physical activities including swimming, racquetball, and tennis. Many of these newcomers to physical conditioning, however, will have a very different motivation from those who have enjoyed athletic activity in the past.

The concern with physical conditioning has been part of a wider trend toward what might be called narcissism, or "selfism." A major factor behind selfism is the feeling that materialism is not a totally fulfilling goal. Selfism results from growing interest in the physical and emotional aspects of life, sought as alternatives to the material. Exercise, dieting, and health fads are all part of this phenomenon. So too are the movements of the mind that emphasize self-analysis and human awareness. Phenomena like the popularity of Erhard Seminar Training (est) and the surfacing of a magazine like *Self—The News You Need to Make a Better You* are just two indicators of the search for completeness in realms far removed from material reward.

Although selfism has risen on the wings of disaffection with materialism, it will go even higher on the frustration of the material satisfaction gap. Selfism has spread with material wealth and the disillusionment with it, but it will now become a refuge for those who become frustrated by the increasingly harsh struggle for material advance. The emphasis on physical and emotional well-being is now a haven not only for those disillusioned with the fruits of materialism, but also for those who find too much pain in the struggle to achieve them.

The trend toward self-examination can assist in the transition to slowth. *The New York Times* writer Richard Eder has noted in an article, "Whatever Happened to the Idea of Progress," that "the emphasis on health and spiritual development, sometimes criticized as narcissism, may in fact be a useful preparation."[6] Eder cites psychiatrist and sociologist Michael Maccorby, the author of *The Gamesman: The New Corporate Leaders.* According to Maccorby, "We've lost the right to unlimited use of our cars, to eating steak four times a week. But it's easier to give up steak because of cholesterol. It's easier to reduce the use of the car in the interests of health, to walk, to bicycle. Narcissism, up to a point, can make us more adaptable."

Another consequence of the struggle to close the satisfaction gap will be smaller families and delayed childbearing. This is an alternative way to cut consumption by reducing the numbers that families with stagnant incomes must support. For some families this means no more than a delay in childrearing; for others it means resorting to having no children at all. For example, Steven Flint is a resident of Des Plains, Illinois, a city that he is now combing in search of an affordable home for his family. He said to *Time,* which inquired about his search, "For $500 I can reserve a place and then work my tail off at two jobs for a year to get the down payment together. I'll have to continue with two jobs after we move in, and my wife will probably have to work all her adult life to support this house. There is a good chance our daughter will be an only child."[7] For other couples the decision in favor of a smaller family will relate less specifically to the cost of housing than the cost of childrearing. One 1977 estimate of the cost of raising a child for eighteen years, including food, clothing, education (not college), and medical expenses, is over $50,000, given a family income of between $16,500 and $20,000.

A feasible means of cutting consumption to cope with slowth is through trimming the size of the family that the budget must support. The current contraction in birth rates is certainly an indication that this is happening. By 1977 only 15 percent of American families had more than two children under 18. Almost half the families had no children at all under that age. "In almost every country, the fertility index is falling dramatically, at speeds never before reached in peacetime,"[8] says Gerald Calot, Director of the National Institute of Demographic Studies in Paris. In 1978 U.S. fertility levels—the average number of births per thousand women of childbearing age—fell to 1.8, well below replacement levels. "Often, both husband and wife work, get used to living well on their joint incomes and are reluctant to surrender all that to raise children," says a feature article in the *Wall Street Journal* that plots the pending population decline in Europe.

Smaller families are one way to reduce claims on the budget. Another is to delay childbearing and even marriage. But the delay, especially in having children, has its cost. The risk of infertility or damage to the reproductive system rises as childbearing is postponed for women over 30 and certainly over 40 years of age. "But when they discover—too late in some cases—that they have problems in conceiving, the psychological consequences for both the man and the woman can be devastating," is the view of Miriam Mazor. In a *Psychology Today* article entitled "Barren Couples," Mazor documents the "sense of helplessness at losing control over one's life plans,"[9] a sense that she herself had experienced during the initial frustration of her childbearing plans. Often it is the couple's effort to provide the desired material life-style by postponing plans for children that leaves them in this desperate state. With slowth, the wait and the risks will be endured by more couples.

Whereas some families may be controlling their consumption by limiting their size, other households are adjusting through the attempt to actually boost their incomes. For some this means continuation of the present trend toward the two wage-earner family. "For the middle class in the United States most, if not all, real increases in the standard of living (indeed, if there have been any at all) in the past decade have come about by a working spouse,"[10] says R. Joseph Monsen, professor and Chairman of the University of Washington's School of Business Administration. Monsen goes on to discuss the primary reason that necessitated a shift toward the two wage-earner family—the price of housing. "Since the cost of housing has been significantly outrunning income gains in recent years, we have witnessed a situation in which only a third or fourth of all families in the United States can afford to purchase homes—a significant drop from a half or more a decade ago."

Economist Herbert Stein has observed the same effect in terms of the degree to which income and consumption have grown despite the dismal productivity performance. He has noted that the women who entered the labor force during the 1970s have allowed the real per capita income to grow by having a larger fraction of the population at work. This is true because if there are more people at work, more income can be generated even with a decline in labor productivity, which is output *per* working person.

The contribution of the working spouse, whether in helping to support the burden of mortgage debt or other pressing family needs, has been impressive. Sociologist Valerie Kincaid Oppenheimer has examined the impact of working wives on the finances of the family. She concludes from the available statistics that wives are being encouraged to work and are making a very positive contribution to family welfare. She suggests, furthermore, that the two wage-earner family is becoming an alternative and common means of living standard advancement. Says Oppenheimer, "Although wives earn considerably less, on the average than husbands, wives' economic contribution to their families can still be highly important enough, in many cases, to provide a functional substitute for upward occupational mobility on the husband's part, or to compensate for a husband's relatively low earnings compared to other men in his occupational group."[11] The importance of that second income is a point that has been driven home to bachelors as well. One American computerized dating agency has observed that whereas the quality of physical appearance was once enough to define the desirable date, earning power and professional status are now also an important quality sought by many males.

But output growth cannot continue indefinitely merely by virtue of adding women to the labor force. Already, by the end of the 1970s, women constituted more than 40 percent of the American work force. There is limited room for continued growth in the number of women who will seek jobs. Beyond that, output growth will cease to benefit from the addition of more and more women to the work force.

Like the delay of childbearing, the route of seeking two incomes does not come without cost. Often the need or desire to work detracts from the task of raising children, a trend that child-development expert Urie Bronfenbrenner sadly mourns. By the mid-1970s more than half the women with children of school age were employed and over a third with children under 6 held down a job. Indeed, over a third with children under 3 went to work. "Fewer and fewer parents are doing their job of caring for children," says Bronfenbrenner, who adds in an interview with Susan Byrne of *Psychology Today* that "if there's any reliable predictor of trouble, it probably begins with children coming home to an empty house, whether the problem is reading difficulties, truancy, dropping out, drug addictions, or childhood depression."[12]

In addition to the growth in two wage-earner families, the work force will swell from yet another source—an increase in the typical age of retirement. Unlike the trend toward wives working, older retirement is a phenomenon that has only just begun to surface as a major force. In the face of slowth, pressure to work to an older age will grow. A key factor behind this push will be a need by people in their middle years to consume a greater portion of their income to satisfy their current demands. Longer working lives will result from financial pressures or the inadequacy of current Social Security and pension provisions. It may be reinforced through pressure of 'grey power' lobbies, which will lend support to people who choose to raise the number of years they continue earning their own income. This movement will swell as long as the level of inflation is uncertain, a condition that leads people to consume without delay and spurn saving for tomorrow.

Individuals will try in other ways to boost their incomes. For some people slowth will act to strengthen the outlook or effort they apply to work. This means not only harder work, longer hours, and increased application of energy and dedication; it may also entail other modern manifestations of the work ethic. Slowth will make some people more willing to move their places of residence in response to job opportunity. They will be forced into responding to the shift in economic growth patterns away from the traditional economic centers of the Northeast in favor of the West and South. This will provide the incentive to move in order to advance or, in some cases, even to maintain living standards. Those who are inclined to redouble their effort in work have other options. They can utilize job training to upgrade work skills. Nighttime courses offer a vehicle for people to acquire business and trade skills. These courses are well suited to individuals beyond the prime schooling age who are struggling to satisfy their living standard aspirations.

The response of college students faced with greater obstacles to their material goals is already in evidence. There is a recognition on campuses across the United States of the harsher economic climate. This has accounted for the growing demand for a more practical education ostensibly afforded by degrees in law, accounting, business, and engineering. The ideal of the liberal arts degree has, for many economically minded students, been eclipsed by the race for the security of the marketable degree. With notable exceptions, the bastions of higher education are being transformed into high-powered vocational institutions.

Conventional vocational institutes, for those not involved in higher education, will also flourish. Schools and courses in a host of trades are now acting as a form of first job experience for those who lack the experience and know-how, but not the ambition, to break into the better paying parts of the job market. A variety of vocational education programs now substitute, for better or worse, for the on-the-job training so difficult to obtain in an economy beset by slow growth. Trade schools and vocational institutes train students for work as, among other things, computer programmers, travel agents, and managers of hotels, motels, and airlines.

Another response to slowth will entail a vastly different type of activity, far removed from the work ethic. Scheming and speculation will represent the income augmenting efforts of certain types of individuals—those who feel that conventional (and taxable) work is an insufficient means of material advancement. Such individuals probably feel that the economic system is stacked against the working person because of seemingly incessant inflation and rising taxes. The only solution, according to this view, is to strive for advancement outside the system.

The weighty matter of taxes appears to be a prime motivator of those participating in the "subterranean economy." This label was applied by economist Peter Gutmann who noted an increase in what he termed "excess cash." He speculated that this was used to support work done "off the books" to avoid taxes. He estimated that in 1976 nontaxable transactions constituted 10 percent of the gross national product. Although this estimate has been disputed as too large, it appears that the subterranean economy has grown along with the magnitude of taxes. In a *Fortune* feature story on the subject, Irwin Ross lists those entities that are likely to do business off the books. "Tax evasion is a common fact of life in retail outlets of all sorts—grocery stores, boutiques, small variety stores, bars, restaurants, antique shops—as well as the construction trades, service businesses, small manufacturing companies, and among the self-employed, including such professionals as doctors. In overall terms, these pursuits represent a substantial chunk of American economic life."[13] It is Ross's contention that tax evasion results from the inflationary spiral of taxpayers' incomes into increasingly higher tax brackets. Whatever the technical reason, more of the citizenry is building other people's garages, working in stores and restaurants, assisting with tax returns, and doing their neighbor's plumbing, all "off the books." In fact it seems as if tax evasion is well on the way to becoming America's number one indoor sport. As such it is the individual counterpart to the political tax revolt and something we should see more of as economic frustrations build alongside slowth.

Another response to the inflationary erosion of the reward for conventional work is the frenzied move by people to own real assets such as gold, art, antiques, and real estate. In a stampede largely toward economic self-defense, land and gold have been snapped up at a frenetic pace. The level of interest in these and other markets will grow as they are seen to represent a vehicle for some form of economic security.

There are many ways available to each of us to narrow the satisfaction gap. For some people, though, the task will not be easy. Those who feel that one spouse must remain at home to care for the children cannot easily add an extra income. The many for whom retraining would be long and expensive cannot move into a new and better paying career. Families must be fed and clothed in the interim. But far more important, even allowing for the many ways we as individuals can overcome slowth by expanding our own real incomes, as a society we cannot do this. The very nature of slowth is that the nation's income will not be growing, at least at the rates experienced in the past. If some individuals by their own cleverness or ingenuity are advancing their standards of living at the old rate, others must be falling further behind. These latter will include the many who are unable to add an extra income, change their pattern of life or work, or play fast and loose in the conduct of their personal economic affairs. Together, the decline in their fortunes will outweigh the income gains of others. This is inherent in slowth.

Others will find that the consumption reducing route is also closed. Many expenditures cannot be trimmed. Households that have incurred a large fixed debt do not have flexibility in cutting what they spend. Mortgages, for example, must be paid despite the assumptions that were made at the time they were incurred. For a number of home buyers, those assumptions included not only higher real incomes, but probably high inflation that among its distortionary ways also would help reduce the real bite represented by fixed mortgage payments. Inflation does enable mortgage holders to retire fixed debt with "cheaper" dollars. Yet with stagnant real incomes, the struggle will be on for mortgage holders to maintain their payments as well as finance aspirations for the future.

The possibility of real income growth for the nation as a whole will not exist because of the very nature of slowth. The prospect of cutting consumption is an option for only certain individuals. The result is that, despite the major life-style adjustments enacted by some, the satisfaction gap will remain a stressful fact of life for a great many Americans.

chapter 16

Less-Stress

"The desire of food is limited in every man by the narrow capacity of the human stomach; but the desire of the conveniences and ornaments of building, dress, equipage, and household furniture, seems to have no limit or certain boundary."[1]

—Adam Smith.

"We don't have a desperate need *to grow. We have a desperate* desire *to grow."*[2]

—Milton Friedman.

Hans Selye, whose work established the existence of the phenomenon known as stress, is fond of telling the story about how he popularized the concept. After writing numerous technical books and articles on the subject, he was asked by his publisher to communicate in simple words a summary of his findings relating to stress. Selye obliged by synthesizing thirty years of research into a mere ten pages. Approving, but still not satisfied, his publisher requested an even more pithy summation. In response, the doctor condensed his findings into this one simple phrase: "Fight for your highest attainable aim but do not put up resistance in vain."[3]

For those attempting to cope with slowth, this advice for dealing with "less-stress" has a great deal of validity. It reflects the fact that for many of us the greatest impact of slowth is in fact psychological. This is particularly true for those unable to effect real lifestyle changes that can be used to narrow the satisfaction gap. For them, the maintenance of material aspirations unrelated to reality is indeed resistance in vain and a source of great distress. In considering how this has developed, it is helpful to examine the psychology of growth. Slowth threatens more than merely the growth of what there is to consume, a development actually welcomed by those who decry our saturation with consumer artifacts. It also threatens to burst the balloon of collective expectations that has floated continually upward to become a distinctive marker hovering over the American landscape.

The notion is hard to dispute: we have become psychologically dependent on steady improvements in living standards, and these standards are now serving as the seeds of our disappointment. Against this background, slow growth creates an ever wider satisfaction gap—the difference between slower improvements in living standards and higher aspirations that are molded by our past experience. On a personal level, slowth is challenging our own aspirations with the threat of disappointment and imposing on many people a futile struggle to somehow narrow that satisfaction gap. We have called this by-product of slowth "less-stress" because the widening satisfaction gap represents a new and painful dynamic to which we must adjust.

The potential for a satisfaction gap, created by continually rising demands, was the subject of much testing by a group of social scientists at the University of Michigan Survey Research Center. These researchers devote their work to understanding the psychological basis underlying economic behavior. The prosperity of postwar America, they contend, has conditioned many of us to continually raise our aspirations, rendering satisfaction with existent material standards difficult to achieve.

"Satisfaction with a product for instance, a car or a restaurant meal, depends not only on the quality of the product, but also on what the person whose satisfaction is studied expects from the product." These are the words of George Katona, a member of the center and a prime contributor to the discipline of psychological economics. "Satisfaction with income or standard of living is likewise affected by the person's expectations and aspirations in addition to what has actually happened to him."[4]

Aspirations, if we accept this premise, constitute the yardstick by which people judge their economic performance. Furthermore, the size of this yardstick is not constant but changes with past accomplishment. This conclusion follows from the work of psychologist Kurt Lewin whose experiments on expectations performed in 1944 are still referred to by those writing about the subject today. Lewin contends that we subject our aspirations to a reality testing based on past performance—with each success leading only to higher aspirations.

Americans have now had their aspirations boosted by successive decades of improved living standards. Material betterment has sometimes even exceeded commonly held levels of expectation. Luxuries such as overseas travel, family multicar ownership, and an ever shorter workweek have served to whet our appetites for a society of even greater comfort—a society that continues to provide more. A measure of the past growth and the affluence it has created is our expenditure of larger portions of our incomes on what we want rather than what we need, a malaise complicated by a growing inability to distinguish between the two.

Katona and his colleagues concluded from their work that society has become psychologically dependent on growth. By means of extensive interview surveys they concluded:

> High expectations of a better material future are characteristic of American culture; low expectations are more often than not symptoms of disappointment, frustration and alienation. A full 63 percent of the employed males in our sample said that they expected progress and change in five years. Americans demand and expect progress and change much more than Europeans. If five years from now their standard of living was the same, almost half of Americans would be somewhat disappointed or even dissatisfied, but this pattern was not found in other affluent societies.[5]

This study, discussed by Burkhard Strumpel of the Michigan Survey Research Center, was conducted in 1972 but little has changed since then. Indeed, according to a 1976 poll by Patomac Associates, a "better or decent standard of living" tops the personal hopes of those questioned. Significantly, this was mentioned more frequently than "good health," a "happy family life," and "peace in the world."[6] Such results are so extreme as to appear implausible. Yet a deep examination of the effects of slowth should be enough to firmly establish the importance of rising living standards in our society.

A key part of growth's importance stems from the way material betterment helps us stave off feelings of depravation. It is not that most Americans fear going hungry or living without adequate shelter or even the prospect of forgoing certain luxuries. Rather it is a fear of *relative* deprivation—the feeling that we are getting less out of the system than others who are perceived to deserve less. This insecurity stems from the concern that the economic system is neither equitable nor just and that we ourselves shall bear the brunt of that injustice. Slowth will accentuate these concerns. This feeling of deprivation will persist until we become convinced that our failure to improve living standards is not confined to ourselves but is instead a problem we all share.

The perversity by which a feeling of deprivation can thrive amid material plenty has led to a good deal of interest on the part of psychologists. The first suggestion of it came in a post-World War II study of life in the U.S. Armed Forces. *The American Soldier* by Samuel Stouffer and his colleagues dealt with promotion and status in the military, but their findings hold relevance to the more general phenomena of wealth, status, and comfort provided by present-day living standards. In their book the authors sought to explain how soldiers in divisions with greater promotional opportunity, such as those in the Air Corps, felt less satisfied about their promotional status than those with less opportunity such as soldiers in the Military Police. The answer, the authors suggested, was the coexistence of men of lower rank with those of a higher rank who served as objects of comparison.

Although growth does not reduce the tendency to compare, it helps those so inclined to live with inequity. "Growth in providing the majority of people with continuously rising income is a palliative that keeps underlying problems in the distribution of income, wealth and consumption from surfacing," is the way Strumpel puts it. Slow growth will widen the satisfaction gap. Our accomplishments will fall short of our aspirations. We will perceive ourselves to be making less progress than others. This is the essence of the more subtle psychological struggle that slowth will impose. For many this state of affairs will be complicated by a much more tangible difficulty—the struggle to make ends meet.

For the average middle-class citizen such problems do not stem from an inability to provide the necessities of life, but instead from the strain of financing a living standard that conforms to expectations rather than to means. The extensive development of instruments of debt have allowed the American consumer to enjoy many goods that can be paid for with tomorrow's income. Self-owned housing is invariably financed by a mortgage. Automobile and consumer appliance sales frequently rely on credit. Indeed, the size and quality of houses and cars that are purchased are not based on real incomes enjoyed today, but on the strength of what past experience leads householders to believe they can afford in the future.

According to Katona and his coauthors, in a study comparing economic motivation in Western Europe and the United States, American consumers are more "dynamic" in this sense: "The dynamic consumer does not live from day to day. He purchases goods that will serve him in the future. He borrows to acquire housing and durable goods suitable to the status he expects to have and geared to his expected income. By . . . committing future income in advance, his needs and wants exert great pressure toward obtaining a higher income."[7]

Financial frustration will be a fallout of slowth. As incomes fail to grow quickly enough to reduce the burden of debt incurred with overly optimistic expectations, cash binds will result. Expenditures will have to be trimmed. In one of a number of stories about the phenomenon labeled inflation, *Time* reporters interviewed people about their frustrations. They quoted a marriage counselor, Gloria Pineles, who maintained that inflation is inimical to family stability. "People are accustomed to living a certain lifestyle, and all of a sudden they find that they cannot take an annual vacation or send their second child to college. This leads to resentment and frustration. Family finances become clouded in secrecy, and neither spouse has a good understanding of where the paycheck is going."[8]

The fixation of politicians and the popular press on inflation has done little to imbue Pineles or any citizen with an understanding of what is really going wrong. Inflation, in contexts such as these, is merely a buzzword used to conjure up images of rising prices and stagnant paycheck buying power, afflictions that most victims have come to understand. Lost, however, in this masquerade is the basic economic cause of reduced buying power—not prices that rise too fast, but supply that fails to rise fast enough. The real and essential problem is not that things cost too much but that collectively we provide too little in the way of goods and services. Inflated prices are the means by which we experience slowth. They are the focus of our anger and attention. Yet it is really the slow growth of production that deprives us of the material things we require to fulfill our aspirations.

Slowth and its resultant inflation are bringing less in the way of material comforts: more of us live in apartments rather than our own homes, drive smaller cars, take local less exotic holidays, and eat fewer full-course restaurant meals. For members of society with low incomes, the situation is yet more critical. The struggle posed by slowth is much more severe.

Less-stress, the pain in adjusting to the satisfaction gap, will be the result of the aspirations we have nurtured. The trend toward less, brought about by slowth, will run counter to those aspirations, making some kind of adjustment imperative. But, as we maintain, only certain people will be capable of making a speedy adjustment by either enhancing their income or cutting consumption. For the rest of us, the adjustment to slowth will be slow and painful and full of frustration and anger.

chapter 17

Managing to Live with Slowth

BUSINESS

Picture this scene at the annual shareholders' meeting of one of America's large corporations. A proud management has distributed all the statistics that summarize the year's results. The president beams, as he points to a chart and says, "Now, Ladies and Gentlemen, I'd like to call your attention to this chart showing last year's sales levels in comparison with those of the previous decade. You will be happy to note that sales have held steady." This is greeted with enthusiasm by those assembled, each of whom owns a piece of the action.

Seems unlikely? Will the era of slowth substitute plateaus and semihorizontal lines on sales charts, which previously pointed toward heaven? It must. The slow growth of aggregate economic output means that the average growth of the components of that output have also slowed. Profits are part of the gross national product (GNP) when expressed in income form. Within a static total, profits can grow only at the expense of the other categories of the national income—wages, salaries, interest, and rents. Growth in profits is unlikely to come from reductions in the values of these other components; pressure from the relevant vested interest groups is too strong. In a similar way, since what is sold is what is produced, domestic sales levels cannot grow if total domestic production levels are constant. The flat charts at the shareholders' meeting, for both profits and sales, are the inevitable consequence of slowth. They cannot be avoided.

This is the source of the manager's satisfaction gap in a world of slowth. Although he or she and everyone else who reads the arguments we present may accept the inevitability of slowth for the entire nation, they see no reason why it should affect *them*. Expectations remain tied to past performance. "Sure," they say, "the economy isn't growing but my firm will continue to grow in sales and profitability." This is the same phenomenon we already observed with individuals holding pessimistic views for the economy while remaining optimistic about themselves. And in just the same way, it must eventually lead to frustration and disappointment among managers and their shareholders.

An economy that fails to grow must have a similar impact on the fate of the elements that make up the economy—the firms, the governments, and the individuals. Slowth will substitute disappointment and dissatisfaction for the dynamic engine that until now has driven our material achievements and ambitions ever upward. Yet, as with the individual, the firm and the government will seek ways of adapting or managing to live with slowth. These means are the subject of this chapter.

The behavior of the firm is much like that of the individual. Increasing success has met with increasingly higher expectations. For the individual, success in monetary terms means income; in material terms it is things like houses, cars, exotic vacations, and nights on the town. For a great many firms, the main measure of success is growth—growth in assets, growth in sales, and growth in profits. Ultimately, profits remain the long-term objective, but in the shortened period over which we recognize merit and assign reward, growth in a firm's size has also been an ingredient of success. It brings not only higher earnings for management but also means control over broader spheres of activity. Managers become upwardly mobile. Growth means new responsibility for departments, product lines, and markets. It creates challenge and excitement.

Slowth will challenge managerial measures of success by undercutting the growth in sales. With the growth ethic not easily satisfied, we could see an exaggeration of the Darwin-like struggle by which continued growth of some firms causes others to fade from existence. This is because the impact of slowth on business will be the same as its effect on individuals whose incomes fail to grow. Static sales will create a satisfaction gap as expectations are formed without reference to the reality set by a stagnant economy. As with the individual, certain firms will be motivated to bridge that gap by being aggressive and seeking a greater share of the pie, leaving less for those who fail to mobilize themselves.

Ultimately, most firms will have to shelve their drive for growth in sales. As they do so, the motivation of managers will change. Like the individual who seeks to close the satisfaction gap by cutting consumption, managers will strive for shareholder satisfaction by cutting costs and operating a more efficient shop. Growth through a rise in profits, though not a rise in sales, will become a common goal even though aggregate success is impossible without less remaining for wages, salaries, rent, and interest. That is because together these make up the national income, or GNP, that will be suffering from slowth.

For clues to how firms will act in a slowly growing economy, we can look at operations confronted with slowly growing markets. The response of firms operating in markets with limited prospects for growth is simple; they go where the action is. This is the behavior that has given rise to the conglomerate and the multinational enterprise. During the 1950s and particularly the 1960s, many American businesses with large shares of certain domestic markets faced limited growth prospects if they remained confined to selling the same products in the United States. Their response to keep growing was to move into new markets that offered greater promise for expansion. They diversified into new products and new countries. Between 1950 and 1970, investment by U.S. firms abroad multiplied sixfold. Much of this outlay was for direct investment—funds expended to obtain control over existing foreign operations or establish new ones from the ground up. A good deal of it went to Western Europe for manufacturing operations. Firms exploiting this outlet sought to break loose from local "mature" markets in which their dominant position limited their growth potential to that of the market itself.

This major move led to a concern by Europeans that was articulated in 1968 by Jacques Servan Schreiber in *The American Challenge*. "Fifteen years from now it is quite possible that the world's greatest industrial power, just after the United States and Russia will not be Europe but *American industry in Europe*." Less than fifteen years after this prediction, the perceptible march of American firms has slowed. Yet the mammoth outfits that Schreiber pointed to are still there: Union Carbide, IBM, Celanese, Standard Oil of New Jersey, Monsanto, Esso, and others. Indeed the investment of U.S. firms overseas continues, although it takes less obvious forms. "Among the reasons that [multinational] growth is less visible now than in the past is that, by the late Sixties most of our large corporations had produced a kind of global grid of producing subsidiaries," says professor Raymond Vernon, a specialist in international business. He goes on so say, almost with shades of Schreiber, "Expansion thereafter has taken place within that grid."[1]

As a result of slowth in the domestic market, some U.S. firms will be laying down their grids. But no longer will this be primarily the result of massive manufacturing firms moving to other industrialized countries. They will not be building or buying plants abroad for manufacturing goods. Rather, they will operate from a home base using, perhaps, relatively small foreign offices. Their products for the most part will not be manufactured goods such as cars and tractors, but instead will be services, especially in the area of information and know-how. The new breed of firms that look abroad for growth will be smaller and maintain a lower profile than their multinational ancestors. The services sold abroad will involve project engineers and managers, management consultants, computer service and software companies, accounting firms, restaurant chains, real estate developers, private educational institutions, and entertainment enterprises.

The pursuit of foreign markets as a means of circumventing slowth can work for these types of firms. Although some service-oriented firms have already established themselves abroad, as a group they are less represented than American manufacturers.

They are also highly developed in an industrialized economy such as ours, a reflection of our advanced movement to a service economy. This will equip them to compete in the developing nations that are undergoing rapid rates of industrial growth. Rising incomes and industrial activity in Mexico, Brazil, Taiwan, Hong Kong, Saudi Arabia, Singapore, and Indonesia are becoming attractive markets for purveyors of American services and knowhow. The propensity to seek markets in developing nations will increase sharply with the advent of slowth at home. Although the modes of operations will vary widely from one industry to another, from one firm to another, the service industries will have one general advantage over their first-generation multinational ancestors in reaching out abroad. They will not require the large investment in foreign plants and equipment that other multinationals have found necessary. This will mean a reduction in the physical investment put at risk in potentially volatile developing nations.

A U.S. firm that holds a unique position in American life, and is both a purveyor of froth and fantasy and one of the best examples of this country's efficient service industries, is Walt Disney Productions. Operators of Disneyland in California and Walt Disney World in Florida, Disney Productions has been fantastically successful with its parks featuring familiar cartoon characters whom so many of us have encountered somewhere along the path to adulthood. But Disney also packs them in at its theme parks because of the advanced technology it employs in successfully attracting, transporting, feeding, and entertaining masses of people. It is a supremely efficient service operation.

Despite the prominent place Disney parks occupy in the United States entertainment industry, the company is not satisfied. It will be facing limits to domestic growth, especially after the completion in 1982 of EPCOT, a new futuristic park adjacent to Walt Disney World's Magic Kingdom. Despite the location of parks on both coasts and their prominence as vacation places, the recurring gasoline convulsions and the growing domestic competition will serve to limit growth.

With the awareness that the theme park market is becoming saturated in the United States, Disney management is taking its show abroad. Together with a firm called the Oriental Land Company, Walt Disney Productions will be developing a $300 million Tokyo Disneyland. The park, to be located on landfill adjacent to Tokyo Bay, will contain features similar to those of its U.S. counterparts. Although Walt Disney Productions has previously been approached a number of times to establish operations in various countries, Tokyo Disneyland will be the company's first venture outside the United States. The reasons for selecting the site were illustrated by the company's marketing personnel, who drew 50-kilometer circles around the points on maps that designate Disneyland, Walt Disney World, and Tokyo Disneyland. Whereas the California site is surrounded by 7.5 million people and the sparse Orlando area that Walt Disney World occupies has 640,000, Tokyo Disneyland will benefit from the proximity of some 22 million people.

The business aspects of Tokyo Disneyland appear to be typical of the American-Japanese business connection. Rather than taking a large equity position, Disney will license its technology, management services, attraction designs, and the rights to employ its famous characters. Walt Disney Productions in turn will receive a royalty. The Oriental Land Company intends to supply the capital and to build and operate the venture, which might be paradoxically labeled a unique imitation. Says Matsumoto Takahashi, "It is not our intention to make a 'carbon copy' of Disney's existing theme parks but to build a new, unique Disney entertainment experience, introducing new technology and creativity that will be enjoyed by the people of Japan and the world."[2]

The prospect of sending Disney characters to Japan may appear to have little relevance to more conventional U.S. businesses. However, the Disney move abroad will be emulated by a number of firms that seek growth despite slowth at home. Like Disney, they will be selling know-how developed in a society with a highly sophisticated service sector. Although Disney theme parks may be appropriate for export to a nation with relatively high disposable incomes, other U.S. firms will be serving the developing world with some far more basic products.

Who is building offshore drilling projects in Africa, Greece, Mexico, and Malaysia, and a huge copper mine in China? Fluor Company of California is a giant process construction and engineering company that makes a very lucrative living by moving small armies of engineers and construction tradespeople around the world to projects such as these. The business is a custom industry, in which each such factory, refinery, or mine is unique. It is a people-oriented business that features highly skilled corps of engineers and sales people at the top of the pyramid and works down to a huge work force of foreign nationals—now estimated at 100,000—who perform the tradeswork such as welding or pipefitting.

Fluor started by building refineries in the United States. It employed its cash flow to enlarge and modernize its work force, anticipating a domestic boom in the 1970s that never developed. Instead, the firm's involvement in the Third World grew, particularly in the Middle East. Fluor's largest job is in Saudi Arabia where it is building a $5 billion natural gas gathering complex that will turn the gas now being flared off into a refined fuel.

The operation of the company is similar to that of its other U.S. process engineering competitors, including Bechtel, Brown and Root, Pullman-Kellogg, and C. F. Braun. Such firms aggressively seek foreign work, which they undertake with staff generally assigned to individual projects. Permanent foreign operational facilities, other than offices, are rarely required. Says company Chairman J. Robert Fluor, "One of my associates describes us as a self-destruct business. Most managers spend a lifetime building up one company. Our work consists of forming companies to get a product out, then liquidating and moving on."[3]

Owing to Fluor's high involvement in the sometimes turbulent Third World, it is not surprising that some of the projects do not work out the way they were supposed to. The company failed to complete a major copper and cobalt mine in Zaire when a variety of conditions, including sabotage and a war in neighboring Angola, put a halt to the project. Completion of an Iranian refinery was prevented by the political upheavals in Iran, although Fluor was ultimately paid. The company has largely been successful in hedging against this kind of risk with contracts that provide for advance monthly billing for its fees and overhead.

Fluor is a success story of rare proportions; it also exemplifies the kind of services that Americans are successfully performing abroad. It will be emulated by other construction, engineering, and architectural firms that are organized, dynamic, competent, and willing, for the sake of growth, to risk operating abroad. It is firms such as these that will grow despite slowth.

Expansion abroad, particularly in developing nations, will be one response by managers to slowth. Domestic stagnation will make this option more attractive to firms that are capable of international competition. Yet this is an option that is limited to a relatively small number of firms. Major corporations, for the most part manufacturers, are already extensively involved abroad. Their continued expansion is limited by a number of circumstances that have developed over the years to erode the competitive advantage of U.S. manufacturing firms. Still other companies lack the size and resources for foreign operations, and others, who may be naturals for foreign expansion, may lack the stomach for risky business in Third World nations.

Columbia University's Stefan Robock, an international business expert, sums it up this way with regard to developing regions: "If you're looking for continued expansion this is the real underdeveloped business area of the world. It comprises the bulk of the world's population, so these areas should be attractive to the multinationals, and yet the marriage is not taking place. One reason is an exaggerated perception of political risk. Another is a reluctance to go into joint ventures."[4] We maintain that the advent of slowth will encourage more firms to take those risks. For those who assess themselves as capable, expansion into foreign markets will be one of the only ways to grow.

Firms that are unable to battle slowth on the foreign front will have to jockey for the faster growing markets at home. The rush will be on to move into the more dynamic sectors of the economy. Diversification, as part of this movement is called, has been a common means of growth in the past. It gave rise to the acquisition sprees of the late 1960s, when growth-minded conglomerates set record levels for merger and acquisition activity. As economic growth slows, even firms with a less zealous dedication to growth will be in the market for dynamic firms and product lines. The corporate scene will be marked by an increasing number of participants competing in a frenetic game of musical chairs for a smaller number of dynamic markets.

That game will be played in a number of ways. Some firms will stick close to their home base, seeking to exploit growth potential in segments of their own market. This is a strategy of complementary growth, of using the same kind of resources and know-how already resident with present management. During the era of slowth we anticipate that managers will target certain more dynamic segments of their market for growth. In terms of consumer goods, the shift will be toward more durable, well-crafted, and perhaps more costly items. "Made to last" is a claim that will assume top advertising billing along with style and price. Certain consumer goods that until now were sold wholesale to retailers and can be direct marketed to final users will also grow in popularity. Automobile parts and household items, like plastic plumbing components, garage doors, and even sections of houses, will be increasingly sold directly to consumers. Thoughtful design of such items will be essential, as they must be capable of being installed by people who are not skilled in the trade. Manufacturing of the product, advertising, and the provision of instructions will be geared to the lay consumer. A corresponding shift in the service and repair industries should take place. Tradespeople will be spending more time on reconstruction and rebuilding, as consumers seek to salvage worth from their present goods. Likewise in the capital goods industries, servicing existing components will be a way of expanding business. As the lives of factories, power plants, or hospitals are extended, those performing repair and maintenance work will benefit. New machines will have more built in flexibility, enabling them to be converted to alternative tasks. The second-generation robots we already noted show the extensive opportunities that exist.

Most industries will have some kind of growth segment. The key question for managers is whether they can recognize such segments and move to take advantage of them. In some cases, the transition and identification of the growth segment can be relatively easy. Take the case of Levi-Strauss, which grew enormously large and successful by putting vast numbers of young people into pairs of jeans. Increasingly, though, Levi-Strauss has been faced with major competition that seeks to drape denim over the bodies of an American populace that grows older each day. The jeans market, in short, is saturated. This realization led to widespread skepticism about Levi-Strauss's growth potential, which was reflected in poor stock performance. Shares that at one time traded at a premium of over 700 percent above book value dropped to less than 50 percent in 1978.

The management of Levi-Strauss is responding to this challenge with an entire line of moderately priced casual and semiformal garments. More Levi-Strauss labels are appearing on shoes, wallets, luggage, briefcases, ski overalls, parkas, and vests. Says Robert T. Grohman, Chief Operating Officer, "What seems to have happened is that the traditional jeans consumer has broadened his wardrobe to sportswear. Well, we can produce anything the consumer wants. We're not a one-product company. You can't relate our future to the future of denim jeans."[5] Like Levi-Strauss, firms faced with static markets, which will be more pervasive with slowth, will have to undertake some major shifts in the products they sell.

Yet, as Levi-Strauss moves into markets for other garments and leisure attire accessories, competition in these areas will also become more intense. Similarly, we expect that competition in a number of dynamic markets and market segments will gain in intensity as a result of slowth. That competition will come not only from firms in the same industry, but also from firms that are diversifying into totally new lines of business in search of the opportunity to grow. Take, for example, one growth market we have already mentioned, automated office equipment and user-oriented computers. This is one of the target markets of a company named Exxon Enterprises Inc., a venture capital company flush with cash provided from its parent, Exxon Corporation. Exxon Enterprises has almost a dozen ventures that include the development and sales of microcomputers, computer-based text editing systems, computer printout machines, telecopiers (which produce hard printed copy from telephone signals), and a number of other high-technology information systems. In developing some of its innocuously named products—one journal calls them "ersatz names"—Exxon Enterprises is challenging some major firms. Qyx is a computer-controlled typewriter that provides direct competition to products of the computer giant, IBM, as well as those of smaller firms producing word processing equipment. In offering a range of information processing equipment, it appears that Exxon Enterprises is preparing itself to join the battle to determine who will equip the automated office.

In entering this competition, Exxon Corporation will encounter one of its fellows in the oil company fraternity, Sun Oil Company. Sun Oil has been diversifying into the computer-related marketplace for some time. It too is in the word processing market with products aimed at small professional offices. The presence of two oil companies in this market is not surprising. And it is not at all curious to find that Sun Oil has bought a grocery chain, an industrial distributor, and a trucking company, or that Mobil Oil Corporation has acquired a giant retailer and papermaker, or that Atlantic Richfield Company has bought Anaconda Company, a major copper producer. Through diversification by merger and acquisition, the oil companies are playing another version of corporate musical chairs with gusto. In the mid-1970s, oil companies made over forty acquisitions of firms that have nothing whatever to do with oil.

The timing of this rush to diversify is easy to understand. Although it was not the industry's first step into nonoil-related fields, acquisition activity picked up after the Arab Oil Embargo, which had a severe impact on the industry. The embargo limited the role of major oil companies to one resembling more a marketer than an owner of the oil and, over the long run, threatened their continued access to the product they sell. In light of this development, as well as the questionable and undoubtedly expensive sources of oil at home, oil company officials are seeing the writing on the wall. Growth in their sales will be increasingly constrained by availability of supply and by the impact of higher prices on demand. Although the Organization of Petroleum Exporting Countries' extraction of higher oil prices imposed an uncertain future on the oil companies, it also provided some of them with the means for effecting change in their business. The enormous leaps in prices have created a situation where the industry is awash with cash. A large portion of these funds are reinvested in oil and gas exploration and development activity; other funds, however, are going to diversify out of the oil business.

"The potential for mergers and acquisition is staggering," says an alarmed Senator Edward Kennedy. "Exxon, for example, could tomorrow buy J. C. Penney, DuPont, Goodyear, and Anheuser-Busch using only its accumulated cash and liquid assets."[6] In 1980 Exxon overtook GM at the top of *Fortune*'s list of the 500 largest companies in the United States. Because of its high profile and the potential alarm that the merger and acquisition approach to diversification would lead to, Exxon has limited this kind of activity. As *Business Week* colorfully put the firm's problems, "For a company as large as Exxon Corp., planning for significant diversification outside the energy business is every bit as difficult as trying to dock a very large crude carrier at a yacht slip."[7]

The efforts at diversification by Exxon and its fellow oil companies may seem specific to one industry, but they serve as big, broad examples of the efforts and problems that other companies will find in adjusting to slowth. A slowing of economic growth will create a chain reaction of sorts. Sales will ease off for a number of firms that sell, for example, frivolous consumer items or extract and sell certain raw materials. Larger and more aggressive companies in these industries will seek new windows on growth. In the face of stagnant sales, management will attempt to diversify into faster growing markets through new product lines or acquisitions. Some smaller firms in these markets will face stiff competition from large and well-financed newcomers. Others will be bought out, willingly or not, by firms in search of growth. In an economy that fails to grow overall, the growth of one firm will be achieved at the expense of others. Slowth, with all things remaining equal, will increase the level of corporate concentration.

Yet all things will not remain equal. Firms seeking diversification through acquisition face a group of politicians, civil servants, and citizens who view any trend toward greater concentration with alarm. A pronounced trend in this direction will provide them with a stick to fight off corporate mergers. Indeed, that invisible stick is now being held over the heads of Exxon managers. "Exxon is so big," observes a financial analyst, "it cannot buy up anybody without getting into trouble with the Government."[8] If Senator Kennedy and John Shenenfield, Chief of the Justice Department Antitrust Division, have their way, the federal government would move to outlaw the mergers of all companies bigger than a certain size and would block the acquisition of firms that represent a substantial share of a given market. This is the essence of what Kennedy's Small and Independent Business Protection Act of 1979 would attempt.

Such a move to limit corporate size would embrace an aspect of U.S. history embodied in the Jeffersonian ideal of a society composed of a large number of small businesses. Attempts at institutionalizing such ideals were made by Congress in passing various pieces of legislation at different points in U.S. history. But the latest antimerger push derives some of its impetus from an uptick in corporate takeover activity that is already underway. During 1978 there were eighty mergers between firms valued at over $100 million as opposed to forty-one in 1977 and fourteen in 1975. The value of reported mergers in 1978 hit a ten-year high of over $34 billion, an amount second only to the intense activity in 1968.

Although the bill sponsored by Kennedy may not pass, it has capitalized on support among politicians and voters for restraining any trend toward larger corporations. While the debate to decide whether corporate bigness is good or bad for the economy and society rages on, some firms will manage to grow and diversify through acquisition. Ultimately, however, any visible trend toward increasing corporate size through acquisition will incite public sensitivities and bring about yet another level of business regulation. The route of growth through acquisition will be an easy one only for smaller, less visible firms.

In summary, the opportunity for the growth of all firms will be threatened by slowth. Some managers will nevertheless succeed in charting a course to higher sales levels, but with constant totals for the economy, others must lose. Certain firms will grow by selling to or working in foreign markets. These will generally be service firms that are willing and able to take the risk of operating in new regions. For other firms, foreign markets will offer limited opportunity. Some of these will push toward growth at home, either by diversifying into growth segments of their own industry or finding less familiar opportunities outside. Owing to slowth, however, competition in growth markets will be even swifter than is normally the case, as larger, more powerful firms seek a domestic window on growth. Although some means to growth do exist, slowth will make it impossible for managers to achieve their objective on aggregate. This means that many businesses will fail.

Are there other goals apart from growth, which managers of a firm can pursue to satisfy its shareholders? The shortage of opportunities for growth will mean that more managers will be placing primary emphasis on cutting costs. This is a path to higher profits different from the pursuit of market domination through growth in size or the attempt to achieve economies of scale through expanding an operation. Operating strategies in the management of a firm intent on cost reduction contrast with those of an organization attempting to achieve higher revenues. Richard G. Hamermesh and Steven Silk, who have devoted themselves to the study of stagnant industries, are emphatic about the need of members of such industries to adopt strategies that face up to the fact of limited growth potential. "Failure to recognize these realities can lead to competitive strategies that seem logical but are seldom successful. This is most likely to occur when stagnant sales are viewed as 'a marketing problem' instead of as a fact of life. Rather than increasing total demand, typical marketing solutions such as brand proliferation and heavy advertising usually result in higher inventory investment, higher manufacturing costs, and lower profitability."[9]

A strategy that recognizes and accepts stagnation in certain markets can lead to higher profits via a lowering of costs from deploying resources more efficiently. Firms that have been enjoying strong growth have typically tolerated a certain amount of inefficiency that has crept into their operations. Probably for a great number of firms higher profits are attainable even with static sales. Indeed, the presence of static markets may be the factor that induces such firms to become leaner, more efficient, and profitable. Higher profits through improved efficiency can come in a number of ways, which might include more effective management of inventories, consolidation of production facilities, faster and lower cost means of distribution, or a better use of personnel.

In managing to live with slowth, a great many firms will be breaking new ground. They will be pushed into the search for new markets or growth segments of their own markets. Prospective product lines or acquisitions will have to be evaluated for their viability in a markedly different economic environment from that which has existed for the past quarter century. If no outlets to growth are chosen, a strategic approach to improving profitability must be devised, involving, perhaps, a survey of operations in search of a means to improve efficiency and cut costs. Sound plans must be drawn up and implemented. All this is less necessary for success in an economy that grows rapidly. Slowth, however, will be bringing new urgency to management.

Slowth is likely to be a boon to a particular industry, management consulting, which assists in managing change in such difficult environments. Within the range of services offered by many such firms are assistance in evaluating the growth potential of new markets and identifying growth segments in older ones, as well as devising strategies for entering markets. Consultants can also help improve the profitability of a firm by identifying, implementing, and monitoring plans to improve efficiency. This might include, for example, a program for improved inventory or maintenance management, rationalizing production operations, or implementing a more efficient management structure or information system. But with or without outside assistance, there are ways for individual firms to adjust.

Slowth, however, imposes definite limits on the abilities of firms when taken together to improve their total profits or sales. These limits stem from the fact that on aggregate, given no or slow growth in the GNP, improvement in profits or sales must come at the expense of other firms or, in the case of profits, at the expense of other sectors of the economy. If businesses succeeded in boosting their total profits in the face of stagnant output, that growth would have to come from increased foreign operations or from a decline in domestic wages and salaries or other elements of national income (rent and interest). Rather, it is more likely that growth in sales and profits of some businesses will dictate that others flounder. Ultimately, the meaning of slowth for the firm will parallel its impact on individuals. This process begins with high expectations that motivate some managers to try harder to measure up to past performance. Although means to do this exist, the goals of growth can be achieved only at the expense of others. A period of skirmishes will ensue that, in the case of business, may mean more intense fights for market share, take-over battles, labor un-rest (as higher profits may be sought at the expense of wages), and some major business failures. Ultimately, some resting point will be achieved that requires managers and shareholders, like individ-uals, to reduce their expectations and learn to live with slowth.

GOVERNMENT

James Davidson, Chairman of the National Taxpayers Union has a cynical view of our elected officials. "Beyond anything else, most Congressmen want to get elected."[10] Davidson's group is trying its best to do away with one tool, deficit spending, that they claim our politicians exploit in their effort to stay in office. The National Taxpayers Union is proposing a constitutional amendment to limit the ability of the federal government to spend funds in excess of those it raises through taxes. In doing so, the group's members no doubt support Davidson's account of the actions of our elected of-ficials. "As a matter of pure logic they improve their chances through deficit spending, which enables them to make the benefits of increased spending immediately evident to special constituencies while disguising the costs with borrowing and inflation." As part of a broader resentment toward and resistance against higher levels of government spending, such views promise tough times ahead for those who manage our affairs of state.

Davidson and his group are doing battle against a political sys-tem that has dictated that its officeholders continually obtain higher spending levels. Political scientist Morris Fiorina examined the reasons for the currently low turnover rate of members of the House of Representatives—a rate that runs about 15 percent as compared with 50 percent in the last century. He found that Con-gressmen commonly achieve reelection by securing more govern-ment spending for their constituents. Fiorina concluded that the electorate demands this kind of pork-barrel approach and assesses its elected officials according to their ability to deliver the goods. In Fiorina's words, "We, the people, weed out those Congressmen whose primary interest is not re-election."[11] The product of this weeding out process is ever higher levels of government spending.

For the civil service that administers government programs, as well as for the politicians who install them, growth in government spending is the key to satisfaction and success. For politicians it means reelection. For civil servants it means promotion and higher salaries as new programs justify the employment of new people to be supervised and bestow the opportunity for enlarged authority on those holding government jobs. Books such as Anthony Downs's *Inside Bureaucracy* document this phenomenon. In his 1967 work, Downs elaborated the reasons why government agencies, or any bureaucracy, has a bias toward growth. He gave these reasons:

- An organization that is rapidly expanding can attract more capable personnel, and more easily retain its most capable existing personnel, than can one that is expanding very slowly, stagnating, or shrinking.
- The expansion of any organization normally provides its leaders with increased power, income and prestige. . . .
- Growth tends to reduce internal conflicts in any organization by allowing some (or all) of its members to increase their personal status without lowering that of others.
- Increasing the size of an organization may also improve the quality of its performance (per unit of output) and its chances for survival.

Growth of the bureaucracy, to which these objectives contribute, goes hand in hand with higher government spending. Both are central to the satisfaction of those who work in any bureaucracy.

Even before the time that Downs wrote his book, politicians and civil servants had been able to satisfy their objectives not only because the economy has been growing, but also because government has been a growing part of the economy. From 1964 to 1979, federal spending as a percentage of the GNP rose from over 18 percent to almost 22 percent. State spending as a percentage of GNP rose even faster from almost 4 percent to over 6 percent. Government's enlarged role within the economy has combined with growth of the GNP to produce today's massive level of spending and proliferation of government programs.

Can government grow during an era of slowth? Will the system of rewarding high spending officials with reelection dictate real growth of government spending in a stagnant economy? A key issue of the slow growth period that lies ahead is whether our citizens will tolerate the growth of government at a time when their own incomes fail to grow. There are clear indications that the answer is no; that while the public wants their services, they demand with increasing militancy that these should be provided without the continual expansion of government within the economy. The efforts of the National Taxpayers Union to ensure a balanced federal budget as well as the flurry of initiatives to limit taxes and government spending that we have witnessed over the past several years represent, according to a National Governors' Association report, "the single greatest burst of activity to control government fiscal powers in the nation's history."[12] It is no accident that it is coming at a time when real personal incomes are not growing.

It is difficult to imagine that an increasingly angry and resentful middle-class electorate will idly tolerate the imposition of spiraling taxes or inflation to finance the growth of government. Tom Bethell of *Harper's* sums it up accurately in saying, "As long as the economy was growing sufficiently, this passing around of money from taxpayers seemed to be a satisfactory way of doing business. Everyone seemed to be living at everyone else's expense, and hardly anyone worried." Today it is the middle class that is clearly worried that other sectors of society are living at their expense. That perception, right or wrong, spells trouble for a government that attempts to increase its spending.

Middle class resentment of slow growth in incomes and the pinch of taxes and inflation was a major factor in bringing down two Canadian governments within one year. Besides ample reservations about the personal leadership style of Prime Minister Pierre Trudeau, Canadian voters were also responding to fundamental economic factors when they defeated his government in May 1979. Chief among these was the perception that the economic policy of Trudeau's Liberal government was adrift and that growth in government spending was doing little good for middle-class voters. After the Liberal defeat, this sentiment was summarized by Jeffrey Simpson, Ottawa Bureau Chief of the *Toronto Globe and Mail:*

The Liberals ran aground when the economic facts of life, in Canada and abroad changed for the worse. . . . They felt the hot political rage of the middle class, whose members' rising incomes had paid for programs designed to spread opportunity in the age of expanding affluence. Sure, some programs failed, and some people got annoyed at their taxpayers' dollars being spent in what they took to be a cavalier way. But everyone was doing well and there was plenty more money all around. But when the spectre, and then the reality of slow growth took hold, the middle class, at least in English Canada, feared for the continuation of that affluence.[13]

It was just a scant nine months later that Canadian voters turned against the minority government of Joe Clark, who had replaced Trudeau. A major reason for the lightning-swift defeat of that government was the image of Clark himself, who was portrayed by the media as less than dynamic and intelligent (this was dubbed the "whimp" factor in the campaign). But the government was also brought down because it was tied to a budget that proved politically indefensible. Although it had an ultimate target of zero real growth in federal spending and lower deficits, a major feature of the budget uppermost in the minds of the voters was a provision for a sharp movement toward the higher world oil and gas prices and an $0.18 per gallon excise tax on gasoline. In proposing that Canadians consume their medicine in one bitter swallow, the "nine months and eighteen cents a gallon" government, as it was dubbed, brought on itself the wrath of an electorate that used its voting power to resist any overt challenge to its standard of living.

Voter resentment of the type expressed in Canada will be a common feature of slowth. It is resentment toward slow growth in personal incomes and toward government policies and programs that threaten, through higher taxes or inflation, to exacerbate the satisfaction gap that is a common experience for many of its citizens. Growth of government and government spending, however financed, will inflame this resentment. This state of affairs places our officials and civil servants in a bind. Voters want the same level of services supplied by a government that does not grow. They will judge the job of their officials by the way these services are delivered while restricting government spending to the same size slice of the same size economic pie.

Such demands are hard to achieve in any but a static society, one whose priorities and needs do not change. But this is not the nature of our society. Despite slowth, our nation will experience a continual shifting of priorities and the growth and diminution of a variety of perceived needs. The current reemphasis on defense spending is just one example. Previous U.S. administrations brought about a relative reduction in the nation's defense spending, which constituted 8.4 percent of the GNP in 1964 and less than 5 percent in 1979. Today a concern for American military security is being stirred by external and domestic political circumstances. Slowth, and the straitjacket it will impose on government, means that financing fancy new conventional weapon systems must be accomplished by the sacrifice of other spending programs.

Higher defense spending is just one example of a number of perceived needs that will arise in the future, creating some tough choices. Governing during slowth will require choices among groups, priorities, and programs and will be coupled with the need to sell these choices to the electorate. The Great Society image of effective government as one that does something about all the nation's problems and fulfills all its needs is behind us. Good management of government during slowth means effective application of resources to programs that are assigned the highest priority.

But the nature of federal spending makes achievement of this task seem almost as impossible for those in Washington as the task of achieving the aims of the Great Society. A large chunk of federal spending is nondiscretionary in the sense that it is mandated by law. This includes spending on the vast majority of social programs that must provide benefits for everyone who meets eligibility requirements. Some programs, such as Social Security, Supplemental Security Income (for the aged, blind and disabled), Medicare, and Medicaid, also have cost-of-living clauses built into them. All such transfer programs, including grants-in-aid to state and local governments and interest on the national debt, constitute roughly two-thirds of federal government spending.

One response of the federal government will be the attempt to regain control over the portion of these transfer payments that go to state and local governments. During the 1980s we are likely to witness a reverse tug-of-war to determine who will pay for key services. A diminution of the funding role of the federal government would mean an about-face in federal-state fiscal relations in which the states (and municipalities) have become increasingly reliant on the federal government. It would also result in greater disparity in the level of services provided by states with differing tax bases. Nevertheless, one means by which federal politicians will attempt to hold down federal spending will be through shifting the responsibility for providing the services the public demands but resents paying for. The federal-state conflict over who pays will be another slowth skirmish. Regardless of which level of government wins, however, managers of the affairs of state at all levels will have to be tough in evaluating the conflicting pressures for limited resources.

This chapter is aimed at both government and business. Slow economic growth and the spending squeeze it will impose dictate that certain functions of government be undertaken in a managerial mode that has been more characteristic of business. This means a greater effort at efficiency in government and a deeper commitment to the example of people like Robert MacNamara who sought to transpose the methods of business to the Defense Department during the early 1960s. This means establishing objective standards of performance for certain functions, as well as measuring that performance on a continual basis. The continued application of funds and personnel will either have to be justified in concrete terms or face reduction or elimination.

One area of government where the introduction of the managerial techniques has already begun is in public education. This has been spurred by alarm among some state officials at the refusal of some voters to approve all educational spending measures placed before them. Against a background of uncertain educational quality, despite skyrocketing costs per pupil, a number of states are placing school funding on a more businesslike footing. Several states have adopted measures that include standardized tests for teachers and students, tying funding to actual measured achievement (instead of to a straight head count), efforts to reduce administrative overhead, and long-range planning. Ongoing experiments with the voucher system is also an example. This system, advocated by Milton Friedman, allows parents to select schools that they feel provide the best educational value for their children. "It's too early to call this a trend but I expect it to gather momentum,"[14] says Russel Vlaanderen, Director of a research organization called the Education Commission of the States, in discussing these approaches to managing education programs. "It's definitely tied to the accountability movement."

One leading state in this accountability movement is New Jersey. There the state legislature passed a law that requires school districts to draw up programs similar to corporate five-year plans. The planning process includes developing goals with community input, fixing educational targets for achievement, and establishing means to evaluate school performance. The state employs former school principals and teachers who act as auditors of each district's adherence to its plan. Each district produces an annual report that gives the result of student testing and outlines plans for educational improvement. Instructional expenses are allocated to specific programs for the purposes of evaluation, and the districts may be called on to state how they are using their plants and equipment. As an overall measure, the New Jersey legislature placed an upward limit, tied to the increase in real estate valuations, on the potential rise in per-pupil expenses.

One management tool that can aid in allocating scarce resources is being applied with a good measure of success. Zero-base budgeting (ZBB) is being used in the United States and Canada by school boards and government agencies as well as by private firms. ZBB is a process by which resources are allocated within an organization without the presumption that the given group of services to which they are applied are justified merely because they existed in past years. The process draws together managers who are asked to specify not only the nature and magnitude of the service they aim to provide, but also different levels or increments in which that service can be provided. This identification of increments of service allows an organization to reallocate resources in response to a changing environment, without either eliminating programs entirely or increasing total spending. Additionally, this method, which was initiated at Texas Instruments in the late

1960s, encourages all levels of management to examine their priorities and consider alternative ways of achieving their goals. When conducted properly, it is a planning, budgeting, and decision-making process, one that will help managers be responsive to the public's changing demand for services without a constant ratcheting upward of government spending.

It is far from clear whether more rigorous managerial methods and the improvement in efficiency that results will be enough to bridge the satisfaction gap experienced by politicians, civil servants, and the public whom they serve. There will still be continual conflict about how slowly growing resources are allocated. But what is the alternative? Slowth is changing the ground rules that enabled a continual rise in government spending. Any government that skirts the hard choices about spending or the disciplined attempt to get more for its existing level of resources will be out of step with its citizenry, who will be forced to do this on an individual basis. Even the old shell game, which enabled federal politicians to buy votes back home without having to risk voter wrath by raising taxes, is now threatened. It is now evident that a large segment of the electorate has become suspicious of where that money comes from. The voters are beginning to point their fingers at government in assigning the blame for inflation.

chapter 18

Victory over Inflation?

A large measure of the anger and frustration of the average American is being directed at the virtually endless prospect of rising prices. Slowth remains invisible to the vast majority of the public. Stagnant real incomes—formed from national aggregate incomes corrected for the population and price level—are statistics reserved for the business page and momentary mention on the evening news. Instead the average citizen measures his or her income against what it costs to live in an obvious and apparently meaningful way: "My income rose last year by 10 percent, but so have prices." The reasoning continues, "If only we could stop prices from going up so fast, my income would stretch further." The conclusion that is reached, "To get ahead we must stop inflation," is shared by many, including some whose training in economics makes it hard to forgive.

This reasoning is wrong. The framework we have developed in the foregoing chapters should clearly establish the fallacy that is involved. Achievement of real living standard improvements is not a monetary phenomenon, but rests with our ability to produce. Slow growing output means little or no change in what is available to buy. Without greater levels of production, higher incomes cannot result in more buying power. Prices become inextricably linked to incomes: as incomes rise, prices *must* rise by the same amount.

217

A 10 percent rise in income in the face of stagnant production means that we face an inflation rate of 10 percent. Clearly, although inflation does have decidedly negative features, it is not the root cause of our most commonly shared economic woe, stagnant living standards.

Indeed, for other powerful reasons inflation, especially when it is unanticipated, deserves the scornful attention it has received. It arbitrarily redistributes wealth and income away from those who have saved money or those whose incomes bear no link to the price of what they buy. It plays havoc with the economically weak, especially the old living on what they scrimped for later life. Correspondingly, unpredictably high inflation bestows favor on those in debt or those in an economic position to benefit from rising prices. This includes people paying fixed interest mortgages and the biggest debtor of them all, the government.

Whereas the beneficial effect of inflation is confined to specific, albeit large, segments of the economy, inflation affects us all negatively in a very powerful way. It injects great uncertainty into our economic future and renders planning an exercise in futility. It stirs concern and anguish among those who have worked and saved, casting severe doubt on the value of their efforts.

There is evidence to suggest that it is not so much high levels of inflation that prove objectionable to the public, but uncertainty induced by the unpredictability of that rate. Economic research carried out by one author of this book, Maurice Levi, sought to determine how economic expectations affected the popularity of U.S. Presidents. It was found that Gallup Poll statistics regarding presidential popularity did not vary significantly with *actual* past inflation levels, but with variability or *uncertainty* about future inflation. The author concluded that there is a reward of popularity for any President and government in achieving stability, not necessarily in prices, but in the rate of price change. "It is important that the government attempt to achieve a world where the paths followed leave inflation predictable." At least we would then know how to plan.

How can governments create a world of predictable inflation and exorcise the national *angst* over inflation? How, alternatively, can they help us live with the inflation that exists? One way is through the indexing of wages, transfer payments, pensions, and instruments of savings to the level of prices. Despite a number of mechanical problems, there is a key political drawback attendant to this kind of measure. Any government making the case for it is admitting defeat in the fight against demon inflation. Rather, there are a number of indications that our government is following a second path, that of attempting to achieve a real victory over inflation.

The suggestion of a concerted and unwavering government campaign of the type needed to beat inflation is enough to incite the cynic in each of us. "Government has backed down before and will again retreat in the face of high unemployment," is one obvious response. Yet, we maintain, there is ample indication that a powerfully fought war against inflation is likely to occur.

The view that inflation is chronic and unavoidable is difficult to substantiate by reading a long span of economic history. A glance at a graph of price level changes reveals a series of high peaks connected by a series of long plateaus. Several periods show an actual decline of prices. In fact, prices in 1950 were virtually the same as those in 1800 for the wide range of goods that constitute the Wholesale Price Index. Despite the markedly higher prices that prevail now relative to the 1950s, the average annual rate of inflation between the end of the Korean War in 1952 and the expansion of the Vietnam War in 1965 is less than 1.5 percent per annum. The Vietnam War marked the watershed of present inflation rates that are now becoming increasingly harder for the American public to accept. A reading of history certainly shows that inflation can be avoided. If there is no war, why do we have inflation?

The American public has found its answer to that question, and it is one that bodes ill for our elected officials. According to political scientist Everett Carl Ladd, Jr., "Americans have changed their thinking about its [inflation's] source. In the 1950's and early 1960's, they blamed inflation mostly on labor and business. Now they are convinced that governmental actions in taxing and spending are the major causes. They hold government responsible and have concluded, moreover, that it is incapable of acting effectively."[1]

A similar account was provided in Congressional testimony by

Albert E. Sindlinger, Chairman of his own marketing and opinion research firm. As a result of his organization's poll of over 20,000 households during 1977 and 1978, he concludes that "during the 1960's until recently, most people cared very little about the deficit because they thought—and, I would add, I think they were educated to think—that somebody else was going to pay the bill and that the deficit is good to make the economy grow. Now, deficit is a dirty word among growing numbers of people from all walks of life and all shades of opinion, all economic strata, who regard the deficit as the primary cause of the Nation's economic dilemma."[2]

The truth underlying these assessments is evident in the electoral moves to force tax and spending restraints on government. Proposition 13 in California, the move afoot to impose constitutional limitations on the federal deficit, or California Proposition 4 (which proposes to limit the growth of government expenditure to the rate of inflation or the growth of real per capita income) are sterling examples of the voting public's resentment toward government and the inflation for which it is being held responsible. Apart from other effects they might have, these movements will help reduce inflation for another reason: they threaten government and the power of elected officials. Populist measures restraining government will encourage politicians to take action themselves on the inflation front. It is the stick that the electorate holds over public officials, and, indeed, there is a carrot not far behind.

"If either political party," says Ladd, "could convince the American people that it could be counted upon for a coherent and effective response [to inflation], it would reap huge electoral dividends." Today there are signs that this message has got across in Washington, D.C. In October 1979 a previously divided Federal Market Committee of the Federal Reserve Board reached a unanimous decision that shook financial markets and made headlines in newspapers around the world. The decision represented a subtle yet fundamental change in the way the watchdog of U.S. monetary policy, the Federal Reserve System, controlled the level of money within the economy. The Federal Reserve Board deemphasized the effort to control credit by manipulating interest rates and announced that henceforth it would attempt to exercise direct control over bank reserves with the view to reaching targeted growth rates in the monetary aggregates. The move held the promise of tighter control over credit creation and made record-high interest rates a certainty. The rate the Federal Reserve charges member banks for funds, the federal discount rate, was raised a full percentage to 12 percent. In February 1980, in a further push to dampen inflation, the discount rate was raised again to 13 percent. In March the rate was "split" above the 13 percent level and set at 16 percent. The rate charged by banks to prime customers quickly rose to 20 percent, making the rates of the credit crunch year of 1974 seem low by comparison. The action, if adhered to, would be "by far the most important and significant change in U.S. monetary policy in a generation,"[3] according to economist Alan Greenspan. It clearly indicated one thing: The Federal Reserve Board meant business in its fight against inflation.

The reaction of the Jimmy Carter Administration has also been significant. One British spokesman said, perhaps alluding to the prospect that credit tightening would be politically damaging in upcoming elections, "It is very courageous for a country that is sliding into recession to increase its discount rate a full point."[4] Whether as a result of courage or good political judgment, President Carter has stood behind the Federal Reserve Board's moves, stating, "The Number One threat to our national economy is inflation." He added, "Whatever it takes to control inflation, that's what I will do."[5] This may have been a touch of bravado used in a circumstance in which the President had no policy options but to tackle inflation. Nonetheless, it may offer a political payoff, reflecting the public's resolute disdain for rising prices. "In years past," as *Newsweek* summed up the October 1979 monetary uproar, "American Presidents forced to choose between stimulus and restraint have generally opted for stimulus, especially in an election year. But public opinion may be shifting, and it is possible Carter will decide that a firm stand against inflation will play well politically. Some observers say the President now has a unique opportunity to wring inflation out of the system by hanging tough."[6] This point is echoed by Ladd, who notes that "in the fall of 1978, an extraordinary 76 percent of all Americans—three-quarters of business and professional people and three-quarters of manual workers—described inflation as the nation's 'most important problem.' "[7] The March 1980 Carter Administration promise to balance the 1981 federal budget was directed at capturing widespread voter support.

The opportunity to beat inflation definitely exists. The large spreads appearing in newspapers and magazines devoted to a relatively arcane shift in the method of administering monetary policy bear testimony to that fact. The public, from financial market participants to members of the lay populace, is displaying an awareness of money matters that, in the United States, is totally new. Part of that awareness stems undoubtedly from the trials of coping with the sting of record-high interest rates. Despite the prospect of the economic carnage these rates invoke, criticism of the monetary tightening became decidedly muted. The most common response, even from political liberals, was that such corrective measures are needed to combat inflation. Characterization of tighter monetary measures as a form of "medicine" for a sick inflation-ridden economy became the common, if almost trite, reaction.

It is not certain whether the policy of slowing growth in monetary aggregates will be adhered to in the face of political pressures generated by high unemployment. But because the public attributes to government the central role in what happens with inflation, the political consequences of appearing to cave in on this issue are far from light. Stagflation will not be an acceptable outcome so long as the public is aware that an alternative—strict monetary control—exists. In the end, the high unemployment headache of the body politic will be weighed by this or some future administration against the illness of inflation. We do not know what weights this group of elected officials will place on the scales. It is apparent, however, that they will need to present their case to a far more knowledgeable public, one educated about the role of money in causing inflation. In itself this sets the stage for an eventual victory over inflation.

Although the citizenry is more aware of the cause of inflation and the means with which to fight it, it is mistaken in attaching high expectations to the prospect of victory. Price stability does not ensure economic growth. As long as substantive impediments stand in the way of production, growth will remain slow. Slowth can live alongside any rate of inflation. The prospects for our medium-term future involves, in our view, a double-sided slowth— slow growth in output and in the price of that output. We are embarked, as we cross the threshold of the 1980s, on a path toward a quiescent economy. Price changes, improvements in living standards, creation of better job and business opportunities, and installation of new technology—all of these will take place at a markedly slower rate than we have enjoyed during recent decades.

Is this all that bad? What does the balance sheet of slowth look like in the way it affects the character of our society? In the realm of economics it means that our living standards will remain almost stagnant. As a nation we will fall behind others for whom production is a preeminent goal. Yet it is possible, with application of some sacrifice and dedication and, most important, an understanding of the nature and presence of slowth, to achieve a steady level of prices. Rising prices, despite the gloom imparted by enervating bouts with stagflation, are not necessarily a part of slow growth.

If that is to be the case—if we are to achieve price stability amid slowly growing output—our personal expectations must still evolve. Psychologically, the widening of the satisfaction gap will be stressful. Until we adjust to slow growth by lowering our expectations, less-stress will result. Unless we adapt to the reality of slowth, conflicting pressures will be placed on government as the pleas for positive action to combat slowth and unemployment conflict with the need for price stability. If the electorate and our officials opt for beating inflation, at least a portion of our economic anxiety will be allayed. Elimination of the uncertainty that hovers over our efforts to work and save will be a welcome counterbalance to less-stress. For despite the difficulty we face in adjusting to stagnant real incomes, we shall know that at least those incomes are *real*.

The way we alter our life-styles in making the adjustment to slowth can, if we choose that path, instill an improved balance. We can narrow our satisfaction gap by becoming more involved in fulfilling our own needs from our own efforts. We can use our leisure time more creatively without prodigious spending. We can cultivate more awareness of the way we consume and acquire skills that substitute our own production for that of the marketplace.

These will help close the satisfaction gap. In the process we can also rechannel our aspirations and maintain a positive creative force in our lives, despite the demise of prospects for further material fulfillment.

Positive life-style alternatives are not open to or will not be chosen by everyone. The resulting frustration and anger will marshal forces for the unfortunate political events we have called the slowth skirmishes. Inherent in the view of the growthers, is the position that we are not doing enough to stimulate and aid economic performance. They seek to restore growth as the number one measure by which we assess our national achievement. We have projected in this book that the slowth skirmishes will result in an eventual standoff. Although we shall go forward at times, and backwards at others, our society will maintain its commitment to improving the quality of existence for the nation as a whole. Our consciousness, we assert, will not be subverted for the sake of restoring growth. The slowth skirmishes, for all their unpleasantness, will attest to the underlying reality that we are choosing a greater balance between our economic well-being and the quality of our lives. The challenge of the days ahead is to maintain that balance and to make the reality of slowth that results one to which we successfully adapt.

Notes

1 Introduction

1   *Time,* June 18, 1979.
2   *Time,* June 12, 1978.
3   *Time,* April 25, 1977.
4   *Time,* July 2, 1979.

2 The Real Essentials

1   *Bulletin of the Northwest Mining Association,* May 1979.
2   Herman Daly, *Toward a Steady-State Economy,* Freeman, San Francisco, 1973.

3 Environmentalism and the Material Input

1   *Ecolibrium* (A Shell Oil publication), Winter 1979.
2   "Man's Control of the Environment," *Congressional Quarterly,* 1978.
3   *Ecolibrium* (A Shell Oil publication), Winter 1979.
4   *Time,* June 26, 1978.
5   *Business Week,* November 26, 1979.
6   *Business Week,* November 26, 1979.
7   Kenneth Boulding, "The Economics of the Coming Spaceship Earth," in *Environmental Quality in a Growing Econ-*

omy, Henry Jarrett, Ed., published for *Resources of the Future* by Johns Hopkins Press, Baltimore, 1966.

8 Chester L. Cooper, *Growth in America,* Greenwood, Westport, Conn., 1976.

9 *The New York Times,* April 19, 1977.

10 *Saturday Review,* February 17, 1979.

11 *Dun's Review,* August 1979.

12 *Saturday Review,* February 17, 1979.

13 Andrew R. Thompson, *West Coast Oil Ports Inquiry,* 1978.

14 *San Francisco Chronicle,* March 28, 1979.

15 *San Francisco Chronicle,* March 28, 1979.

16 *San Francisco Chronicle,* March 28, 1979.

17 *San Francisco Chronicle,* March 28, 1979.

18 *Forbes,* December 11, 1978.

19 Data Resources, Inc., *Impacts of Clear Cutting Restrictions in National Forests on the Softwood Sector of the U.S. Forest Products Industry* (Study for the U.S. Department of Commerce), Washington, D.C.

20 *Fortune,* November 5, 1979.

4 People Power: Living with Compassion

1 *Time,* June 12, 1978.

2 *Vancouver Sun,* July 12, 1978.

5 People Power: Taxes and the Incentive to Work

1 *Newsweek,* June 19, 1978.

2 Abraham Maslow, *Motivation and Personality,* 2nd ed., Harper & Row, New York, 1970.

3 *Business Week,* June 4, 1979.

4   *Psychology Today,* May 1978.
5   *Psychology Today,* May 1978.
6   *Business Week,* June 4, 1979.
7   *Canadian Business,* June 1978.
8   *Time,* February 21, 1977.

6   Our Machinery Input

1   *Financial Analysts Journal,* September–October 1978.
2   *Review, Federal Reserve Bank of St. Louis,* September 1979.
3   *Business Week,* July 3, 1978.
4   *San Francisco Chronicle,* March 28, 1979.
5   *Time,* November 27, 1978.
6   *The Economist,* April 14, 1979.
7   *Industry Week,* August 6, 1979.
8   *Business Week,* July 3, 1978.
9   *Business Week,* October 17, 1977.
10   *Business Week,* October 17, 1977.
11   *Business Week,* July 3, 1978.
12   *Business Week,* May 28, 1979.
13   *Research Management,* March 1977.
14   *Time,* October 2, 1978.
15   *Research Management,* March 1978.
16   *Forbes,* March 6, 1978.
17   *Business Week,* July 3, 1978.

7   Blocking the Technological Path to Change

1   *Congressional Quarterly,* March 11, 1978.
2   *Business Week,* December 25, 1978.

3   *Congressional Quarterly,* November 24, 1979.

4   *Business Week,* December 25, 1978.

5   *International Herald Tribune,* April 12, 1979.

6   *Fortune,* May 7, 1979.

7   *Business Week,* December 25, 1978.

8   *Dun's Review,* August 1978.

9   *Congressional Quarterly,* March 11, 1978.

10   *Business Week,* December 25, 1978.

11   *Congressional Quarterly,* March 11, 1978.

12   *Congressional Quarterly,* November 24, 1979.

13   *Science,* September 1969.

14   Beatrice Trum Hunter, *The Mirage of Safety.*

15   Ross Hume Hall, *Food for Naught, The Decline in Nutrition,* Random House, New York, 1976.

16   Samuel S. Epstein, *The Politics of Cancer,* Doubleday, New York, 1979.

17   Gerald Gall, University of Alberta, "Address delivered to the 21st Annual Conference of the Canadian Institute of Food Science and Technology," June 26, 1978, unpublished paper.

18   Samuel S. Epstein, *The Politics of Cancer,* Doubleday, New York, 1979.

19   *Barron's,* July 31, 1978.

20   Beatrice Trum Hunter, *The Mirage of Safety: Food Additives and Federal Policy,* Scribner, New York, 1976.

21   *Congressional Quarterly,* April 22, 1978.

22   *Congressional Quarterly,* April 22, 1978.

23   *Business Week,* October 17, 1977.

24   Thomas Berger, "Northern Frontier/Northern Homeland," in *Berger Commission Report,* Government of Canada, Ottawa.

25   Jacob Bronowski, *A Sense of the Future,* MIT Press, Cambridge, Mass., 1977.

8 Working for More Output

1 *Advertising Age,* April 16, 1979.
2 *Editor and Publisher,* July 22, 1978.
3 *Editor and Publisher,* July 22, 1978.
4 *Business Week,* March 26, 1979.
5 *Business Week,* March 26, 1979.
6 Otto Hagel and Louis Goldblatt, *Men and Machines.*
7 *Harvard Business Review,* July–August 1977.
8 *Industry Week,* February 19, 1979.
9 *Canadian Labour Comment,* February 10, 1978.
10 *Data Management,* May 1979.
11 *FIET Conference on Computers and Work,* November 17–18, 1978.
12 *Saturday Review,* June 23, 1979.
13 *International Labour Review,* Winter 1978.
14 *Congressional Quarterly,* March 17, 1979.
15 *Industry Week,* July 9, 1979.

9 The Productivity Puzzle

1 *Business Week,* February 13, 1978.
2 *Wall Street Journal,* January 29, 1979.
3 *Newsweek,* May 28, 1978.
4 *Newsweek,* May 28, 1978.
5 *Economic Report of the President,* U.S. Government Printing Office, Washington, D.C., 1979.
6 *Economic Report of the President,* U.S. Government Printing Office, Washington, D.C., 1979.

7   *Fortune,* August 14, 1978.

8   *Business Week,* January 28, 1980.

9   *Economic Report of the President,* U.S. Government Printing Office, Washington, D.C., 1979.

10 *Challenge,* May/June 1979.

11 *Fortune,* September 11, 1978.

12 *Fortune,* September 11, 1978.

10   The Slowth Backlash

1   *Newsweek,* December 6, 1976.

2   *Newsweek,* May 29, 1978.

3   *Newsweek,* May 29, 1978.

4   *Fortune,* December 3, 1979.

5   *Fortune,* September 11, 1978.

6   *The Economist,* February 10, 1979.

7   *Fortune,* September 25, 1978.

11   Learning from Land

1   Russell Train, "Growth with Environmental Quality," in *Management and Control of Growth,* Vol. 1; Randall W. Scott, Ed., Urban Land Institute, Washington, D.C., 1975.

2   *San Francisco Bay Guardian,* April 1972.

3   *Urban Land,* November 1973.

4   "The Use of Land: A Citizen's Guide to Urban Growth" (A Task Force Report Sponsored by the Rockefeller Brothers Fund), in *Management and Control of Growth,* Vol. 1.

5 Joint Committee on Housing and Urban Development Association and the Alberta Department of Housing and Public Works, *Report to the Minister of Housing and Public Works,* June 29, 1978.

6 *The New York Times,* February 6, 1977.

7 *The New York Times,* March 4, 1977.

8 *Management and Control of Growth,* Urban Land Institute.

9 *Urban Land,* February 1978.

12   Slowth and the Growth Debate

1 Daniel Bell, "Are There 'Social Limits' to Growth?" in *Prospects for Growth,* Kenneth D. Wilson, Ed., Praeger, New York, 1977.

2 Daniel Bell, "Are There 'Social Limits' to Growth?" in *Prospects for Growth,* Kenneth D. Wilson, Ed., Praeger, New York, 1977.

3 Robert Theobald, "Managing the Quality of Life," in *Prospects for Growth.*

4 Robert Theobald, "The Steady-State Economy," in *Prospects for Growth,* Kenneth D. Wilson, Ed., Praeger, New York, 1977.

5 Robert Theobald, "The Steady-State Economy," in *Prospects for Growth,* Kenneth D. Wilson, Ed., Praeger, New York, 1977.

6 Daniel Bell, "Are There 'Social Limits' to Growth?" in *Prospects for Growth,* Kenneth D. Wilson, Ed.

7 Robert K. Merton, *Social Theory and Social Structure.*

8 John Maynard Keynes, "Economics for Our Grandchildren," in *The Collected Writings of John Maynard Keynes,* Elizabeth Johnson, Ed., Macmillan, London, 1971.

13 The Inevitable State of Slowth

1 *Time,* July 14, 1975.

2 *The Economist,* April 7, 1979.

3 *The Northern Miner,* July 26, 1979.

14 The Looming Battle

1 Burkhard Strumpel, *Economic Means for Human Needs,* University of Michigan Press, Ann Arbor, 1976.

2 *Fortune,* December 18, 1978.

3 *Wall Street Journal,* March 29, 1979.

4 *Newsweek,* June 4, 1979.

5 *The Economist,* October 14, 1978.

6 *The New York Times,* December 30, 1979.

7 *Newsweek,* March 19, 1979.

8 *San Francisco Chronicle,* April 20, 1977.

9 *The Daily Californian,* May 23, 1979.

10 *Fusion: Magazine of the Fusion Energy Foundation.*

11 *The Daily Californian,* April 9, 1979.

12 *The Daily Californian,* April 9, 1979.

13 *Business Week,* January 28, 1980.

14 *Dun's Review,* August 1979.

15 *Observer,* June 10, 1979.

15 Slowth and the American Way of Life

1 *Psychology Today,* October 1978.

2 *The New York Times,* December 30, 1979.

3   *Saturday Review,* May 26, 1979.

4   *Time,* December 3, 1979.

5   *The UC Employee,* April 1979.

6   *The New York Times,* December 30, 1979.

7   *Time,* July 23, 1979.

8   *Wall Street Journal,* August 23, 1979.

9   *Psychology Today,* May 1979.

10 *California Management Review,* Spring 1979.

11 "The Sociology of Women's Economic Role in the Family," *American Sociological Review,* June 1977.

12 *Psychology Today,* May 1977.

13 *Fortune,* October 9, 1978.

16 Less-Stress

1   Chester L. Cooper, *Growth in America,* Greenwood, Westport, Conn., 1976.

2   Milton Friedman, Donahue, television interview, December 9, 1979.

3   Hans Selye, *The Stress of My Life: A Scientist's Memoirs,* Van Nostrand Reinhold, New York, 1979.

4   George Katona, *Psychological Economics,* Elsevier, New York, 1975.

5   Burkhard Strumpel, *Economic Means for Human Needs,* University of Michigan Press, Ann Arbor, 1976.

6   Roper Public Opinion Research Centre, *Current Opinion,* September 1977.

7   George Katona, Burkhard Strumpel, and Ernest Zahn, *Aspirations and Affluence; Comparative Studies in the United States and Western Europe,* McGraw-Hill, New York, 1971.

8   *Time,* January 15, 1979.

17   Managing to Live With Slowth

1   *Forbes,* June 25, 1979.
2   Press Release, Walt Disney Productions, April 30, 1979.
3   *Fortune,* February 26, 1979.
4   *Forbes,* June 25, 1979.
5   *Forbes,* August 21, 1979.
6   *Business Week,* April 24, 1978.
7   *Business Week,* April 24, 1978.
8   *Oil and Gas Journal,* November 13, 1978.
9   *Harvard Business Review,* September–October 1979.
10   *Dun's Review,* May 1979.
11   *Fortune,* May 7, 1979.
12   *Congressional Quarterly,* August 25, 1979.
13   *Toronto Globe and Mail,* November 16, 1979.
14   *Dun's Review,* June 1978.

18   Victory over Inflation?

1   *Fortune,* December 18, 1978.
2   Testimony before the Senate Subcommittee on Taxation and Debt Management Generally, January–February 1978.
3   *Time,* October 22, 1979.
4   *The New York Times,* October 9, 1979.
5   *The New York Times,* October 10, 1979.
6   *Newsweek,* October 22, 1979.
7   *Fortune,* March 26, 1979.

Bibliography

Arthur Anderson & Co., *Cost of Government Regulation Study for the Business Roundtable, (Executive Summary)*, March 1979.

Bacon, Robert W., and Walter Eltis, *Britain's Economic Problem: Too Few Producers*, Macmillan, London, 1976.

Bronowski, Jacob, *A Sense of the Future*, MIT Press, Cambridge, Mass., 1977.

Brooks, Harvey, and Edward Ginzton, Chairmen, *Energy in Transition*, U.S. Department of Energy, Washington, D.C., January 1980.

Callenbach, Fred, *Ecotopia*, Bantam Books, New York, 1977.

Daly, Herman, *Toward a Steady-State Economy*, Freeman, San Francisco, 1973.

Denison, Edward F., "Where Has Productivity Gone," in *Contemporary Economic Problems*, William Fellner, Project Director, American Enterprise Institute for Public Policy Research, Washington, D.C., 1979.

Edison Electric Institute, *Economic Growth in the Future: The Growth Debate in National and Global Perspective*, McGraw-Hill, New York, 1976.

Epstein, Samuel S. *The Politics of Cancer*, Doubleday, New York, 1979.

Grubel, Herbert G., and Michael Walker, Ed., *Unemployment Insurance: Global Evidence of Its Effects on Unemployment*, The Fraser Institute, Vancouver, 1979.

Hall, Ross Hume, *Food for Naught, The Decline in Nutrition*, Random House, New York, 1976.

Kahn, Herman, William Brown, and Leon Martel, *The Next 200 Years: A Scenario for America and the World*, Morrow, New York, 1976.

Katona, George, *Psychological Economics*, Elsevier, New York, 1975.

Katona, George, Burkhard Strumpel, and Ernest Zahn, *Aspirations and Affluence; Comparative Studies in the United States and Western Europe*, McGraw-Hill, New York, 1971.

Keynes, John Maynard, "Economics for Our Grandchildren" in *The Collected Writings of John Maynard Keynes,* Elizabeth Johnson, Ed., Macmillan, London, 1971.

Maccorby, Michael, *The Gamesman: The New Corporate Leaders,* Simon & Schuster, New York, 1976.

Maslow, Abraham, *Motivation and Personality,* 2nd ed., Harper & Row, New York, 1970.

McGregor, Douglas Murray, *Leadership and Motivation,* Essays edited by Warren G. Bennis and Edgar H. Schein, with the collaboration of Caroline McGreggor, MIT Press, Cambridge, Mass., 1966.

Meadows, Donella H., and others, *The Limits to Growth, A Report for the Club of Rome's Project on the Predicament of Mankind,* Universe Books, New York, 1972.

Mishan, Ezra Joshua, *The Costs of Economic Growth,* Praeger, New York, 1967.

Mishan, Ezra Joshua, *The Economic Growth Debate, An Assessment,* G. Allen & Unwin, London, 1977.

Oppenheimer, Valerie Kincade, "The Sociology of Women's Economic Role in the Family," *American Sociological Review,* June 1977.

Schumacher, Ernst F., *Small is Beautiful: A Study of Economics as If People Mattered,* Blond & Briggs, London, 1973.

Scitovsky, Tibor, *The Joyless Economy: An Inquiry into Human Satisfaction and Consumer Dissatisfaction,* Oxford University Press, New York, 1976.

Scott, Randall W., Ed., *Management and Control of Growth,* Urban Land Institute, Washington, D.C., 1975.

Smith, Adam, *An Inquiry into the Nature and Causes of the Wealth of Nations,* W. Straham, & T. Cadell, London, 1976.

Stouffer, Samuel A., and others, *The American Soldier,* Princeton University Press, Princeton, N.J., 1949.

Strumpel, Burkhard, *Economic Means for Human Needs,* University of Michigan Press, Ann Arbor, 1976.

Tiger, Lionel, *Optimism: The Biology of Hope,* Simon & Schuster, New York, 1979.

A Time to Choose, America's Energy Future, Final report of the Energy Policy Project of the Ford Foundation, Ballinger, Cambridge, Mass., 1974.

Turner, James S., *The Chemical Feast: The Ralph Nader Study Group on Food Protection and the Food and Drug Administration,* Grossman, New York, 1970.

Index

Abalone Alliance, 71
Absenteeism, 49-50, 95
Accounting firms, 196
Acid rain, 25, 73-75, 155
Africa, 198
Age Discrimination in Employment
    Act, 1967, 100
Agricultural land, United States,
    134
Agricultural Reserve, British Columbia,
    134
Air:
    clean, 18
    emissions, 5
    pollution standards, 26
    quality, 20
Air Quality Resources Board, California, 29-30
Alaska, 10, 27, 28, 168-169
    gas, 85
    land preservation, 29
    mineral reserves, 34
    North Slope, 123
    oil pipeline, 10, 20, 30, 85, 123
    oil transportation, 29
    protected wilderness, 10
    resource potential, 28
Alberta, 75
American Dream, 119, 148
American Indian Movement, 167
American Industrial Health Council, 82
American Nuclear Energy Council, 68
Anaconda Company, 203
Angola, 199

Anheuser-Busch Company, 204
Appalachia, 25
Arab Oil Embargo, 20, 26, 111, 143,
    203
Arctic regions, 85
Arctic Wildlife Refuge, 28
Arizona, 28
Asbestos, 82, 84
Aspirations, 1, 14, 151-152, 165, 168,
    172, 173, 175, 188-189, 192
Association of Bay Area Governments,
    San Francisco (ABAG), 132
Atlantic Richfield Company, 28, 203
Automatic:
    office equipment, 202
    typesetting process, 88-90
Automation, 87-100
    auto industry, 91-93
    newspapers, 87-90
    offices, 96-100
    service industry, 96-100
    shipping, 93

Babin, Charles, 51, 58
Baby-boom, 130
Bacon, Robert, 112
Balance of payments, 2, 113-114,
    123, 151
    deficits, 15, 106, 122-123, 165
    United States, 124, 151
Balance of trade, 2, 3, 124
Baltimore Canyon, 27
Banks, Dennis, 167
Barkdoll, Gerald, 82

237